Doris Lessing and the Forming of History

Doris Lessing and the Forming of History

Edited by Kevin Brazil, David Sergeant and Tom Sperlinger

EDINBURGH
University Press

Edinburgh University Press is one of the leading university presses in the UK. We publish academic books and journals in our selected subject areas across the humanities and social sciences, combining cutting-edge scholarship with high editorial and production values to produce academic works of lasting importance. For more information visit our website: edinburghuniversitypress.com

Edinburgh University Press Ltd
The Tun – Holyrood Road, 12(2f) Jackson's Entry, Edinburgh EH8 8PJ

Typeset in 10.5/13 Adobe Sabon by
Servis Filmsetting Ltd, Stockport, Cheshire,
printed and bound in Great Britain by
CPI Group (UK) Ltd, Croydon CR0 4YY

A CIP record for this book is available from the British Library

ISBN 978 1 4744 1443 2 (hardback)
ISBN 978 1 4744 1444 9 (webready PDF)
ISBN 978 1 4744 1445 6 (epub)

Contents

Acknowledgments   vii

Timeline   ix

Introduction   1

1. Early Lessing, Commitment, the World   10
   Adam Guy
2. 'I'm an adolescent. And that's how I'm going to stay':
   Lessing and Youth Culture 1956–1962   26
   Nick Bentley
3. Sequence, Series and Character in *Children of Violence*   39
   Kevin Brazil
4. The Politics of Form: *The Golden Notebook* and Women's
   Radical Literary Tradition   56
   Rowena Kennedy-Epstein
5. Readers of Fiction and Readers in Fiction: Readership and
   The Golden Notebook   71
   Sophia Barnes
6. From *The Grass is Singing* to *The Golden Notebook*:
   Film, Literature and Psychoanalysis   84
   Laura Marcus
7. 'A funny thing laughter, what's it for?': Humour and Form
   in Lessing's Fiction   97
   Cornelius Collins
8. Lessing and the Scale of Environmental Crisis   111
   David Sergeant
9. Lessing and Time Travel   128
   David Punter

10. Lessing's Interruptions   137
    Tom Sperlinger
11. Lessing's Witness Literature   152
    Elizabeth Maslen
12. A Catastrophic Universe: Lessing, Posthumanism and Deep
    History   164
    Clare Hanson

Select Bibliography   181
Notes on Contributors   202
Index   204

Acknowledgements

Stephanie Codsi's editorial work was invaluable in preparing this collection for publication, especially on the bibliography and in completing the index. We would like to thank the Faculty of Arts and the Department of English at the University of Bristol for funding towards both permissions and editorial work. Jackie Jones and Adela Rauchova at Edinburgh University Press have provided supportive advice throughout. We are grateful to Susan Watkins, who helped to find this collection such a suitable home. The idea for this book and some of its chapters originated in *Doris Lessing 2014: An International Conference*, held at Plymouth University in September 2014. We would like to thank the School of Humanities and Performing Arts at Plymouth for funding the conference, the Doris Lessing Society for funding a drinks reception, and all the delegates for their stimulating contributions.

The quotations in this volume from the following published works by Doris Lessing are reprinted by kind permission of Jonathan Clowes Ltd, London, on behalf of The Estate of Doris Lessing, and HarperCollins Publishers Ltd: *Martha Quest* © 1952 by Doris Lessing; *A Proper Marriage* © 1954 by Doris Lessing; *A Ripple From the Storm* © 1958 by Doris Lessing; *Landlocked* © 1965 by Doris Lessing; *Going Home* © 1968 [1957] by Doris Lessing; *The Temptation of Jack Orkney and Other Stories* © 1972 by Doris Lessing; *The Summer Before the Dark* © 1973 by Doris Lessing; *The Memoirs of a Survivor* © 1974 by Doris Lessing; *Shikasta* © 1981 [1979] by Doris Lessing; *The Marriages Between Zones Three, Four and Five* © 1980 by Doris Lessing; *The Making of the Representative for Planet 8* © 1982 by Doris Lessing; *The Wind Blows Away Our Words* © 1987 by Doris Lessing; *A Small Personal Voice* © 1994 by Doris Lessing; *The Four-Gated City* © 1990 [1969] by Doris Lessing; *Under My Skin* © 1994 by Doris Lessing; *The Summer Before the Dark* © 1995 [1973] by Doris Lessing; *Play With a Tiger and Other Plays* © 1996 by Doris Lessing; *Putting the Questions*

Differently © 1996 by Doris Lessing; *The Golden Notebook* © 1999 [1962] by Doris Lessing; *Mara and Dann* © 1999 by Doris Lessing; *Ben, in the World* © 2000 by Doris Lessing; *The Fifth Child* © 2001 by Doris Lessing; *The Sun Between their Feet* © 2003 by Doris Lessing; *Alfred and Emily* © 2008 by Doris Lessing.

The quotations from the unpublished typescripts for *The Summer Before the Dark* and *The Marriages Between Zones Three, Four and Five* in Chapter 10 are © 1973 and 1980 respectively by Doris Lessing. They are reprinted here by kind permission of Jonathan Clowes Ltd, London, on behalf of The Estate of Doris Lessing, and the Harry Ransom Center at the University of Texas at Austin. The research on Lessing's typescripts in that chapter was supported by a 2013/14 Hobby Family Foundation Endowment from the Ransom Center.

Timeline

Year	Lessing's Life	Historical Events and Notable Literary Works	Publications
22 Oct. 1919	Doris Tayler born, Kermanshah, Persia.		
1922	Harry Tayler born, Kermanshah, Persia.	British coup against Shah Qajar in Persia. Eliot, 'The Waste Land'.	
1923		Crown Colony of Southern Rhodesia founded.	
1924	Tayler family move to Banket, Lomagundi, Southern Rhodesia.	Lenin dies; Stalin leader of the USSR. Forster, *A Passage to India*	
1925		Woolf, *Mrs Dalloway*	
1927	Attends convent school in Salisbury.		
1929		Wall Street Crash. Woolf, *A Room of One's Own*	
1930		Land Apportionment Act enforcing racial segregation in Southern Rhodesia.	
1932	Works as au pair in Salisbury.	Huxley, *Brave New World*	
1933		Hitler becomes German Chancellor.	
1935	First newspaper stories published.	Nuremberg Laws; Italy invades Ethiopia.	
1936		Spanish Civil War. Orwell, *The Road to Wigan Pier*	

Year	Lessing's Life	Historical Events and Notable Literary Works	Publications
1937	Moves to Salisbury to work in the telephone exchange; writes 'two bad apprentice novels'.	Stapledon, *Star Maker*	
1939	Marries Frank Wisdom; John Wisdom born.	Second World War begins. Joyce, *Finnegans Wake*	
1941	Jean Wisdom born.	Japan bombs Pearl Harbour.	
1942	Becomes active in Communist groups in Salisbury.	Siege of Stalingrad; Nazi Party implements the 'Final Solution'.	
1943	Divorces Frank Wisdom; marries Gottfried Lessing; begins publishing poetry in *New Rhodesia*.		
1944	Publishes political journalism in *Labour Front*.	Eliot, *Four Quartets*	
1945		Atomic bombing of Japan; Second World War ends. George Orwell, *Animal Farm*	
1946	Works for Hansard in Rhodesian Parliament; Peter Lessing born.	Churchill's 'Iron Curtain' speech; Cold War begins.	
1947	Sends 'unashamed agitprop' play to Bertolt Brecht.	Independence of India and Pakistan.	
1948		Apartheid begins in South Africa; State of Israel founded; assassination of Gandhi.	
1949	Arrives in London with Peter Lessing; divorces Gottfried Lessing.	Foundation of People's Republic of China; foundation of NATO. Orwell, *Nineteen Eighty-Four*	

Year	Lessing's Life	Historical Events and Notable Literary Works	Publications
1950	Moves to Kensington to live with Joan Rodker; begins psychoanalysis with Toni Sussman.	Korean War.	*The Grass is Singing*
1951	Joins the Communist Party of Great Britain.		*This Was the Old Chief's Country*
1952	Visits the Soviet Union; MI5 begins spying on Lessing, to last for twenty years.	Mau Mau uprising in Kenya; Queen Elizabeth II ascends to British throne. Ellison, *Invisible Man*	*Martha Quest*
1953		Stalin dies. Southern Rhodesia joins Central African Federation.	*Five: Short Novels*
1954	Moves to Warwick Road, SW5; meets Clancy Sigal. Receives the Somerset Maugham Award for *Five*.	US tests hydrogen bomb. Golding, *The Lord of the Flies*; Tolkein, *The Lord of the Rings*	*A Proper Marriage*
1955	Travels to Southern Rhodesia.	Bandung Conference. FLN uprising in Algeria. Beckett, *Waiting for Godot*; Nabokov, *Lolita*	
1956	Banned from entering Southern Rhodesia and South Africa; leaves the Communist Party.	Twentieth Party Congress of the USSR; Hungarian Uprising; Suez Crisis. Osborne, *Look Back in Anger*	*A Retreat to Innocence*
1957	Joins editorial boards of *The New Reasoner* and *Universities and Left Review*. Begins relationship with Clancy Sigal.		*The Habit of Loving; Going Home*
1958	Attends Aldermaston Marches; moves to Langham Street, W1.	Achebe, *Things Fall Apart*	*A Ripple From the Storm*
1959		State of Emergency declared in Southern Rhodesia.	*Fourteen Poems*

Year	Lessing's Life	Historical Events and Notable Literary Works	Publications
1960	Attends inaugural meeting of anti-war Committee of 100.	Sharpeville Massacre in South Africa; ANC outlawed. R.D. Laing, *The Divided Self*	*In Pursuit of the English: A Documentary*
1961	Relationship with Clancy Sigal ends.	Eichmann Trials in Jerusalem. Heller, *Catch-22*	
1962	Moves to 60 Charrington Street.	Cuban Missile Crisis. Burgess, *A Clockwork Orange*	*Play With A Tiger* *The Golden Notebook*
1963	Jenny Diski, aged 16, comes to live with Lessing in London.	Civil Rights Marches in USA; John F. Kennedy assassinated; independence of Kenya, Zanzibar. Plath, *The Bell Jar*	*A Man and Two Women*
1964		Nelson Mandela imprisoned; Civil Rights Act, USA; ZANU outlawed in Rhodesia. Shah, *The Sufis*	*African Stories*
1965		Unilateral Declaration of Independence of Rhodesia sparks civil war; US begins bombing campaign in Vietnam.	*Landlocked*
1966		Cultural Revolution in China; British Colonial Office dissolved.	*The Black Madonna; Winter in July*
1967			*Particularly Cats*
1968		Martin Luther King assassinated; 'May Events', Paris; USSR invades Czechoslovakia; Civil Rights Marches in Northern Ireland.	
1969		Neil Armstrong walks on the moon. Vonnegut, *Slaughterhouse Five*	*The Four-Gated City*

Year	Lessing's Life	Historical Events and Notable Literary Works	Publications
1970		Rhodesia becomes a republic. Independence of Gambia.	
1971		Bantu Homelands Act in South Africa; independence of Bangladesh. Naipaul, *In a Free State*	*Briefing for a Descent into Hell*
1972		Bloody Sunday in Derry.	*The Story of a Non-Marrying Man and Other Stories*
1973		US withdrawal from Vietnam. Yom Kippur War. Pynchon, *Gravity's Rainbow*	*Collected African Stories*
1974		Three-day week in Britain.	*The Memoirs of a Survivor*
1975		'Emergency' declared in India.	
1976	Prix Médicis	Piercy, *Woman on the Edge of Time*	
1977	Refuses offer of an OBE.		
1978		McEwan, *The Cement Garden*	*Collected Stories Volume 1* *Collected Stories Volume 2*
1979		Iranian Revolution; USSR invades Afghanistan; 'Winter of Discontent' in Britain. Carter, *The Bloody Chamber and Other Stories*	*Shikasta: Re: Colonised Planet 5*
1980		Independence of Zimbabwe; Iran-Iraq War; Solidarity protests in Poland.	*The Marriages Between Zones Three, Four, and Five*

Year	Lessing's Life	Historical Events and Notable Literary Works	Publications
1981		Rushdie, *Midnight's Children*	*The Sirian Experiments*
1982	Austrian State Prize for European Literature and the Shakespeare Prize (Hamburg).	Falklands War	*The Making of the Representative for Planet 8*
1983		Famine in Ethiopia. Coetzee, *Life and Times of Michael K*	*Documents Relating to the Sentimental Agents in the Volyen Empire; The Diary of a Good Neighbour*
1984		IRA bombs British government; Miner's Strike in Britain; Indira Gandhi assassinated.	*The Diaries of Jane Somers*
1985		Iran-Contra Affair; *glasnost* and *perestroika* in USSR. Atwood, *The Handmaid's Tale*	*The Good Terrorist*
1986	W. H. Smith Literary Award and the Mondello Prize in Italy for *The Good Terrorist*	Chernobyl explosion, USSR. Coetzee, *Foe*	
1987	Palermo Prize.		*Prisons We Choose To Live Inside; The Wind Blows Away Our Words*
1988	Collaborates with composer Philip Glass on the opera *The Making of the Representative for Planet 8*, performed by the Houston Grand Opera.	USSR withdraws from Afghanistan. Rushdie, *The Satanic Verses*	*The Fifth Child*

Year	Lessing's Life	Historical Events and Notable Literary Works	Publications
1989	Honorary degree from Princeton University.	Tiananmen Square Massacre; Communism collapses in Eastern Europe. Ishiguro, *The Remains of the Day*	
1991		Disintegration of USSR; apartheid ends in South Africa.	
1992	Refuses DBE; John Wisdom dies of a heart attack in Zimbabwe.		*The Real Thing: Stories and Sketches; African Laughter*
1994		Democratic elections in South Africa; civil war in Rwanda.	*A Small Personal Voice; Under My Skin: Volume One Of My Autobiography, to 1949*
1995	Honorary degree from Harvard University. James Tait Black Prize for *Under My Skin*.		*Spies I Have Known and Other Stories; Playing the Game*
1996	Idries Shah dies.		*Love, Again*
1997	Collaborates with Philip Glass on the opera, *The Marriages Between Zones Three, Four and Five*	Roy, *The God of Small Things*	*Walking in the Shade: Volume Two of My Autobiography, 1949–1962*
1999	Order of the Companion of Honour. XI Annual International Catalunya Award.	Coetzee, *Disgrace*	*Mara and Dann: An Adventure*
2000	Nominated for International IMPAC Dublin Award for *Mara and Dann*	Smith, *White Teeth*	*Ben, In The World*

Year	Lessing's Life	Historical Events and Notable Literary Works	Publications
2001	Prince Asturias Prize; David Cohen Prize. Companion of Honour from the Royal Society of Literature.	September 11 attacks in US; US invades Afghanistan.	*The Sweetest Dream*
2002	S.T. Dupont Golden PEN Award.		*On Cats*
2003		US and UK invade Iraq. Atwood, *Oryx and Crake*	*The Grandmothers*
2004			*Time Bites*
2005			*The Story of General Dann and Mara's Daughter, Griot and the Snow Dog*
2007	Awarded the Nobel Prize for Literature.		*The Cleft*
2008			*Alfred and Emily*
17 Nov. 2013	Dies in London on 13 October, four weeks after the death of Peter Lessing.		

Introduction

Kevin Brazil, David Sergeant and Tom Sperlinger

'It's a question of form' (1993: 418). So declares frustrated writer Anna Wulf, in what remains Lessing's most celebrated novel, *The Golden Notebook*. As this volume shows, the attempt to find forms which might record, model and engage historical change and all that it entails is one that persists throughout the six decades spanned by Lessing's writing. The chapters that follow attend to the full weight of Anna's statement: when Lessing's writing turns towards history it is not simply a question of finding the literary form that might best represent it; rather it involves questioning the very relationship between form and history, as they are brought together afresh in each new work. These questions might be common to literary criticism, but the chronological breadth of Lessing's career, and its sheer variety and productivity, makes them both particularly pressing and particularly enlightening in her work. As she moves from colonial Rhodesia to post-war Britain, and from war-torn Afghanistan to our posthuman future, her work employs the full panoply of techniques, modes, genres and effects that we refer to as forms: short stories, realism, serial fiction, documentary, drama, jokes, Sufi tales, reportage – and more.

But to what, exactly, does Lessing's writing turn, when it turns towards history? This is another question to which there is neither a single nor a simple answer. Two contradictory understandings of history can be seen to run throughout Lessing's work, and it is the irresolvable tension between them that makes the question of history, as much as the question of form, such a persistent and unifying theme in her oeuvre.

On the one hand, there is the notion of history as a teleological and determining process, one which guides the actions of the living, and whose logic can be grasped by those perceptive enough to see it. The most significant source for this belief was, of course, Marxism – or rather, a version of Marxism seized upon for offering the only vision of anticolonial resistance and anti-racist humanism to a young critic of colonial Rhodesia. But just as Lessing later argued that Marxism's utopianism, and its attempt at a 'world-mind, a world ethic' (1993: 14), was but one secular manifestation of an enduring pattern, so too this understanding of history as a meaningful process in itself, whose shape it was the task of the visionary writer to perceive, appears in multiple guises in Lessing's work. Such a blending of sacred and secular utopianism provides one of the most vivid images of this concept of history, recorded in Anna Wulf's Red Notebook on 28 August 1954: 'time has gone and the whole history of man, the whole history of mankind, is present in what I see now, and it is like a great soaring hymn of joy and triumph in which pain is a small lively counterpoint' (270).

Against this determinism, however, stands Lessing's belief in 'what a great influence an individual may have, even an apparently obscure person, living a small quiet life. It is individuals who change societies, give birth to ideas, who, standing out against tides of opinions, change them' (1994: 91). This belief grants to the individual's agency the capacity to 'give birth' to new ideas, and so shape the history that is shaping them. Lessing has spoken of this double view in relation to her own life: 'While there is something in me which I recognize is uniquely me, and which obviously interests me more than other things and which I am responsible for, at the same time I have a view of myself in history, as something which has been created by the past and conditioned by the present' (1996: 76).

It might be tempting to resolve these two attitudes into a biographical narrative of youthful conversion followed by mature disillusion – but this risks simplifying both positions into a naïve faith in Marxism followed by a sober liberalism, as well as enforcing a deceptive linearity to Lessing's thinking. As Nick Bentley's chapter in this volume shows, Lessing had a much more nuanced understanding of how youthful commitment may evolve and be critiqued in later life. Lessing also continued to experiment with these questions right up to her final book, *Alfred and Emily* (2008), in which her parents are released from the Great War, which had long been seen as overdetermining their marriage and Lessing's childhood. By imagining an alternative history in which that war did not happen, Lessing grants to each of her parents an agency that they did not have in their lives, separated from one another, and removes herself from history altogether. Yet this fictional alternative is balanced by a sober re-telling of how things actually turned out. A more productive procedure for literary criticism is thus, following *Alfred and Emily*, to rethink the relationship between these two understandings of history and how they might generate each other. This was one of the exercises that preoccupied Hannah Arendt's thought, and bringing

Arendt and Lessing together can do much to illuminate the complexities of Lessing's understanding of history.

The concept of history as a teleological and meaningful process has been subject to much scepticism, and has been reduced often to caricature, so that what it entails and why it appeals can be difficult to perceive. Indeed, Lessing herself expressed this scepticism in her satirical portrayal of Klorathy's belief in 'the logic of history' in *Documents Relating to the Sentimental Agents in the Volyen Empire* (1983: 23). It is for this reason that Arendt's careful unfolding of what is distinctively modern about Marx's concept of history is so useful, especially since it is one she herself, like Lessing, ultimately rejects. For Arendt, what was distinctive about Marx's inversion of Hegel's philosophy of history was that his resulting materialist philosophy of history incorporated two elements. Firstly, the notion that history is a process that is the product of human activity, one in which repetitions cannot occur. Secondly, the belief that this process has an eventual and final outcome, one which can be known in advance as a plan, according to which mankind can act in order to 'make history' and by so doing, paradoxically, end history (2006: 76–86). Thus in Lessing's work, right from the outset, we have repeated attempts to depict a scale commensurate with this process of history unfolding – whether that be the world, the universe, or evolutionary time – interspersed with visions of the ideal and meticulously fabricated city towards which this process is heading.

However, for Arendt the problem with this concept of history is that it relies upon mistakenly viewing the ability to act in history as a form of making: 'neither freedom nor any other meaning can ever be the product of human activity in the sense in which the table is clearly the end-product of the carpenter's activity' (2006: 78). Such a belief was nevertheless persuasive, for in it 'we can detect the age-old attempt to escape from the fragility of human action by construing it in the image of making' (79). For all that Lessing's work is a powerful testament to the ways in which we desire to escape from this knowledge of our fragility, her work is just as powerfully committed to our ability to act in the world in ways unforeseen by any teleological vision. And one way in which we can do so is through the stories we tell about our actions.

For Arendt, the story is what mediates between the actions that make up history, and works of art, among them works of literature. No action can ever achieve its intended purpose, since we are all born into an 'already existing web of human relationships, with its innumerable, conflicting wills and intentions'; therefore our actions produce 'stories with or without intention as naturally as fabrication produces tangible things. These stories may then be recorded in documents and monuments, they may be visible in objects or art works, they may be told and retold into all kinds of material' (1958: 184). We tell ourselves stories all the time: in their ability to reveal the meaning of action in its retrospection, the 'story reveals the meaning of what otherwise would remain an unbearable sequence of sheer happenings' (1970: 104). Stories thus 'in their living reality, are of an altogether different nature' from the form they are given in art, for artworks are products of making, of fabrication: while they may be 'thought things . . . this does not prevent their being things' (1958: 169). As things made, they give a form to the story that is history, but not a form to history itself: and the form they give this story is the most significant thing about them.

An attention to form is thus vital for a number of recurring debates in Lessing criticism, as the contributors to this volume demonstrate. Susan Watkins has neatly summarised the difficulties faced by critics wishing to relate Lessing's work to third-wave or post-feminism, in part 'occasioned by Lessing's own increasingly articulate distancing of herself from feminism' (2010: 171). Rowena Kennedy-Epstein in her chapter deftly recovers Lessing's innovations in *The Golden Notebook* from the author's own retrospective reading of the book: 'Lessing's assertion [in 2007] that the text's value is more political and historical than literary shows how much she herself must have been inculcated into the genre norms of mid-century, even while she broke them' (see p. 59). Similarly, Laura Marcus shows, in the first ever analysis of the impact of film on Lessing's work, the way in which what she terms Lessing's 'cinema mind' anticipated much of the interweaving of psychoanalysis and cinema that proved so productive for later generations of feminist film theorists. Such approaches make it possible to disclose the conflicting intentions in Lessing's work, while still reading it as formally radical.

This view of the relationship between form and history gifts agency to the writer, the ability to 'give birth' to ideas, as Lessing wrote. Arendt suggests: 'Only insofar as the end product of fabrication' – the literary work – 'is incorporated into the human world, where its use and eventual "history" can never be entirely predicted, does even fabrication start a process whose outcome cannot be entirely foreseen and is therefore entirely beyond the control of its author' (2006: 60). In Lessing's writing the making of the work itself is often in evidence, as Kennedy-Epstein and Tom Sperlinger show in different ways in their chapters. Here we see why Lessing's own hard-won commitment to the agency of her stories in relation to history is intermittently accompanied by an insistence that once they are written they will make their own way in the world; and that we, as readers, must remain open to the unpredictable effects that literature can have on us. This may have a particular resonance at this moment in Lessing criticism. Roberta Rubenstein (2010) has described Lessing as a 'protean' writer, and claims that particular privileges were available to those who 'followed the author's evolution one book at a time' as she 'anticipated and anatomized the contemporary *Zeitgeist*' (18). This collection, like Rubenstein's essay and Susan Watkins's recent monograph (2010), is part of a new phase in criticism of Lessing's work, as it begins to respond to an oeuvre that is no longer evolving.

Such a conceptualisation of the place of history in Lessing's work, and the relationship of history to form, places the approach of this volume partially in concert with, and partially at a distance from, recent calls to move beyond modes of 'symptomatic reading', exemplified above all by Fredric Jameson *The Political Unconscious* (1981), that posit history as the unknowable but ultimately determining cause of a literary text. Such calls include Stephen Best's and Sharon Marcus's account of the possibilities entailed by various kinds of 'surface reading' (2009) or by Rita Felski's recent declaration of the 'limits of critique' (2015). Indeed, as the chapters that follow show, a plurality of ways of reading and a testing of the limits of critique are already present in Lessing's work: for instance, in her concern with the didactic utility of literature, seen in both her turn to reportage, as Elizabeth Maslen describes it, and her varied and evolving use of humour, as traced by Cornelius Collins. Similarly, Sophia Barnes's chapter illuminates how *The Golden Notebook*'s exploration of a range of historically specific cultures of reading forces us to question the practices of academic literary criticism.

The responsiveness of Lessing's work to these approaches might have something to do with the focus on scale which this volume reveals as an urgent and constantly evolving presence in her work: with connections and breaks between the individual and collective, the local and global, as well as between surface and depth. As Adam Guy, Kevin Brazil and Nick Bentley detail, the demands of scalar thinking were integral to the post-war, communist literary milieu in which Lessing started out; while David Sergeant and Clare Hanson show them to be – in a different but related guise – just as pressingly relevant to the world in which we currently live, faced with a global environmental crisis that demands a rethinking of our relationship both to other humans and to the non-human lives beyond (or beside) them. How might individuals, and individual literary works, scale up to the dauntingly multiple and global context in which they take their place? And what happens to individual action and experience, or the individual work, when they do?

As Mark McGurl has observed, an often fraught negotiation of these questions of scale has been central to the re-emergence of world literature as a critical category in literary studies (2012). The viewpoint of world literature requires for Franco Moretti (2000) a distant reading of synoptic histories, or by networked servers; for Pascale Casanova (2004), a scale of achievement keyed to the judgement of Paris; for Wai Chee Dimock (2006) an expansion into deep time. Yet each critical attempt to scale up or out has been accompanied by a counterclaim to attend to the granular difficulties of translation (Apter 2013), or to the still living violence of imperialism – whose child Lessing always claimed she remained – that lurks behind the fact that world literature is an English-language literature (Mufti 2016). It may be tempting to claim Lessing as an exemplar of world literature in an attempt to settle what Susan Watkins has aptly described as her complicated relationship to theories of postcolonialism (2010: 172–6). But, on the contrary, it is Lessing's foregrounding of the problems of scale and form involved in any concept of the world that relates the concerns of this volume to the ongoing debates over whether there should be a world literature. Or even if there could: as Sergeant and Hanson also show, in extending its range beyond and within the human, the world of Lessing's writing came to be one in which humans and their literature were only one agent, and an increasingly threatened one at that.

In 1972, Margaret Drabble wrote that Lessing was a 'prophet who prophesises the end of the world', though she was 'not much heeded' (50). In the same essay, Drabble claims that Lessing is 'not obsessed with form but with content' (51). Drabble quotes from *A Ripple on the Storm* (1958), in which the protagonist claims that she imagines the future to be 'short and violent' and that to be a communist is to be a 'dead man on leave' (50). Lessing had renounced communism by the time Drabble wrote this, but her vision of the future in the novel that Drabble focuses on, *The Four-Gated City* (1969), remained a distressing one. The World War Three that Lessing imagined in that novel – with Martha Quest dying on an island contaminated by nuclear war in 1997 – is a reminder that some of Lessing's futures must now be read historically. There may be risks, however, in reading her work too literally as either failed or successful prophecies. As more than one contributor to this volume notes, Lessing's writing is less prophetic than visionary: interested in conceptualising and imagining different futures, shaping them in ways that are neither productionist nor proprietary. In this sense, too, Drabble – and later critics such as Rubenstein, who claims Lessing 'is not one to whom [readers] go for her craft' (15) – underestimate the extent to which the content of Lessing's visions are always determined in part by questions of form.

What does it mean, therefore, that the future begins to appear in Lessing's work in a different form? In his discussion of time travel in Lessing's work, David Punter utilises Derrida's distinction between two kinds of future: that which is predictable and predicted, and *l'avenir*, 'which refers to someone who comes whose arrival is totally unexpected' (Derrida, Kirby and Kofman 2005: 53). Punter reads *Memoirs of a Survivor* (1974), with the arrival of the child Emily, as an instance of just such an unexpected occurrence. As Lessing's career progresses, her fiction manifests an increasing tendency to make space for the new and unexpected. Her imagination still tends towards catastrophe when it considers the future – not least in the worlds of *The Making of the Representative for Planet 8* (1982) or *Mara and Dann* (1999), each overcome by ice – and yet in each case the capacity for human survival remains: there is some transmission of knowledge to (another) future. Thus in her late work Lessing also comes to ruminate about not only endings but beginnings too. Just as in *Alfred and Emily* she imagines a different beginning for herself (in which her life did not begin), in *The Cleft* (2007) Lessing imagines an alternative myth or story of human origins. The narrator, a Roman senator, is aware that the story he is recovering involves remaking history anew, by telling it differently.

As Lessing's vision of the future shifted its focus in her later years, from the utopian collective that promised an end to history – be it the four-gated city or the benevolent Canopeans – to the individuals who might survive the relentless destruction of never-ending historical process, so she placed increasing emphasis on oral storytelling and the survival of stories. This had curious implications for her conception of literary form, as the great novels of the European tradition are envisioned surviving in the post-cataclysmic future of *Mara and Dann* only ('only'?) as archetypal stories equivalent to those derived from opera and drama, and all of them stripped of their enabling form: Mam Bova (*Madame Bovary*) and Ankrena (*Anna Karenina*), Rom and Jull (*Romeo and Juliet*) and Mam Bedfly (*Madame Butterfly*). Similarly, Lessing's Nobel Prize acceptance speech converted perhaps the archetypal novel *Anna Karenina* (1877) into a narrative consumed in a non-conventional fashion akin to oral narrative: as a section dislocated from a larger whole and passed across boundaries of geography, culture and class by chance, to be consumed by an African, that recognisable locus for oral storytelling culture (Lessing borrowed the West African term griot – one who amalgamated roles such as historian and storyteller – for a character name in another late novel, *The Story of General Dann and Mara's daughter, Griot and the Snow Dog* (2005)).

Tolstoy and the other nineteenth-century European realists had been the touchstone for literary excellence for Lessing from the early days of her career, as in 'The Small Personal Voice' (1957), and continued to be so until the very end, in her final book *Alfred and Emily* (2008). The reasons for this seem to change as often as she mentions them, but while Tolstoy's work continues to shape her view of literature and the world, what she never mentions is the particularity of his use of literary form – even as it is this use which must guarantee his value to her. While Lessing's genres might change (once again) in the latter part of her career, she does not become a storyteller in the sense in which she often seemed to imagine the role. Thus, while in cannibalising *Anna Karenina* she seems to imagine the survival of its nourishing parts (as it were) in a different and unexpected form, it remains one predicated on the print culture that both she and Tolstoy wrote out of. At the same time, Lessing performs this act of transformation on receipt of the world's premier literary prize, as if she were subverting the notion of authorial longevity that such a prize suggests. Lessing's own conception of the future of literature – including, implicitly, her own – might thus be seen as perpetuating the breach she struggled so productively to anneal throughout her entire career: between the unique instance and the generic subsumption, between the individual and the collective, the intentional and the unexpected.

Works Cited

Apter, Emily (2013), *Against World Literature*, London: Verso.

Arendt, Hannah (1958), *The Human Condition*, Chicago: University of Chicago Press.

—— (1970), *Men in Dark Times,* London: Harcourt Brace.

—— (2006), *Between Past and Future: Eight Exercises in Political Thought,* London: Penguin.

Best, Stephen and Marcus, Sharon (2009), 'Surface Reading: An Introduction', in *Representations*, 108: 1 (Fall 2009), 1–21.

Casanova, Pascale (2004), *The World Republic of Letters,* trans. M. B. DeBevoise, Cambridge, MA: Harvard University Press.

Derrida, Jacques, Dick, Kirby, and Kofman, Amy Ziering (2005), *Derrida: Screenplay and Essays on the Film*, Manchester: Manchester University Press.

Dimock, Wai Chee (2006), *Through Other Continents: American Literature Across Deep Time*, Princeton: Princeton University Press.

Drabble, Margaret (1972), 'Doris Lessing: Cassandra in a World Under Siege', in *Ramparts Magazine* (Feb.), 50–4.

Felski, Rita (2015), *The Limits of Critique*, Chicago: University of Chicago Press.

Jameson, Fredric (1981), *The Political Unconscious: Narrative as a Socially Symbolic Act,* London: Methuen.

Lessing, Doris [1974] (1957), 'The Small Personal Voice', in Paul Schlueter (ed.), *A Small Personal Voice: Essays, Reviews, Interviews,* New York: Alfred A. Knopf, pp. 3–21.

—— (1958), *A Ripple from the Storm*, London: Michael Joseph.

—— (1969), *The Four-Gated City,* London: MacGibbon & Kee.

—— (1974), *The Memoirs of a Survivor*, London: Octagon Press.

—— (1982), *The Making of the Representative for Planet 8*, London: Cape.

—— (1983), *Documents Relating to the Sentimental Agents in the Volyen Empire*, London: Jonathan Cape.

—— (1993), *The Golden Notebook*, London: Flamingo.

—— (1994), *Prisons We Choose to Live Inside*, London: Flamingo.

—— (1996), *Putting the Questions Differently: Interviews With Doris Lessing, 1964–1994*, London: Flamingo.

—— (1999), *Mara and Dann: An Adventure*, London: Flamingo.

—— (2005), *The Story of General Dann and Mara's Daughter, Griot and the Snow Dog*, London: Fourth Estate.

—— (2007), *The Cleft*, London: Fourth Estate.

—— (2008), *Alfred and Emily*, London: Fourth Estate.

McGurl, Mark (2012), 'The Posthuman Comedy', *Critical Inquiry*, 38:3, 533–53.

Franco Moretti (2000), 'Conjectures on World Literature', *New Left Review* 1 (January–February), 4–68

Mufti, Aamir R. (2016), *Forget English: Orientalisms and World Literatures*, Cambridge, MA: Harvard University Press.

Rubenstein, Roberta (2010), 'Notes for Proteus: Doris Lessing Reads the *Zeitgeist*', in Debrah Raschke, Phyllis Sternberg Perrakis and Sandra Singer (eds), *Doris Lessing: Interrogating the Times*, Columbus: Ohio State University Press, pp. 11–31.

Watkins, Susan (2010), *Doris Lessing,* Manchester: Manchester University Press.

Chapter 1

Early Lessing, Commitment, the World

Adam Guy

In a section on commitment in the novel, the programme for the first Edinburgh International Literary Festival quotes the American writer and activist Dwight Macdonald:

> The question of 'commitment' was settled for me in the thirties when we on *Partisan Review* struggled against the communists, who were trying to slip that particular strait-jacket over American poets, novelists and critics. Since they didn't have state power, they failed. I also remember M. Sartre's sophisticated absurdities on the subject. The issue has been settled a long time ago and that the English should still be kicking it around is an interesting example of cultural lag. (Hook 1962: 44)

In its select coordinates Macdonald's broadside is emblematic of discussions of its time – both positive and negative – on literary commitment. In these discussions, commitment is a phenomenon of the left, and the left as defined at its communist pole; political ideology is caricatured as dogma; Jean-Paul Sartre's notions of *littérature engagée* are evoked; and overall, the issue of commitment is cast in relation to a specific historical temporality, often leading out of a mythic and prelapsarian 1930s.

Doris Lessing's 1957 essay 'The Small Personal Voice' is another such discussion of literary commitment. Less willing to equate commitment *tout court* with the phenomena that Macdonald describes, Lessing's essay is still troubled by the potential of these phenomena to represent committed writing. So, for example, Lessing's historical temporality is more nuanced than Macdonald's – both more expansive and less simply linear – although the iconic, originary charge of the 1930s remains. This said, Lessing's points of reference diverge from those of Macdonald regarding Jean-Paul Sartre. 'The Small Personal Voice' evokes the Sartre not of *littérature engagée*, but instead an earlier Sartre, included in a list alongside Albert Camus, Jean Genet and Samuel Beckett as evincing a 'pleasurable luxury of despair' – an 'acceptance of disgust', which is 'as much a betrayal of what a writer should be' as doctrinaire socialist realism and its 'acceptance of the simple economic view of man' (Lessing 1994: 15). Lessing's omission is in many ways remarkable: Sartre's notions of commitment were not only the most prominent – and most thoroughly theorised – of the post-war period, but also intersect at key points with 'The Small Personal Voice'.[1]

As such, this chapter begins by mapping the intersections between Lessing's earlier notions of commitment and those of Sartre, both as for-mulated by Sartre himself, and as circulating widely beyond his purview. Rather than proposing some kind of schematic reading of Lessing's work according to Sartrean principles, this chapter offers up Sartre as a productive comparator for Lessing's thinking by first staging an encoun-ter between the two writers and their ideas – both in her non-fiction and her fiction – about the meaning and purpose of writerly commitment in the period after 1945. In particular, a shared 'worlding' of the notion of commitment is central for both Lessing and Sartre. Regarding Lessing, the chapter names an *early* Lessing in order to map a route towards *The Golden Notebook* – a locus for critical discussion of writerly commit-ment in her work (Bentley 2009; Hargreaves 2012). Instead of focusing on her most famous novel, this chapter asks instead how Lessing *begins* to think about commitment, and how such concerns might resonate with her fiction of the 1950s and early 1960s.

The notion of writerly commitment articulated in 'The Small Personal Voice' proceeds from Lessing's statement that 'the highest point of lit-erature was the novel of the nineteenth century, the work of Tolstoy, Stendhal, Dostoevsky, Balzac, Turgenev, Chekhov; the work of the great realists' (8). Lessing then recounts reading a contemporary novel and finding it lacking:

> I was looking for the warmth, the compassion, the humanity, the love of people which illuminates the literature of the nineteenth century and which makes all these old novels a statement of faith in man himself. (10)

For Lessing, a return to these 'qualities' would generate a committed literature: 'It is these qualities which I demand, and which I believe spring from being committed; for one cannot be committed without belief' (10). In Lessing's tautological formulation here, it is the literary epiphenomena – warmth, compassion, and so on – of the phenomenon of commitment that must be demanded rather than the phenomenon itself. But at the same time, this epiphenomenal link is only sustained by belief, a belief that itself has commitment as an epiphenomenon. So belief generates both commitment and the literary manifestations of this commitment; Lessing's commitment, therefore, begins on non-empirical grounds, reached only at a remove through the will of belief.

But if Lessing's notion of commitment begins with an abstract ethical 'demand' for certain 'qualities', it ends with the concrete political gesture of the decision. Mid-way through 'The Small Personal Voice', Lessing presents a literary middle-ground between the two poles noted above of a 'pleasurable luxury of despair' and a doctrinaire socialist realism: 'Somewhere between these two, I believe, is a resting-point, a place of decision, hard to reach and precariously balanced. It is a balance which must be continuously tested and reaffirmed' (15). Though belief re-enters here at a rhetorical level, and though the emphasis is on precariousness and provisionality, Lessing also shows how commitment requires a point of decision. For the rest of the essay, Lessing seeks, through subtraction, to establish this dialectic between commitment's ethical demands and its political decisions. So, for example, her definition must exclude on the one hand the 'inner censor' (16) manifested in contemporary Soviet communism – a political decision made in bad faith; and on the other, this definition must also negate the approach of the Angry Young Men, which, though 'refreshingly derisive', is overly 'bounded' by an 'immediate experience of British life and standards' – an originary ethical demand limited by the borders of the nation and the nation state (19).

Explicitly addressed across a number of works over a number of years, Sartre's notion of commitment is articulated at greater length than Lessing's. At its core this notion might be summed up in the title of Sartre's essay of 1948, 'Writing for One's Age' ('Écrire pour son époque') – communicated in a more philosophical vocabulary in its final sentence as: 'We stand for an ethics and art of the finite' (Sartre 1967: 238). But given Sartre's longstanding investment in the figure of the committed writer, Sartrean commitment might more substantially be understood in two interrelated ways. First, Sartre formulates notions of commitment from the Second World War onwards in a body of writing that finds its most enduring legacy in the essays collected together in 1948 as *What is Literature?* (*Qu'est-ce que la littérature?*), as well as in other pieces such as 'The Nationalisation of Literature' ('La Nationlisation de la littérature', 1945), and 'Black Orpheus' ('Orphée noir', 1948). But at the same time, Sartre's commitment played out in his actions and interventions as a public figure. Through the numerous causes he supported from 1945 onwards, through the resolutely political tenor of his journal *Les Temps modernes*, through the meetings that he and Simone de Beauvoir held with Fidel Castro and Che Guevara, and through his advocacy for figures such as Patrice Lumumba and Albert Memmi, Sartre's commitment was put into practice. The point of interrelation between these two aspects of Sartre's commitment is in evidence, for example, in the mutual exchange and influence he shared with intellectuals and artists like de Beauvoir, Frantz Fanon and Aimé Cesaire. Perhaps ultimately, therefore, Sartrean commitment is better thought of beyond its Sartrean prefix – as a form of praxis emerging from a broader network.

As with Lessing's critique of the national limitations of the Angry Young Men, one important aspect of this network is that it was fundamentally global. For Rebecca L. Walkowitz, Sartre saw committed literature as 'the necessary and strategic response to the international problems of the postwar era'. But Walkowitz also shows that Sartre's understanding of the particular prerequisites of a committed literature shifted precisely in relation to their global conditions. 'Black Orpheus' is exemplary in this respect: Walkowitz suggests that the essay casts a different light on Sartre's earlier writings on commitment, with their assumption of 'a shared community of readers and writers [. . .] always at home in the language they are using'; for Walkowitz, the notions of *négritude* discussed in 'Black Orpheus' modify this former assumption, and allow for the development of a truly cosmopolitan form of committed writing (Walkowitz 2012: 23, 25). Lessing's notion of commitment converges with Sartre's precisely at the point at which such a global background is inscribed. Indeed Walkowitz's account of this developing globality in Sartre's thinking on commitment accords with Lessing's formulation of a commitment constantly in motion – one 'continuously tested and reaffirmed'.

For both Lessing and Sartre, the work of thinking a global background for the committed writer begins in showing the different dimensions of this background. Hence, in a Western context where Cold War struggles often stood in for any concerns beyond the nation or the nation state, Lessing and Sartre evoke the Cold War situation closely alongside that of the end of empire, conjuring their global background by accumulation and juxtaposition, rather than by referencing any singular, totalising category. So, for Lessing, the 'insistence of our rulers on spending so much of the wealth we produce on preparations for a war against communism; a war which will take place if and when the United States decides' is set alongside the potential of a 'disciplinary war against a dissident colony', to which 'the young men obediently march off' (19–20). Similarly, for Sartre, the 'fate of the bourgeoisie was tied up with European supremacy and colonialism', but it 'is losing its colonies at a time when Europe is ceasing to govern its destiny' in a world-system that no longer sees 'little kings carrying on wars for Rumanian oil or the Bagdad [*sic*] railroad', but instead two 'world powers, neither of which is bourgeois and neither of which is European' that are 'disputing the possession of the universe' (Sartre 1967: 182).

Categories of scale and mass are important for both writers. In particular, in his rhetorical gradient – class, colony and continent builds to 'world powers', and then to the 'universe' – Sartre displays the very *literary* calculations that support an attempt to render a global background for the committed writer. For Sartre, the concise singularity involved in simply evoking a totality or a whole does not suffice: a rhetorical strategy is sought to stand in for the sheer multiplicity and granularity of thinking on a global scale. Here, Wai Chee Dimock's work might provide a suitable gloss, as she relates such concerns to Benoit Mandelbrot's fractal geometry, which offers literary criticism a frame where '[s]calar opposites [. . .] generate a dialectic that makes the global an effect of the grainy', a geometric imaginary that goes 'all the way up and all the way down, all the way out and all the way in', and that 'loops the gnarled contours of the globe through the gnarled contours of every single node' (Dimock 2006: 77–8).

In one of the central passages of 'The Small Personal Voice', a similar process of description takes place:

> Everyone in the world now, has moments when he throws down a newspaper, turns off the radio, shuts his ears to the man on the platform, and holds out his hand and looks at it, shaken with terror. The hand of a white man, held to the warmth of a northern indoor fire; the hand of a black man, held into the strong heat of the sun: we look at our working hands, brown and white, and then at the flat surface of a wall, the cold material of a city pavement, at breathing soil, trees, flowers, growing corn. We think: the tiny units of the matter of my hand, my flesh, are shared with walls, tables, pavements, trees, flowers, soil . . . and suddenly, and at any moment, a madman may throw a switch, and flesh and soil and leaves may begin to dance together in a flame of destruction. We are all of us made kin with each other and with everything in the world because of the kinship of possible destruction. And the history of the last fifty years does not help us to disbelieve in the possibility of a madman in a position of power. We are haunted by the image of an idiot hand, pressing down a great black lever; or a thumb pressing a button, as the dance of fiery death begins in one country and spreads over the earth; and above the hand the concentrated fanatic stare of a mad sick face. (13, ellipsis original)

If the threat of nuclear apocalypse brings with it the threat of an all too singular image of globality – a single bomb, a single world destroyed – then here Lessing seeks to recover the granular aspect of that globality. Lessing's structuring figure is the synecdochic evocation of bodies, beginning with the ear, and moving through a multitude of hands, before finally reaching a single face – all as a means of spanning a wide spectrum of difference and denoting a multitude of people across a broad geography, to the end of expressing the multiplicity of the world under threat.

But to further develop her image of globality, Lessing also needs to find a form for the inevitable incommensurabilities that will arise from trying to generate such a broad image. And so, the hands, the walls, the tables, the pavements, the trees, the flowers, the soil in the passage above not only become an accumulated assemblage, standing in for a broader multiplicity, but also generate the oscillations between similarity and difference that are central to Lessing's task. As noted above, on the one hand, these elements are named in all their difference and multiplicity, but on the other, they are equally shown to be reducible in the abstract to the same – perhaps molecular – 'tiny units', which elide their differences. Moreover, if a 'switch' is thrown, this reducibility is literalised, as the differences between the listed elements are removed in the unity of destruction: Lessing's descriptive economy becomes commensurate with an atomic bomb in its capacity to convey the similarities between different things.

The seductive potential of a reduction to mere identical 'units' plays out at a formal level too in the passage above. Rhetorically, in its structure of listing, in its patterns of hands and fire, and in its functionally identical 'switch', 'button' and 'lever', the passage seems almost overdetermined in its formal efforts. In this form pointedly presenting itself as *form*, Lessing offers a model of any given text reduced down to a balanced equation, made up of weighable 'units'. Elsewhere in 'The Small Personal Voice', such a model is taken to its extreme. As Lessing criticises Colin Wilson's writing for its lack of global reach, she deploys the most legible form of reducible unit – number – to mount this critique:

> Mr Wilson has every right to be anti-humanist and anti-materialist; but it is a sign of his invincible British provincialism that he should claim to speak for his generation. The fact is that outside the very small sub-class of humanity Mr Wilson belongs to, vast numbers of young people are both humanist and materialist. Millions of young people in China, the Soviet Union, and India for instance. And the passions that excite the young African nationalist, five years literate, watching the progress of dams building in India and China, because he knows that what goes on in other countries intimately affects himself, have little in common with the passions of Mr Wilson. (22)

Lessing's critique of Wilson operates at two levels. First, Wilson's rejection of humanism and materialism is portrayed as unrepresentative in a statistical sense when viewed from a global perspective – Wilson is out of keeping with 'vast numbers of young people'. Second, the very manner in which such an unrepresentative view is achieved is also unrepresentative: while Wilson is portrayed as a narrow British provincial, the exemplary 'African nationalist' exists in a networked world-system, their passions excited by dam-building in India and China. Such a point of comparison articulates Lessing's position, and the type of background against which her notion of commitment is inscribed. But as this passage shows, it is through the rhetorical stringing together of numbers that Lessing builds up her own picture of something so substantial as an entire world – numbers first simply 'vast', then shown from different angles and scales, with 'millions' of people, but also the single African nationalist, with his precisely articulated 'five years' of literacy; and all – as with the passage about the hands – built from the developmental, steady accounting of a repetitious, unfolding rhetoric.

Moving back to Sartre from here, there is an irony to be detected. In 'The Small Personal Voice', Colin Wilson represents the most prominent local example of the 'pleasurable luxury of despair' and 'acceptance of disgust' that Lessing sees exemplified by Sartre and his contemporaries. However, in one way, Lessing shares a certain provincialism and anachronism with Wilson in the fact that both ascribe to Sartre and his like a caricatured 'existentialism' – traditionally opposed to the kind of 'humanism' Lessing espouses – and nothing more. This unencumbered, abstract existentialism derives (albeit in broad strokes) from Sartre's more apolitical pre-war writing, while ignoring the manner in which it carries through as the philosophical basis for his later notions of commitment. By summarising Sartre's achievement thus, Lessing and Wilson seem wholly typical of their time and place – a context dominated by what Alan Sinfield calls the 'conservative interpretation of existential freedom' seen, for example, in the writings of W. H. Auden, Thom Gunn and William Golding (Sinfield 2004: 104). And yet, though Lessing does not share Sartre's philosophical reference points, in mounting her critique of his provincial British proxy (Wilson) in the name of writerly commitment, she does so precisely on the same conceptual and rhetorical grounds on which Sartre's notion of commitment unfolds. Lessing is closer to Sartre than 'The Small Personal Voice' allows.

In his essay 'Situation of the Writer in 1947', though Sartre's picture of a world-system is more melancholic than Lessing's – it is a potential glimpsed, but not yet fully achieved – his means are the same:

> the plays of Cocteau, of Salacrou, and of Anouilh are being performed everywhere. I could cite any number of works which have been translated into six or seven languages less than three months after their publication. Yet, all this is brilliant only on the surface. Perhaps we are read in New York or Tel Aviv, but the shortage of paper has limited our editions in Paris. Thus the public

has been dispersed more than it has increased. Perhaps ten thousand people read us in four or five foreign countries and another ten thousand in our own. Twenty thousand readers – a minor pre-war success. These worldwide reputations are far less well established than the national reputations of our elders. (Sartre 1967: 179)

This passage studiedly oscillates between numbers of different sizes, and at different scales – 'any number of works' against 'six or seven languages', 'ten thousand people' in 'four or five foreign countries'. As Sartre's argument progresses, its formal elements remain the same: a single 'London stage' putting on a performance of Sartre's 1944 play *No Exit* (*Huis Clos*) would not achieve an audience of 'more than twenty to thirty thousand spectators', while a BBC radio broadcast achieves 'a half-million'; a single columnist's 'three hundred thousand readers' generates only 'a few thousand' readers of his deeper, more sustained works, while the rest 'will learn his name from having read it a hundred times on the second page of the magazine' (Sartre 1967: 180). As with Lessing, number here is a legible means of making a granular picture of grand global proportions. And equally like Lessing, the recitation of numbers becomes a device to bind together this picture, an apparently simple and consistent rhetorical surface that in fact shifts perspective and scale at each iteration, steadily tracking the connection between individual parts and their encompassing global whole.

Lessing and Sartre share both a central theory (a conception of a committed writer whose commitment plays out against the background of an unfolding world-system) and a means of expounding this theory (a rhetoric that uses number as a legible means of approaching the enormity of their global background). Such convergences show how Lessing's early work can be opened up to a context beyond contemporary anglophone discussions of writerly commitment like those of Dwight Macdonald discussed at the start of this chapter. But in one way, that such a gesture results in a comparison with Sartre seems decidedly majoritarian – replacing the context of one newly postcolonial metropole and its language with another. The gesture is partially redeemed, however, at the points at which Lessing and Sartre converge. Both writers share an insistence on thinking globally, and working through the literary challenges of delineating this globality as the necessary route to formulating writerly commitment in the post-war world. In the studied globality of both writers' thinking on commitment, therefore, Lessing and Sartre accord precisely at the point at which their comparison might seem insufficient – the global is shored up against colonial-type thinking determined by binaries like major/minor or centre/periphery.

First published in Lessing's 1963 short story collection *A Man and*

Two Women, 'A Letter from Home' begins midway through a letter from a writer, Martin du Preez, in which du Preez's recent reacquaintance with the poet Johannes Potgieter is recounted; the addressee is unclear, though it is implied that he or she might be another writer, or at least someone who spent time among writers (Lessing 2003: 226). The panorama offered by 'A Letter from Home' seems in many ways paradigmatic of what has come to be called the world literary system, as well as its various discontents, staging the tension Emily Apter sees in a very different context, where '[l]iterary history's cartographic catalogue is [. . .] either constrained by the national habitus, or thrown into the vast agglomerative catchall of "world literature"' (Apter 2008: 582). Given the alternatives of the strictly (and strictly policed) national, and the emptily global, Lessing's story asks whether a more serious scaling-up can be achieved.

'A Letter from Home' portrays a literary system that seems seductively global: if the epistolary form stands as a potential symbol of free expression and ease of communication across great distances, then the story's formal dimension follows through on this potential in its linguistic fluidity. Written in English, but drifting variously into Afrikaans, 'A Letter from Home' accumulates different means of being multilingual, as shown by du Preez's repeated phatic utterances – sometimes only in English ('Right'), at others only in Afrikaans ('*Goed*'), but also in succession, as a kind of staging of the act of translation ('Right. *Goed*.'). The writers in 'A Letter from Home' appear also to exist within a mobile, networked literary space of the kind that joins up easily with the story's linguistic fluidity. All three writers mentioned in the story (du Preez himself, Potgieter, and another, Dick) have had employment in universities, while du Preez is 'made' editor of a literary periodical called '*Onwards*', which leads him to get back in touch with Potgieter (see Lessing 2003: 226–7).

Lessing's portrayal of the university, however, refuses to realise its potential as a site of cosmopolitan exchange. Dick – mentioned only in passing at the start of the story – is said to have

> a poetry Scholarship from a Texas University and he's lecturing the Texans about letters and life too in Suid Afrika, South Africa to you (forgive the hostility) and his poems are read, so they tell me, wherever the English read poetry. (226)

At the level of narrative detail, here Lessing evokes a notional cosmopolitan internationalism – an American university sponsoring a South African poet who is widely disseminated in English. But the ideal shades into the real in the strict geographical designations of Texas against

South Africa, which themselves conceal an even more negative global equivalence – with both places segregated similarly along racial lines. In the absence too of anything dialogic in Dick's mere 'lecturing', and in the linguistic politics of the passage – where an act of translation ('Suid Afrika, South Africa to you') suggests an act of 'hostility' that must be 'forgive[n]' – Lessing suggests that in the world-system of 'A Letter from Home', violent divisions and borders between people and places must still remain.

The prehistory to the main events narrated in 'A Letter from Home' folds in both du Preez's and Potgieter's relationship to the institution of the university. Du Preez relates the fact that Potgieter once 'got a type of unofficial grace-gift job at St – University on the strength of those poems of his'. In his capacity as a 'sort of unofficial Laureate at that University', Potgieter is said to have

> produced a book of poems which had the whole God-fearing place sweating and sniffing out heresy of all kinds, sin, sex, liberalism, brother-love, etc., and so on; but, of course, in a civilized country (I say this under my breath, or I'll get the sack from my University, and I've got four daughters these days, had you forgotten?) no one would see anything in them but good poetry. (226–7)

After 'the good country boys from their fine farms and the smart town boys from their big houses all started looking sideways and making remarks', du Preez says that Potgieter resigned and withdrew to 'live in Blagspruit in the Orange Free, where his Tantie Gertrude had a house' (227). Alongside its careful patterning of centres and peripheries – town and country, the connected university and the remote hometown – the general detail here implies that, unlike with Dick, both Potgieter's and du Preez's involvement is with South African universities. And while the urge to translate still runs through the fluid texture of du Preez's prose (even within the same language: 'etc., and so on'), his parenthetical remark about his own position in a university shows a more rigid complicity with the status quo. Therefore, in the world picture built up at the start of 'A Letter from Home', the received boundary lines of the nation and its incumbent proprieties endure, and are policed effectively, from without and within any potentially offending subjects. The story is quick to set out its dominant rhythm, where forms of literary/political openness, on local and global scales, are proffered and then withdrawn. Transcendent literary value, and its expanding dissemination through translation are forestalled, for example: 'those poems of [Potgieter's] [. . .] God they were good. Not that you or any other English-speaking domkop will ever know, because they don't translate out of Afrikaans'

(226). And in the political realm too, the editorship of the progressive-sounding periodical *Onwards* leads du Preez merely to seek out 'our indigenous poets': the racialised overtones here show that the struggles the story portrays are those of white writers automatically privileged within the system of apartheid; the only black voice heard, sketchily, in the story is of Potgieter's cook, Esther.

'A Letter from Home' is thus the pessimistic mirror image of 'The Small Personal Voice'. Where Lessing's earlier essay speaks from outside a set of closed systems to present an open, global alternative, her later story speaks from within a set of closed systems, merely confirming their insurmountability. And so whereas in 'The Small Personal Voice', writerly commitment, set on a global stage, takes place at the intersection of the ethical demand and the political decision, in 'A Letter from Home' commitment is merely an unintended consequence of its national conditions. Discussing Potgieter's resignation and retreat to the country, du Preez gives one reason as the fact that

> our Hans, he was reduced to pap, because he's not a fighter, Hans, he was never a taker of positions on the side of justice, freedom and the rest, for to tell you the truth, I don't think he ever got round to defining them. (227)

In the ideal 'civilized country', 'good poetry' can be fully realised in its ideal autonomous form, a form that is preliminary to politics, with its taking of positions and definitions of 'justice, freedom and the rest'. But in more inopportune conditions, mere 'good poetry' takes on other, seemingly committed, resonances. As the 'God-fearing place' of 'St – University' is in South Africa, a primary alertness to religious taboo ('sin, sex') quickly shades into political taboos coded along racial lines – 'liberalism' and 'brother-love' are impossible under apartheid. Indeed, Lessing leaves a near blind spot in the story as to whether the writers she portrays personally advocate justice and equality at all; certainly du Preez's letter gives itself away in part with a parenthetical reference to 'the kaffir church down in the Location' (230) – the only explicit irruption in the story of South Africa's violent determinations of space and language along racial lines.

In what becomes, from one perspective, a scathingly ironic allegory for the struggle of the individual writer's vision against the demands of the community, the main body of the story has du Preez relate a visit to remote Blagspruit to see Potgieter. After du Preez contacts Potgieter for some poems for *Onwards*, he eventually receives a reply that mentions nothing of poetry, and is written 'in a sort of Gothic print, each letter a work of art, like a medieval manuscript' (227). So on a trip back from Johannesburg, du Preez decides to 'drop in' on Potgieter at

Blagspruit, finding Potgieter's house run by the stern, religious Esther, and his days dedicated to running a store and maintaining good standing with his fellow townspeople (228). After a period of heavy drinking, Potgieter reveals a manuscript to du Preez, written in the same ornate script as his earlier letter, he says, to prevent anyone in the town reading his work. The two then proceed to the veld to destroy the manuscript, although ineffectually, as in the morning du Preez sees Potgieter 'chasing about after screws of paper that were whirling around among the dust and stuff' in the morning wind (235). After du Preez returns home, he receives another letter from Potgieter, this time in 'ordinary writing, like yours or mine, but rather unformed and wild', warning that he has escaped Blagspruit to head North, as '[t]hey know me now' (236–7).

The story's central symbol reaches its fullest expression with the destruction of du Preez's manuscript, but is set up earlier. Initially, out in the veld, the two men come by a 'butcher-bird's cache', where every thorn of a thorn tree has 'a beetle or a worm or something stuck on it'. Potgieter's attention is drawn to one beetle that manages to extract itself from its thorn. As the beetle is 'trying to up itself' from its back on the ground, Potgieter

> *bent down, picked up the beetle and stuck it back on the thorn.* Carefully, you understand, so that the thorn went back into the hole it had already made, you could see he was trying not to hurt the beetle. (231, italics original)

Dismayed, du Preez pleads, 'Hans, man, for God's sake!', to which Potgieter says, 'reproachfully, "The ants would have killed it, just look!" Well, the ground was swarming with ants of one kind or another, so there was logic in it' (231). This symbol of obsessive conservatism, of the preference for solitary defeat rather than defeat at the hands of the mass is then transfigured in reverse at the culmination of the story. The manner in which du Preez and Potgieter destroy Potgieter's work is to go to another thorn tree on the veld 'and we tore out the pages from his manuscript and we made them into little screws of paper and we stuck them all over the thorns'. The two then 'wept for the state of our country and the state of poetry' and 'drank a lot more brandy, and the ants came after it and us, so we staggered back down the gleaming sleeping main street of Blagspruit' to bed (234). But whereas the beetle is given a solitary death on a thorn rather than a ravaging by the ants, Potgieter's writing is cast back to the potential attack of his community by the wind. The two writers recapture 'perhaps a third' of the screwed-up manuscript pages, and while du Preez sees the event as a drunken accident rectifiable in literary terms – 'you could write them down again, couldn't you? You couldn't have forgotten them surely?' – Potgieter's worries are personal and social: 'anyone can read them now, don't you see that, man?' (235).

Moving from Potgieter's withdrawal to a remote town, through his use of a cipher to disguise his poetry, to his failed act of destruction, and then his eventual and open-ended escape, 'A Letter from Home' tracks the escalating decisions of a writer in his attempts to reach a position of complete non-commitment. Lessing shows these decisions to be not only ethically dubious, but also an impossibility; the charged political atmosphere and oppressive culture of South Africa creates a demand that must be answered, and all writing becomes committed writing of some sort – even if, as hinted, that commitment is to the status quo of apartheid. Moreover, the idea of apartheid as status quo seems all the more potent given the publication date of 'A Letter from Home'. In 1961 – only two years prior to the publication date of Lessing's story – South Africa became a sovereign republic, but still legislated to maintain the regime of apartheid. In relation to the dialectic set up in 'The Small Personal Voice', it could be said that 'A Letter from Home' dramatises the unavoidability of the ethical demand of writerly commitment, and parodies the attempt of its central figure to put off his moment of political decision. But equally, the story of Potgieter seems not only more nationally determined than 'The Small Personal Voice', but also less reminiscently Sartrean in the terms on which it approaches questions of commitment. Indeed, Potgieter's desire to create an autonomous artwork, and du Preez's insistence on the abstract value of Potigeter's work seems more like the *'avant-garde* abstraction' formulated in Theodor W. Adorno's famous critique of Sartrean commitment, which, contra Sartre, 'has nothing in common with conceptual or logical abstraction', and is unavoidably 'a reflex response to the abstraction of the law which objectively dominates society' (190).

At the same time, 'A Letter from Home' and 'The Small Personal Voice' are still consistent with each other in the sense that both stage an encounter between aesthetics and politics with a global horizon, and in the same manner. 'A Letter from Home' is geared to convince about its truthfulness. In particular, Lessing shows du Preez's realism to be structured by number. In the story's first paragraph, for example, du Preez relates that it has been ten years since Potgieter lost his job at St– University – an oft-repeated detail in the story; in the second paragraph, 'when I counted up the years it was eight since I'd even thought of him, even counting those times when one says drunk at dawn: Remember Hans? Now, there was a poet . . .' (Lessing 2003: 226, 227 (Lessing's ellipsis)). But as the latter example shows, in one way or another, du Preez's reliance on number is a reliance on an unreliable system. Ultimately, the story's basis in number equates to an assemblage of imprecise drunken counting, aimless temporal markers ('And half an hour later he'd say' (229), 'about an hour later' (232), 'I was working away there an hour or more' (233)), precisely measured racial profiling (Esther 'stood about six feet high' seen first holding a lamp 'up in one great black fist' (228)), and rhetorical aggrandisement ('Hans, you're right. You're right a thousand times.'(233)). Number might provide a nominal baseline of discrete units – as shown in the story's central image, with each individual thorn of a thorn tree impaled with an individual page of manuscript – but when summed up and totalled, all that remains is the architecture of oppression and the muddle of anecdote. Yet at the same time, the descriptive economy of 'A Letter from Home' matches that of 'The Small Personal Voice'. Both pieces put number into the service of *placing* the writer, drawing in a range of scales to show the extension of the writer's endeavours.

Therefore, when literature is discussed in 'A Letter from Home', the function Lessing assigns to number is exposed most clearly. Consider first, at the start of the story, du Preez's calculations regarding the literary value of Potgieter's work:

> Meanwhile, a third of the world's population or is it a fifth, or to put it another way, X5Y59 million people speak English (and it's increasing by six births a minute) but one million people speak Afrikaans, and though I say it in a whisper, man, only a fraction of them can read it, I mean to read it. But Hans is still a great poet. Right. (226)

And then later in the story, when du Preez has read Potgieter's manuscript, the manner in which he relates its contents:

> A kind of chronicle of Blagspruit it was, the lives of the citizens – well, need I elaborate, since the lives of citizens are the same everywhere in the world, but worse in Suid Afrika, and worse a million times in Blagspruit. (232–3)

In the first passage, du Preez's uncertain statistics and his strange quasi-algebraic formulation ('X5Y59') initiate an abruptly truncated act of numerical division that short-circuits its inevitable conclusion – that not many people would be able to appreciate Potgieter's work – to a statement of Potgieter's value as a poet. Here, the break in the mathematical logic exposes, at best, an internally inconsistent rhetorical gloss. And, in the second passage, following the same trajectory of the global scaling down to the local, number enters for emphasis, but malfunctions again, offering radically inconsistent grounds for the comparison at work – 'same' shifts to 'worse', and then to 'worse a million times'. If 'The Small Personal Voice' attempts to manage scale by thinking from a baseline of weighable, manipulable units, then 'A Letter from Home' demonstrates a similar impetus in order to stage its failure.

'A Letter from Home' bears an intrinsic – if negative – relation to 'The Small Personal Voice'. Both pieces take for granted the fact that a writer's work cannot avoid a political commitment, and that this commitment has a global horizon. Lessing makes clear too that an acknowledgement of this insight is not enough – it must be worked through and properly expressed as well. But in du Preez's abruptly interrupted and faulty equations, 'A Letter from Home' shows the difficulties – and the abuses – that can come with such working through. In keeping with the manifesto-like force of its rhetoric, 'The Small Personal Voice' is more squarely invested in the imperative to find a form for inscribing a global background to the writer's commitment. But in 'A Letter from Home', this inscription of globality is failingly warded off, and so is in many ways all the more present.

Ultimately, then, in these two early attempts to think at a world scale, Lessing is concerned with the problems that can occur therein – foreshadowing the ideas explored in later works like *The Four-Gated City* (1969) and *Shikasta* (1979). Both 'A Letter from Home' and 'The Small Personal Voice' consider in different ways the notion that scaling-up suffers from being performed in terms of abstract notions of freedom, existentialism and value, rather than by attending to the specific transnational networks and institutions that constrain but also enable global commitment. But Lessing is equally concerned with pursuing these problems to the point at which they become specifically literary problems. In different ways, the two texts approach the benefits and pitfalls of a scaling-up achieved through the accumulation of number, with this numerical form becoming the basis for a literary rendering of a global commitment. Talking of his notion of the 'world picture', Martin Heidegger notes that

> as soon as the gigantic in planning and calculating and adjusting and making secure shifts over out of the quantitative and becomes a special quality, then what is gigantic, and what can seemingly always be calculated completely, becomes, precisely through this, incalculable. (Heidegger 1977: 135)

It is the point before the 'shift' that Heidegger isolates that Lessing works to describe, and to hold in check. Hers is a formal means of establishing the ground for the 'shift' that Heidegger describes, in order to best convey the true bigness – and the equally big ethico-political pull – of the world.

Note

1. This chapter uses the word 'commitment' as an English translation of the 'engagement' of Sartre's French.

Works Cited

Adorno, Theodor (1980), 'Commitment', trans. Francis McDonagh, in *Aesthetics and Politics,* London: Verso, pp. 177–95.

Apter, Emily (2008), 'Untranslatables: A World System', *New Literary History,* 39:3, 581–98.

Bentley, Nick (2009), 'Doris Lessing's *The Golden Notebook*: An Experiment in Critical Fiction', in Susan Watkins and Alice Ridout (eds), *Doris Lessing: Border Crossings,* London and New York: Continuum, pp. 44–61.

Dimock, Wai Chee (2006), *Through Other Continents: American Literature Across Deep Time,* Princeton: Princeton University Press.

Hargreaves, Tracy (2012), '". . . to find a form that accommodates the mess": Truth Telling from Doris Lessing to B. S. Johnson', *Yearbook of English Studies,* 42, 204–22.

Heidegger, Martin (1977), 'The Age of the World Picture', trans. William Lovitt, in *The Question Concerning Technology and Other Essays,* New York: Harper & Row, pp. 115–54.

Hook, Andrew (ed.) (1962), *Edinburgh International Festival 1962: 'The Novel Today',* Edinburgh.

Lessing, Doris (1994), 'The Small Personal Voice', in *A Small Personal Voice: Essays, Reviews, Interviews,* ed. Paul Schlueter, London: Flamingo, pp. 7–26.

—— (2003), 'A Letter from Home', in *The Sun Between Their Feet: Collected African Stories Volume Two,* London: Flamingo, pp. 226–37.

Sartre, Jean-Paul (1967), *What is Literature?,* trans. Bernard Frechtman, London: Methuen.

Sinfield, Alan (2004), *Literature, Politics and Culture in Postwar Britain,* revised ed., London: Continuum.

Walkowitz, Rebecca L. (2012), *Cosmopolitan Style: Modernism Beyond the Nation,* New York and Chichester: Columbia University Press.

Chapter 2

'I'm an adolescent. And that's how I'm going to stay': Lessing and Youth Culture 1956–1962

Nick Bentley

The mid-to-late 1950s saw an explosion of youth subcultures in Britain – teenagers, Teddy Boys, jazz fans, hipsters, beatniks, mods and rockers, each of which generated a combination of moral panic and media fascination. In Doris Lessing's writing in the late 1950s and early 1960s youth is a recurring theme, including in her plays *Each to His Own Wilderness* (1959) and *Play With a Tiger* (1962), her critical essay 'The Small Personal Voice' (1957), and her novels *A Ripple From the Storm* (1958) and *The Golden Notebook* (1962). This chapter will trace Lessing's engagement with youth culture in her writing and argue that she articulates concerns within the New Left and British culture more broadly and reveals some of the tensions and fears concerning youth, while holding on to the hope that youth could still offer a committed and collective form of resistance to dominant ideologies. Her work will be read against contemporary cultural commentary from the New Left, and against other fiction and commentary on youth from the period, including works by Lynne Reid Banks, Anthony Burgess, Shelagh Delaney, Nell Dunn, Richard Hoggart, Colin MacInnes, Alan Sillitoe and Muriel Spark.

The British New Left were split on whether to see these new youth groups as indicative of a consumer-led Americanisation of traditional working-class British culture or as potential sites for cultural (and political) rebellion. Several writers associated with this group entered this debate about the economic and cultural contexts for the rise of youth subcultures in the 1950s, including Derek Allcorn, Michael Kullman, Stuart Hall, Clancy Sigal, and on the margins of this group Richard Hoggart, Colin MacInnes, Alan Sillitoe, Colin Wilson and Lessing (see Bentley 2005). All of these writers were interested, to differing degrees, in the way that the 1950s economic boom was changing established frameworks of social class in both cultural and political terms, and, in particular, how this trend was affecting youth (Allcorn 1958; Kullman

1958; Sigal 1958; Hoggart 1957; Hall 1959a; Williams 1961; MacInnes 1959). The New Left journal *Universities and New Left Review*, of which Lessing was a member of the editorial board, was a prime site for the articulation of these ideas, and as Greta Duncan and Roy Wilkie observed of the representation of youth in the mainstream media: 'Teenagers are accused not only of lacking a sense of responsibility, but of having no respect for their elders [. . .] It is striking that most people talk of teenagers in negative terms' (24). Duncan and Wilkie, however, aimed to counter this misrepresentation by surveying Glasgow teenagers in one of a series of articles that appeared in this journal in the late 1950s. In another article, Stuart Hall noted that the 'problem' of youth was associated with changing historical contexts in the 1950s, with their political sensibilities affected by a new sense of individualism fuelled by post-war patterns of consumerism. As Hall writes: 'Instinctively, young working-class people are radical. They hate the stuffiness of the class system, though they cannot give it a political name [. . .] they feel and experience these things in private, emotional ways, for this is how adolescents encounter the world' (1959b: 2). This confused mix of apparent political apathy and potential radicalism is seen in the differing responses to youth in much of the literature of the period. In Anthony Burgess's *A Clockwork Orange* (1962) the main character Alex reads in a 'gazetta' 'a bolshy big article on Modern Youth (meaning me, so I gave the old bow, grinning like bezoomy) by some very clever bald chelloveck [. . .] it was nice to go on knowing one was making the news all the time' (32). Lessing would have been aware of these debates due to her connections to the New Left as documented by Jenny Taylor (1982) and Sandra Singer (2015); as she explains in her autobiography *Walking in the Shade*, she lived during this period 'just a short walk away from the New Left and their purlieus [. . .] and sometimes they dropped in' (288).

One of the key figures presenting a critical evaluation of youth subcultures in the 1950s is Richard Hoggart, who discusses what he calls the 'Juke-box Boys' in *The Uses of Literacy* (1957): a group who hang around in milkbars and whose attempt at cultural rebellion is actually a manifestation of the insidious effects of an Americanised consumerism:

> this is all a thin and pallid sort of dissipation, a sort of spiritual dry-rot amid the odour of boiled milk. Many of the customers – their clothes, their hairstyles, their facial expressions all indicate – are living to a large extent in a myth-world compounded of a few simple elements which they take to be those of American life. (248)

Lessing's *Each His Own Wilderness* resonates with similar attitudes to this New Left writing on youth. The play sets up several scenes in which the main character, Myra, who is in her late forties and has been involved with left-wing political groups for many years, argues with Tony, her son, who has just completed his national service. These arguments are often generational; for example, when Myra learns of Tony's plan to leave university and become an electrician she responds in terms that echo Hoggart: 'I suppose you'll spend jolly evenings in the local coffee bar, join a skiffle group, become a scruffy little bohemian, one of the neo-conformists, enjoying all the postures of rebellion from safe positions of utter respectability' (178). Similarly, Tommy in *The Golden Notebook* (son of Anna Freeman's friend Molly and her divorced husband Richard) is associated with coffee-bar drop-out culture; Richard speculates that Tommy's reluctance to join his father's business will result in him becoming 'some sort of a coffee-bar bum' (57). Both Myra and Richard, as representatives of a parent culture, seem to be responding to the contemporary moral panic about the apathy and potential delinquency of youth. In the play, it is apparent that Tony has reached a position of political apathy after much thought, unlike Hoggart's teenagers who it is assumed are apolitical; nevertheless, it reveals Lessing's desire to engage in a critical debate about youth. Similarly, Tommy shows he has a far more reflective consideration of his parents' cultures than the accusation that he will blindly follow the most visibly demonised youth cultures of the period suggests. In contrast, in *Play With a Tiger*, Lessing corroborates concerns about contemporary youth as apolitical and overly individualised, its passions spent on subcultural in-fighting rather than challenging the system. As Dave, a rootless American drifter in his thirties, describes: 'At the street corners the kids are not prepared to fight the world. They fight each other. Everyone of us, we were prepared to take on the whole world single-handed. Not any longer, they know better, they're scared' (37). However, Dave's opinions are far from endorsed by the play as a whole.

This criticism of the perceived apathy of contemporary youth was extended by some commentators to concerns about the direction certain youth cultures were taking. Colin MacInnes's *Absolute Beginners* (1959) (which does have many positive things to say about contemporary youth) identifies the development of right-wing racist attitudes amongst some aspects of youth culture, especially the Teds; the novel includes one character called 'the Wizard', who joins a neo-fascist group called the White Protection League, and another nicknamed 'Ed the Ted' whose random acts of violence are often directed towards the non-white population of London. Although the 'White Protection League' is fictional it almost certainly refers to the White Defence League formed in Britain in 1957 and run by the neo-Nazi Colin Jordan from an office

in Notting Hill. The novel culminates with the media misrepresentation of acts of violence meted out by youths on black people in Notting
Hill in 1958 as a 'race riot'. It is not clear if Lessing knew MacInnes's
novel, but she would have known the Notting Hill area well, having
lived there for a short period when she first arrived in London. *Each His
Own Wilderness* was first performed in March of 1958, so the 'riots'
are not mentioned, but the play does enter into debates on the political
commitment of youth. Myra comments: 'The young are so boring. I've
come to the conclusion I can't stand anyone under the age of 35' (131),
and criticises youth for being politically apathetic, challenging Tony as
representative of his generation: 'I do wish young people would join in
these demonstrations. Why don't you? – we're such a middle aged lot.
Why do you leave it all to us?' (109). Tony declines to respond to this
directly, however, his indifference to (and implicit critique of) Myra's
political activism suggests a rejection of his mother's call to arms. The
play frequently returns to the differing attitudes to political activism represented by the older and younger generations, but ultimately it rejects a
satisfying resolution of a way forward out of this impasse.

Lessing's discussion of youth in terms of generations resonates with
Karl Mannheim's essay 'The Problem of Generations', which would
have been known in the New Left circles with which she was involved;
Mannheim's essay was republished in 1952 and is mentioned by Charles
Taylor in a 1958 issue of *Universities and Left Review*. Mannheim identifies a process of history that is developed in terms of new generations
in cycles of around thirty years. He places his theory of generations
between two traditions – the rationalist approach dominant in French
philosophical thought and a German tradition based on a 'romantic-
historical' formulation. The former he sees as based primarily on a
quantifiable analysis of the changes between generations; the latter as
qualitative which, as he notes following Wilhelm Dilthey, complicates
the idea of progress: 'Every moment in time is therefore in reality more
than a point-like event – it is a temporal volume having more than one
dimension, because it is always experienced by several generations at
once' (283).[1] Similarly, Lessing sees the 'problem' of the generations as
a mixture of concrete responses by the younger generation to specific
social and political contexts mixed with a broader sense of the development of progressive generations, and a specific (political) attitude to
the present. It is the balancing of these two views that allows Lessing,
through characters whose views are endorsed by the work as a whole,
to criticise youth for not responding actively to contemporary political issues, while at the same time identifying a permanent radical spirit
associated with youth which transcends material notions of age. It is this

latter approach that is encapsulated in a comment that Anna, the main character in *Play with a Tiger*, makes: 'I'm an adolescent. And that's how I'm going to stay' (49).

Lessing and MacInnes are not the only novelists who address concerns with youth during this time. Alan Sillitoe's characters are often seen as the quintessential Angry Young Men of the period and in his two central works of the late 1950s, *Saturday Night and Sunday Morning* (1958) and 'The Loneliness of the Long Distance Runner' (1959), he explores the same shifting terrain of class and youth; while the identification of youth culture with transgression and violence reaches its extremity in Anthony Burgess's 1962 novel *A Clockwork Orange*, in which the violence and deviancy associated with youth cultures is preferable to a society in which all forms of transgression are eradicated. Muriel Spark's *The Ballad of Peckham Rye* (1960) differs from Hoggart and Sillitoe in that her novel is sensitive to the ways in which youth culture is coded along gender lines that reinforce patriarchal power relationships. The outsider figure Dougal Douglas, an impish hyperreal character typical of Spark's fiction of this period, is contrasted with the representative Teddy Boy Trevor Lomas, who far from being a radical youth figure, is representative of the prevailing dominant culture. Spark's representation of Lomas's subculture echoes Hoggart's anxieties over contemporary youth as prey to the shiny barbarism of consumer capitalism: 'Most of the men looked as if they had not properly woken from deep sleep, but glided as if drugged, and with half closed lids, towards their chosen partner' (76). The fight that ensues between Lomas and Douglas is parodied by the novel (and indeed by Douglas) as a typical homosocial contest for the position of kingpin amongst the youth of the area. This awareness of the gendered structures of youth culture is also lacking in much of the other fiction on youth culture of the period, particularly that associated with Angry Young Men writers like Sillitoe, John Braine, John Osborne and David Storey, who, as Lynne Segal (1990) and Alice Ferrebe (2005) have noted, tended to reinforce these conventional patriarchal gender positions. In contrast, in texts by female writers such as Lynne Reid Banks (for example, in her 1960 novel *The L-Shaped Room*), Shelagh Delaney (in the play *A Taste of Honey*, 1959), and Nell Dunn (*Up the Junction*) the intersection of the politics of gender and class (and race and sexuality in the case of *A Taste of Honey*) is framed against the backdrop of youth cultures and concerns. As Sandra Singer has identified in Delaney's play in particular, 'Generational conflict is evident in the sharp dialogue between Helen and Jo' (the central mother-daughter relationship in the play) with respect to discourses of race and sexuality (84).

Lessing is also aware of the gender context for youth cultures, in particular as it is manifest in the jazz subculture associated with several of her male characters. In *The Golden Notebook*, Saul, who becomes Anna's lover, is associated with jazz; as he explains, 'my character was formed by Armstrong, Bechet and Bessie Smith' (558). However, Lessing's novels are far more suspicious of the gender politics implied in the celebration of the freedoms of the jazz subculture in works by male writers of the period such as MacInnes. Anna in *The Golden Notebook* describes jazz as being initially 'good humoured and warm and accepting [. . . but] It's got nothing to do with us, we aren't like that' (558). She goes on to equate jazz with the idea of the *mensch*, a fixation in the modern (American) male with his resistance to any form of restraint, which in practice results in men being unable to commit to relationships with women: 'I'm a mensch. I'm not a woman's pet, to be locked up' (560). This identification of women as inherently part of the forces of containment for the resistant male is something Segal identifies in much of the Angry Young Man writing of the period. See, for example, Jimmy Porter's fear of being tied down by his middle-class wife in *Look Back in Anger*. As Alice Ferrebe notes, 'in the England of the 1950s jazz's attendant ambience was rather one of beer and blokes, a rebellion that satisfyingly combined machismo with being in-the-know' (42). Lessing also presents this kind of *mensch* figure in characters such as Dave in *Play With a Tiger* and, to a certain extent, Philip in *Each His Own Wilderness*.

Jazz, and similar subcultures referred to by Lessing were associated with left-wing politics in the 1950s. The reference to Tony joining a skiffle group in *Each His Own Wilderness* and becoming a scruffy little bohemian connects him to the 1950s British folk revival movement that included singer songwriters such as Ewan McCall and A. L. Lloyd, both members of the Communist Party of Great Britain. However, it is presented by Lessing's Myra as leftist posturing, an emphasis on style over practical engagement. A similar character appears in MacInnes's *Absolute Beginners*, nicknamed Ron the Marxist by the novel's teenage narrator and described as being 'closely connected with the ballad-and-blues movement' (143). Both characters bemoan how the jazz scene is being commercialised by local impresarios, though it still carries the progressive prospect for a resistance to the prevailing forces of capitalism as they manifest themselves in the 1950s in divisions across class, gender, ethnicity and sexuality. As the teenager writes:

> But the great thing about the jazz world, and all the kids that enter into it, is that no one, not a soul, cares what your class is, or what your race is, or

what your income, or if you're boy, or girl, or bent, or versatile, or what you are – so long as you behave yourself, and have left all that crap behind you, too, when you come in the jazz club door. (68–9)

This is not a politics of organised parties, but one that reflects an organic, lived ideology of cultural practices and what Raymond Williams (1961) was theorising in this period as structures of feeling. Jazz is also the sub-culture of choice for Jimmy Porter, the breaking of traditional musical forms in jazz improvisation made analogous to his resistance to the constraints placed upon him by conventional mores related to class, gender and sexuality.

In terms of literary and intellectual contexts, jazz was often associated with the philosophical existentialism of Jean-Paul Sartre and Albert Camus during the 1950s, or at least a popular understanding of it. In a British context, Colin Wilson's *The Outsider* had gained a certain amount of attention when it was published in 1956 as an existential exploration of contemporary culture that was particularly associated with youth. For Lessing, however, this kind of self-searching introspection stultifies any potential radicalism of youth culture, and as Adam Guy describes in this volume, she critiques Wilson in her 1957 essay, 'The Small Personal Voice'. Lessing uses youth to detail the debilitating cultural climate that is stifling effective political resistance in Britain in the later 1950s. Speaking from the position of a writer entering middle age (Lessing was in her late thirties when she wrote the essay) she identifies two main, interrelated contexts for the new generation: imaginative writing and the contemporary socialist discourse. For the former, she cites Wilson as an example of a new generation's outlook:

> There is Mr Colin Wilson, who sees no reason why he should not state that: 'Like all my generation I am anti-humanist and anti-materialist.' Mr Wilson has every right to be anti-humanist and anti-materialist; but is a sign of his invincible British provincialism that he should claim to speak for his generation. The fact is that outside the very small sub-class of humanity Mr Wilson belongs to, vast numbers of young people are both humanist and materialist. Millions of young people in China, the Soviet Union, and India for instance. And the passions that excite the young African nationalist, five years literate, watching the progress of dams building in India and China, because he knows what goes on in other countries intimately affects himself, have little in common with the passions of Mr Wilson. Mr Wilson may find the desire of backward people not to starve, not to remain illiterate, rather uninteresting; but he and people like him should at least try and understand it exists, and what a great and creative force it is, one which will affect us all. (25)

Lessing internationalises the idea of youth and critiques a brand of British localism that has deserted the possibility of a new generation becoming actively political. The distinction between different conceptions of youth in different parts of the world also chimes with Mannheim's emphasis on the specific spatial and historical locations of generations:

> Only where contemporaries definitely are in a position to participate as an integrated group in certain common experiences can we rightly speak of a generation. Mere contemporaneity becomes socially significant only when it also involves participation in the same historical and social circumstances. (298)

This attitude is bound up with what Lessing sees as the crisis on the Left and its inability to appeal to a new generation of British youth, who are unsatisfied with prevailing ideologies but have no confident form of political resistance. As she explains in the essay:

> The other day I met a girl who said she envies me because I had had at least ten years of being able to believe in the purity of communism; which advantage was denied to her generation. All of us, she said, were living off the accumulated fat of the socialist hump. She was a socialist herself, but without any enthusiasm. (26)

For Lessing, the crisis of communism is an initially collective solidarity subdividing into factions and subgroups, each with their own nuances of cultural expression. This theme is pursued in *A Ripple from the Storm* (1958), the third part of the *Children of Violence* quintet, with specific reference to the context of Southern African politics during the Second World War. This novel, like Anna's Black Notebook, describes a subcultural group of characters in their early twenties who are brought together by their affiliation to the Communist Party. For several of these characters joining this group is also a distancing from their parent culture: Jasmine Cohen's parents have 'officially disowned her' (although she still lives at home) and the protagonist Martha Quest's 'own mother had also cast her off' (11). At the beginning they are 'talking about the difficulties of "re-educating the older generation to socialist ethics", and what sort of work would be best suited to [their] capacities . . . work which would release them into being much better and nobler people than they were now' (11). As in *The Golden Notebook* the Left is increasingly subdividing into different factions: '"Bloody social democrats," said Jackie. "You're as bad as the Left book club crowd"' (14). Martha has

> ceased to feel a secret disquiet because of the way people fell automatically into groups: a law expressed in this instance, by the way audiences for Help Our Allies, Sympathizers of Russia, or the Progressive Club could be recognized at a glance, all drawn together by some invisible bond, although they

thought that an individual act of will had made them choose this or that allegiance. (11)

This 'invisible bond' is similar to the way in which several critics have suggested youth subcultures cohere internally. As Albert K. Cohen was arguing in a period coterminous to Lessing's novel 'all human action [. . .] is an ongoing series of efforts to solve problems' and 'that all [. . .] factors and circumstances that [. . .] produce a problem come from [. . .] two sources, the actor's "frame of reference" and the "situation" he confronts' (51). In Lessing's case, the situation relates to the specific sociopolitical contexts pertaining in Southern Rhodesia during the Second World War, which are negotiated differently by groups, each with their own specific ideological interests, and frames of reference.

The Golden Notebook also develops Lessing's exploration of how small cultural groups behave, and resonates with theories from the period about the formation and practice of subcultures. The clearest example can be seen in the description of the socialist circles in which Anna and Molly move. Anna describes three sets of letters she receives separately from three men involved in communist party politics; one set before the Twentieth Congress of the Communist Party (during which Stalin's purges were officially reported), one set after, and then a third set after the quelling of the Hungarian rebellion. Anna is struck by the interchangeability of these letters: 'in phraseology, style, tone, they were identical' (67). This example of group expression unsettles Anna and encourages her to consider the ways in which subcultures develop that repress individual singularities, leading her to speculate, 'Well, surely the thought follows – what stereotype am I? What anonymous whole am I part of?' (67).

Elsewhere in the text, the novel's organisation allows Anna to reflect back to her youth in Southern Rhodesia, and although the group described in these sections is not of the form of youth subcultures that were appearing in Britain in the late 1950s, it has similarities in terms of its internal constitution, collective cultural behaviours and practices, and a self-aware acknowledgement of difference from the prevailing (adult) culture amongst white Rhodesians of the mid-twentieth century. Ken Gelder defines subcultures as:

> groups of people that have something in common with each other (i.e. they share a problem, an interest, a practice) which distinguishes them in a significant way from the member of other social groups [. . . They] have come to designate social groups which are perceived to deviate from the normative ideals of adult communities. (2)

This section of the novel retraces themes covered in *A Ripple from the Storm*; however, the complex set of narrative frames allows Lessing, through Anna, a certain distance from which to critique and ironise aspects of the group.

Perhaps the most important reflection on the formation of alternative youth subcultures comes in the narrative associated with Tommy in the first two Free Women sections of *The Golden Notebook*. Tommy is clearly suffering from an existential crisis brought on by a number of factors, including the difficulty of finding meaning in any of the career options he has been offered by his father and his mother; he is 'suffering from a paralysis of the will' (261). He finds his father's business culture ethically and politically suspect, partly from his exposure to Molly and Anna's socialist politics during his upbringing; however, at this moment of late adolescence, Tommy finds that the ideals which he has imbued from Molly and Anna are now breaking apart. This leaves him fractured and uncertain how to proceed. He is critical of the contemporary manifestations of left-wing groups as he describes his friend Tony's involvement with

> the group of new socialists – mostly Oxford Types? They are going to start a magazine, *The Left Review,* or something [. . .] They shout slogans [. . .] They use that awful jargon [. . .] Because they're young. I suppose you are going to say, but it's not good enough [. . .] They rush around sticking up posters and shouting slogans. (270)

Tommy is here, of course, referring to the New Left that itself was attempting to cope with the fallout of the revelations about the Stalinist purges and the crackdown on the Hungarian revolution. Tommy's critique of the New Left is not supported by Anna but his sentiment recognises that the new brand of socialist activity has an element of self-promotion and performativity that resonates with the way in which alternative youth subcultures of the period are being formed. Tommy attempts to kill himself shortly after this conversation, revealing the impasse he has reached with respect to identifying a viable future: both the parent culture and the youth subcultures that are available to him have been found to be lacking.

Lessing's concerns, therefore, seem to centre on the paucity of options open for people entering adulthood who feel inclined to resist the ideologies of the dominant parent culture, but whose means of resistance seem to be limited to either joining apolitical, fashionable subcultures that tend to value music and fashion above politics, or a New Left that itself is going through an ultimately unproductive period of introspection. Although her reading of contemporary youth is more complex than that offered by a writer such as Richard Hoggart, her various works of this period similarly reveal the crisis of the Left as inextricably bound up with concerns about the direction of youth culture and the lack of opportunities for a meaningful and committed form of resistance to the prevailing forms of capitalism and consumerism that are driving the period. Nevertheless, Lessing does not abandon the idea that it is with youth that the potential for a re-envisaged society is possible. Myra's statement in *Each His Own Wilderness,* quoted in the title of this chapter, reveals a conviction that it is important to hold on to the sense of idealism associated with youth while at the same time recognising that for this desire to achieve a successful form of rebellion the adolescent spirit has to be collectivised in meaningful ways.

In this context, it is interesting to turn to comments Lessing makes on youth in her 1971 Preface to *The Golden Notebook*. Here, the topic is addressed in two ways: one showing positive development and a sense of generational change in aspects of contemporary culture a decade after the original publication of the novel; and one that seems to suggest a defeat in the potential of youth to change prevailing attitudes. The young have 'created a culture of their own' that has rejected the image of the 'monstrously isolated, monstrously narcissistic' figure of the artist that Lessing felt was one of the themes of *The Golden Notebook* and a reflection of a particular attitude to creative practice in the late 1950s. This new creative youth culture has 'abolished that isolated, creative, sensitive figure – by copying him in hundreds of thousands' suggesting that there has indeed been a generational shift (of the order identified by Mannheim) between the immediate post-war generation and youth cultures that have emerged on the other side of the 1960s. The tenor of this achievement lies in the possibility for a new sense of connectivity between (young) people based on expressions of their (creative) individuality. The second way of addressing the topic, however, is less optimistic in its reference to the 'recent student rebellions' of 1968 which initially seemed to offer a radical change in how the hierarchical structures of education could be challenged by students developing their own syllabuses. According to Lessing these produced classes that were 'emotional, sometimes violent, angry, exciting, sizzling with life', with the implication that this challenge of the educational system might usher in more broad shifts in future power relationships in society. However, from the vantage of 1971, Lessing suggests that 'it seems as though the rebellion is over'.

These two seemingly contradictory readings parallel the ambivalence she registers towards youth cultures in the late 1950s. On the one hand, the old power relationships seem to be difficult to jettison, as evidenced by her reference to the failed student rebellions. Nevertheless, the potential for youth cultures to bridge the gap between the individual and the collective through new literary and aesthetic practices seems to offer the chance for a genuine generational shift. It is perhaps significant that the rebellion Lessing refers to here is specifically cultural and aesthetic, despite there being relatively little change in dominant economic and political structures over the same period. This could be seen to crystallise the changed generational attitudes anticipated by the New Left in which the rates of development in cultural and economic terms are divorced. For Lessing's generation, as evidenced in the debates she dramatises in *The Golden Notebook*, cultural revolution and political revolution are ineluctably connected; for the generation that emerges at the end of the 1960s, one could be achieved without the other.

Note

1. Mannheim makes reference to Dilthey's 'Über das Studium der Geschichte der Wissenschaften vom Menschen, der Gesellschaft und dem Staat' [1875], in *Gesammelte Schriften*, vol. 5 (1924), 36–41.

Works Cited

Allcorn, Derek (1958), 'The Unnoticed Generation', *Universities and Left Review*, 4, 54–8.

Banks, Lynne Reid [1960] (1962), *The L-Shaped Room*, London: Penguin.

Bentley, Nick (2005), 'The Young Ones: A Reassessment of the British New Left's Representation of 1950s Youth Subcultures', *European Journal of Cultural Studies* 8:1, 65–83.

Burgess, Anthony [1962] (2013), *A Clockwork Orange*, London: Penguin.

Cohen, Albert K. (1955), *Delinquent Boys: The Culture of the Gang*, New York: Free Press.

Delaney, Shelagh (1959), *A Taste of Honey*, London: Methuen.

Dilthey, Wilhelm [1875] (1924), 'Über das Studium der Geschichte der Wissenschaften vom Menschen, der Gesellschaft und dem Staat', in *Gesammelte Schriften*, vol. 5, 36–41.

Duncan, Greta, and Roy Wilkie (1958), 'Glasgow Adolescents', *Universities and Left Review*, 5, 24–5.

Dunn, Nell [1963] (2013), *Up the Junction*, London: Virago.

Ferrebe, Alice (2005), *Masculinity in Male-Authored Fiction, 1950–2000: Keeping it Up*, Basingstoke: Palgrave.

Gelder, Ken (2005), 'General Introduction' in Ken Gelder (ed.), *The Subcultures Reader*, 2nd edn, London: Routledge, pp. 1–15.

Hall, Stuart (1959a), 'Absolute Beginnings', *Universities and Left Review*, 7, 17–25.

Hall, Stuart (1959b), 'Politics of Adolescence?', *Universities and Left Review*, 6, 2–4.

Hoggart, Richard [1957] (1958), *The Uses of Literacy: Aspects of Working-Class Life*, Harmondsworth: Penguin.

Kullman, Michael (1958), 'The Anti-Culture Born of Despair', *Universities and Left Review*, 4: 51–4.

Kullman, Michael, Derek Allcorn, and Clancy Sigal (1958), 'The Face of Youth' *Universities and Left Review*, 4: 51–65.

Lessing, Doris (1957), 'The Small Personal Voice', in Tom Maschler (ed.), *Declaration*, London: MacGibbon & Kee, pp. 11–28.

—— (1966), *Play with a Tiger and Other Plays*, London: Flamingo.

—— [1962] (1973), *The Golden Notebook*, London: Grafton.

—— (1997), *Walking in the Shade: Part Two of My Autobiography, 1949–1962*, London: Harper Collins.

MacInnes, Colin (1986), *England, Half English*, London: Chatto & Windus.

—— [1959] (2011), *Absolute Beginners*, London: Allison & Busby.

Mannheim, Karl [1923] (1952), 'The Problem of Generations', in Paul Kecskemeti (ed.), *Karl Mannheim: Essays*, London: Routledge, pp. 276–322.

Segal, Lynne (1990), 'Look Back in Anger: Men in the Fifties', in *Slow Motion: Changing Masculinities, Changing Men*, London: Virago, pp. 1–25.

Sigal, Clancy (1958), 'Nihilism's Organization Man', *Universities and Left Review*, 4, 59–65.

Sillitoe, Alan [1959] (1985), 'The Loneliness of the Long Distance Runner', in *The Loneliness of the Long Distance Runner*, London: Panther.

—— [1958] (1994), *Saturday Night and Sunday Morning*, London: Flamingo.

Singer, Sandra (2015), 'Feminist Commitment to Left-Wing Realism', in Alice Ridout, Roberta Rubenstein, and Susan Singer (eds), *Doris Lessing's* The Golden Notebook *After Fifty*, New York: Palgrave, pp. 73–95.

Spark, Muriel (1960), *The Ballad of Peckham Rye*, London: Macmillan.

Taylor, Charles (1958), 'The Poverty of the Poverty of Historicism', *Universities and Left Review*, 4, 77–8.

Taylor, Jenny (1982), 'Introduction: Situating Reading', in Jenny Taylor (ed.), *Notebooks/Memoirs/Archives: Reading and Rereading Doris Lessing*, London: Routledge, pp. 1–43.

Williams, Raymond (1961), *The Long Revolution*, London: Chatto & Windus.

Wilson, Colin (1956), *The Outsider*, London: Gollancz.

Chapter 3

Sequence, Series and Character in *Children of Violence*

Kevin Brazil

In her final book, *Alfred and Emily* (2008), Doris Lessing returned to a character who had been represented repeatedly and in different ways over her long writing life: the mother. The second part of *Alfred and Emily* – a memoir following a fictional reimagining of her parents' lives – opens with the claim: 'I have written about my father in various ways; in pieces long and short, and in novels. He comes out clearly, unambiguously, all himself' (152). Of her mother, in contrast, she writes:

> Nothing that she ever told or was said about her, or one could deduce from her in that amazing girlhood, so busy, so full of achievement, or of her nursing years, about which we had the best of witnesses, my father himself, or the years in Persia, so enjoyable and so social, nothing, anywhere, in all this matches up with what my mother became.
> Nothing fits, as if she were not one woman but several. (156)

That the self, especially the female self, is not one but several, is one of Lessing's most pervasive themes. But the syntax of the first sentence here specifies one particular way in which multiple selves are conceptualised. It begins by negating three ways of learning about her mother (telling, deducing, witnessing), before listing a series of stages in her life, 'girlhood', 'nursing years', 'Persia', each given two attributes, the first and last echoing through the repetition of 'so . . . so . . .', with the knowable father whose act of 'witness' is not enough at the centre. The nascent paratactic sequence is then terminated by the repetition of 'nothing', returning us to the beginning of the sentence, while the dispersing 'anywhere' implies that this repetitive series could nevertheless continue, possibility infinitely.

This structuring of her mother's unknowability in the form of a sequence which fails to cohere is accentuated by the inclusion within *Alfred and Emily* of a number of photographs, mostly of her parents, some of which had already been published in the autobiographies *Under*

My Skin (1994) and *Walking in the Shade* (1997). Their reappearance in a book exploring the differences and relationships between biography, autobiography and fiction, alerts the reader to how the photographs in *Alfred and Emily* exceed their expected function in conventional modes of life writing – a strategy Lessing shared with a number of writers at the turn of the twenty-first century, such as W. G. Sebald, Jamaica Kincaid and Monika Maron. Facing photographs of Alfred and Emily appear before the 'novella' begins; 'Part Two' begins with a photograph of Alfred and Emily together; photographs of oxen and the family home are succeeded by three facing photographs (208–9). The photographs pass in a sequence from Alfred and Emily before marriage, to life together, to life with children, mimicking the presentation of a family album. As Marianne Hirsch has written of the family photo album, '[a]s photography immobilizes the flow of family life into a series of snapshots, it perpetuates familial myths while seeming merely to record actual moments in family history' (7). Running covertly through *Alfred and Emily*'s two sections of 'novella' and 'memoir' is another form of auto/biography, the bourgeois family photo album, a form with its own logic of mechanically repetitive seriality, and its own blurring of the lines between lived and desired lives.

Alfred and Emily exposes a knot of interrelated topics: the construction of literary character; the relationship of character to autobiography; the forms of the bourgeois family; and the intermingling of concepts of sequentiality, seriality, repetition, reproduction and inheritance. Each can be detected throughout Lessing's oeuvre, but they are first tied together in the *Children of Violence* series of novels: *Martha Quest* (1952), *A Proper Marriage* (1954), *A Ripple from the Storm* (1958), *Landlocked* (1965), and *The Four-Gated City* (1969). Limning the threads of this knot can show how Lessing was concerned with the form of literary character from the very beginning of her writing. Claire Sprague has proposed that 'the Martha of *Landlocked* and *The Four-Gated City* is a different person from the Martha of the first three volumes' (63; see also Jouve 1982: 87). This is an important insight, accounting for many, if not all, of the perplexities raised by the narrative's ironic exposures of Martha's lack of memory, self-understanding, and inability to give a viable account of her actions. This attention to character also enables a more accurate situating of *Children of Violence* in history, because Lessing's subsequent dismissal of her investment in realism was concomitant with her glossing over of the extent to which the realism of the early volumes in the sequence was situated within a global post-war communist culture, while the latter volumes were linked to the specifically British New Left which emerged from it. As a character anchoring an extended novel sequence, who herself raises questions about the sequentiality or seriality of personhood, Martha Quest thus has an important place within debates about theories of character and the history of global and transnational forms of realism, and about the relationship between the device of literary character and political representation and action.

Can a literary character be not one person but several? Lessing's work responds with a resounding yes, whether this multiplicity takes the form of role playing, doublings, repetitions, mythical recurrence or breakdown. But the nature of the relationship between the textual effects that come together to form a fictional character, and the conception of personhood with which it is aligned, is not so easily affirmed. Character, as John Frow has written, is 'both the central category of literary theory and its least understood piece of equipment' (25). In order to move beyond the dichotomy that has dominated theoretical accounts of literary character, Frow argues that we should approach it neither as an ideologically suspect product of textuality unmasked by 'structuralist reduction', nor the freely self-governing liberal form of personhood assumed by 'humanist plentitude' (17), but rather 'as a complex conceptual entity . . . the set of relations formed by the interaction of all of these dimensions' (25). Thinking character in this way involves dealing with connections between two moving targets: adjusting our sense of which textual conventions designate a fictional character, while also adjusting our understanding of what gets defined as a person, or what a person defines. Character, you might say, is what you see when the windows of these two passing trains momentarily align.

While the final destinations of these two histories are yet to be determined, the transformation of events into a sequence is a necessary condition for the ascription of character – as an ever-shifting set of relations – to any narrative. Uri Margolin has proposed a minimal set of logical conditions for the emergence of character from narrative, but as he admits, '[l]iterary narrative . . . represents a temporal succession of states of affairs involving change, and this immediately raises the question of individual continuity between any two neighboring states as well as over the whole series of states' (117). In fact, the proposition of any logical conditions for the presence of character in narrative is dependent upon the ability to transform events into a sequence, a parallel (and a consequence) of the inability to reconstruct a *fabula* from a discourse, even if the *fabula* is somehow logically prior. If the establishment of continuity between events through the forming of a sequence is a condition for the emergence of character, the same process has been seen as necessary for establishing an account of the identity of a person.

As Amélie Oksenberg Rorty has written, philosophical attempts to 'define conditions for distinguishing successive stages of a continuing person from a successor or descendant person', are the grounds for determining the capacity for action and judgement, as well as legal and moral responsibility (2). Working against the predominantly liberal tradition summarised by Rorty, theorists such as Deleuze and Foucault have stressed, in contrast, the ethical implications of the impossibility of relying on continuity when responding to what Judith Butler has called the demand to 'give an account of oneself' (2005). The sequential nature of literary character, at first sight a dry and technical formulation, in fact gives narrative fiction a purchase on wider questions of identity, responsibility and freedom. And of all of the forms of narrative fiction, the character-based novel sequence seems best equipped to grip these questions tight.

The character-based novel sequence is a relatively late development in the long history of the serial publication of narrative fiction, a practice which reached the height of its popularity in the middle of the nineteenth century (Hughes and Lund 1991). In contrast to the serially published narrative that ended with its final instalment, as established by Dickens and Eugène Sue, Balzac's *La Comédie humaine* was the first series of individual novels to form part of a larger, unified sequence, the temporal punctuation so characteristic of serialisation thus occurring between individual novels rather than within them. In the early twentieth century, in Romain Rolland's *Jean-Christophe* (1904–12), Marcel Proust's *In Search of Lost Time* (1913–27), and Dorothy Richardson's *Pilgrimage* (1915–38), the novel sequence moved away from the analysis of society to the tracing of the development of an individual life, building on the long-established tradition of the *Bildungsroman*. As Jules Romains put it in the 1932 preface to his sequence *Les hommes de bonne volonté*, the unifying object of the novel sequence had drifted inward: from a society, to the generations of a family, to the individual hero. But Romains noted that expanding a *Bildungsroman* across the broader temporal and spatial range enabled by a novel sequence risked reversion to the picaresque, with the unifying protagonist appearing more and more as an 'artifice de composition' (x). The fusion of these two intertwined legacies, of social analysis and the chronicling of an individual life – with the implication that the former can be representatively explored through the latter – can be traced in a range of post-war literary projects, which also manifest an increasingly self-reflexive exploration of the central protagonist as an 'artifice de composition': for instance, John Updike's *Rabbit Angstrom* sequence, C. P. Snow's *Strangers and Brothers* and Philip Roth's *Zuckerman* novels. *Children of Violence* belongs with these projects – with the added distinction that it is the only one focused around a woman.

Especially after Proust, whose influence on *Children of Violence* is flagged in an epigraph to Part Three of *Martha Quest*, the character-based novel sequence in the twentieth century adopts some of the motivations and characteristics of serial autobiography. Of particular note in relation to *Children of Violence* is what Sidonie Smith and Julia Watson have described as the tendency to adopt 'several models of identity in succession or in alternation to tell a story of serial development' (40), the narratological consequence of which is a change in the relationship of the narrator to the narration: '[a]s one narrative, and its narrative moment and occasion, displaces another, stories from the past may be rerouted through different narrating "I's"' (75). This characteristic of serial autobiography, the routing of the narrative through a succession of narrating agents, is also a feature of *Children of Violence*, the obvious difference being that the narrative agent is not in its case an 'I'. Neither is the narrator Martha at some future date: as becomes retrospectively clear when her death is reported towards the end of *The Four-Gated City*. Nor is the narrator Lessing herself: as she insistently pointed out, an 'extremely autobiographical' work of fiction is still not an autobiography, but exists in a close and complicated relationship to one (1996: 105). This is a difference explored in *The Golden Notebook*, after which the relationship to autobiography in the subsequent *Children of Violence* novels 'just all shreds apart', as the discussion of autobiography within *The Four-Gated City* shows (1996: 230). Nevertheless, we might propose as a heuristic that the heterodiegetic narrating agent of *Children of Violence* changes its identity and relationship to both Martha and the narrative moment as though it were the successively changing 'I' of a serial autobiography. Recognising this technique, and its literary historical antecedents, does much to explain the disconcerting shifts and inconsistencies in narrative position and focalisation that have troubled many of the critics who have tried to provide the unity which *Children of Violence* pointedly refuses.

A final characteristic of the character-based novel sequence is the impact of its publication form on the temporality of reading: the alignment of a narrative pause with material access to the text. For Wolfgang Iser, '[t]he serial narrative, then, results in a special kind of reading. The interruptions are more deliberate and calculated than those occasioned by random reasons to the reader of a book' (17). What is true of the serialised novel is equally true of the novel sequence. The material episodicity of the overall narrative emphasises gaps and discontinuities; rather than being ignored, they can be exploited, as in serial autobiography, to signal a changed narrating agent. This puts pressure on the logic binding the successive episodes together, and when the subject of that logic is a character, both character and narrative are joined in that which orders them, the 'artifice de composition' relating textual representation and a conception of personhood. Sequentiality or seriality simultaneously order narrative and character: but what kind of person lives their life as a sequence or series, and what in *Children of Violence* is at stake in the difference between them?

When it was first published in 1952, the author's note to *Martha Quest* announced that '[t]his book, *Martha Quest*, is planned as the first of a series, to be known as *Children of Violence*' (320). With characteristic ambition, the epigraph to Part Three from Proust's *The Guermantes Way* establishes Proust as a precursor. Equally important evidence for how *Children of Violence* positions its form with regard to the novel sequence is the epigraph to Part One of *Ripple from the Storm*, from Louis Aragon's *Aurélien* (1944), the fourth novel in his sequence *Le Monde Réel* (1934–51). As a work of realism produced by a Communist Party member, this series is close in form and intent to the initial aims of *Children of Violence*; however, by the time of *Ripple from the Storm* (1958) the epigraph can only be read as an ironic qualification of Martha's own sentimental education in political action, Aragon's frenzy for the absolute having been tempered by the Hungarian uprising of 1956. In interviews, Lessing emphasised that *Children of Violence* had been planned from its inception as a series: 'I knew almost at once that it was five books, roughly sketched out in my mind. I didn't know how it was going to end, of course' (1996: 60). But she also stressed that 'halfway through the series I wrote *The Golden Notebook*, which completely changed me. It wasn't that I wrote five volumes one after another' (89). Lessing's changing political and aesthetic commitments, effected in other contexts and other novels, determined the alteration of the narrative style of the *Children of Violence* novels; a pivotal event being the interrogation of the realist concept of character that takes place within *The Golden Notebook*.

If *Children of Violence* ends by taking leave of the literary realism that had been the anchoring aesthetic mode of Lessing's career to date – even, albeit negatively, in *The Golden Notebook* – the sequence begins in that realism. If the novel sequence is an aspect of *Children of Violence* that must be understood in its historical context, so too must its developing relationship to realism. Lessing defined realism in the 1950s as 'art which springs so vigorously and naturally from a strongly held, though not necessarily intellectually defined, view of life'. This is as vague as what links her to the 'great realists': 'Tolstoy, Stendhal, Dostoevsky,

Balzac, Turgenev, Chekov'; what they had in common was that 'they were humanists'. Humanism as a moral position defines realism in this essay: it is the necessary condition that allows the novel 'to enlarge one's perception of life', and that ensures the writer's 'committed' situation of 'responsibility' (1994a: 8–9). While this remains vague, it does show that Lessing's 'realism' partakes of what distinguishes all claims towards realism: that it can simultaneously mark an aesthetic, epistemological and moral position, assuming that neither can be separated from the other.

These definitions of realism were influenced by 'the "agonized reappraisals" that [were] going on everywhere in the socialist movements' (8); indeed, their very vagueness makes them part and parcel of them. Jenny Taylor's account of Lessing in the 1950s clarifies a period that in Lessing's autobiography is dispersed into vignettes and distorted by her later communist apostasy. This distortion is all the more disserving for not only occluding Lessing's public activity and influence at the time – she savaged Conservative Home Secretary R. A. Butler on BBC's *Panorama* in 1958 – but for also obscuring the intellectual contexts so crucial to the early volumes of *Children of Violence*. Lessing had joined the British Communist Party in 1949, publicly positioned herself as a member of it, and visited the Soviet Union in 1952; in 1956 she contributed to the internal Party journal *The Reasoner*, whose publication precipitated an exodus of dissidents who went to form the New Left. She sat as the only woman on the editorial boards of *The New Reasoner* and *New Left Review*, was an investor in the Partisan Coffee House in Soho, co-organised and spoke at the first Aldermaston March, and commented upon and debated with leading New Left thinkers such as John Berger and Raymond Williams. In short, as Taylor writes, 'she appears to have been associated with almost every aspect of [this] complex cultural and political configuration, though always ambiguously' (26).

As Nick Bentley has argued, the 'agonized reappraisals' in the Left after 1956 that led to rethinkings of realism were significantly effected by the impact of the writings and theatrical practice of Georg Lukács and Bertolt Brecht on British cultural debate in the 1950s, which in turn influenced British critics such as Berger and Williams (Bentley 2009). Although such debates about realism began in 1930s Germany, they continued to be elaborated in the writings of Lukács and Theodor W. Adorno through the 1950s and 1960s, thus overlapping with Lessing's own interrogations of realism in the same decades (Lukács 1963; Adorno 1974). Lukács's critical writings first became available in English in the 1930s through the Soviet journal *International Literature*, but after the war, his reception was shaped by the publication of another body of 1930s essays, in *Studies in European Realism* (1950). This provided a succinct summary of Lukács's theory of realism in the novel: its emergence from bourgeois society, the importance of *Weltanschauung* (world view), humanism, the analysis of the individual personality as a social being, the difference between appearance and essence, and, above all, the theory of character. This is at the heart of Lukács's realism: 'The central category and criterion of realist literature is the type, a peculiar synthesis which organically binds together the general and particular in both characters and situations' (1950: 6). Lukács's ideas were disseminated in the influential art criticism of John Berger, who wrote that the realist painter should focus not on 'appearances' but on the underlying 'facts of the world' in order to deduce a *'typical* truth' (1). Lessing became close to Berger through their membership of the 'Geneva Club', a New Left discussion group, and organisation of the Aldermaston marches (Lessing 1997: 201–2). Lukács's work was familiar enough in the British context to be cited by C. P. Snow in his 1963 'Second Look' at his infamous definition of 'Two Cultures'. Snow had championed *Children of Violence* throughout the 1950s as an exemplary realist work, and his understanding of realism as being exemplified by Lessing and theorised by Lukács, indicates the ways in which Lessing's writing, and career more broadly, was situated within the cultural field of 1950s Britain.

Lukács's criticism shows why it is important to historically contextualise Lessing's realism when discussing her use of literary character, for Lukács's realism is a theory of just that: a theory of literary character. The typical character shows the dialectical relationship between man and social life to be a complete totality between subject and object, a dialectic which is Lukács's own Marxist definition of reality. While Catharine R. Stimpson has argued that 'Lessing's commitment to the expansion of consciousness tempts one to call *Children of Violence* an example of Lukács's theory of the novel' (191), defined in the early *Theory of the Novel* (1914–5) as 'the adventure of interiority, the story of a soul that goes to find itself' (86), it would be more accurate to relate *Children of Violence* to Lukács's later Marxist revision of his theory of the novel and its typical character, and to how these were later revised again for the era of the Cold War and decolonisation. Lessing's statement in 1957 that *Children of Violence* was above all a 'study of the individual conscience in its relations with the collective' (1994a: 18) is close to Lukács's claim, in 1955, that the 'tensions and contradictions both within the individual, and underlying the individual's relation with his fellow human beings . . . must form the subject matter of contemporary realism' (1963: 75). Lessing's assertion that she was searching for a 'resting point ... precariously balanced' (1994a: 15), between the isolated individual of Genet and Beckett and the collective man of social realism, replays Lukács's presentation of critical realism as a 'third way' between modernism and socialist realism, as well as the geopolitical claim, significant for Lessing's role as a transnational writer, that this third way navigates between Cold War polarisation. In her editorial work for *The New Reasoner*, the journal's advocacy for a position between Stalin's 'Two Camps' was described as a 'mediating "Bandung"' role, confirming her definition of realism and its rhetoric of precarious independence and individuality, as Adam Guy has shown in Chapter 1, as existing in a reciprocal relationship with global postcolonial geopolitics ('Editorial' 1957: 3).

Lessing's valorisation of the nineteenth-century realist novel raises a similar question to that which dogged Lukács's criticism: what could a critical realism achieve in the era of the Cold War and Bandung? Was it always, as Lukács argued of Thomas Mann – a writer whom Lessing consistently praised at this time – to be the melancholic working through of a declining form? Lukács's answer, in 1955, situates the first phase of *Children of Violence* spatially and historically within a global literary project:

> Is there, in fact, anything left for the critical realist to write about?
> I would say: yes. We must not forget the remnants of the old order, and of the old consciousness, linger on and continue to inform many people's experience. (1963: 107)

'The critical realist', Lukács continues, 'following tradition, analyses the contradictions in the disintegrating old order and the emerging new order ... though he tends – again following tradition, to emphasize the contradictions rather than working towards reconciliation' (114). If we take imperialism as a remnant of the old order, and the analysis of its contradictions as the core of *Children of Violence* in the form of Martha herself, then Lessing's series can be positioned within Lukács's framework as an actively critical work of realism. As she asked herself in *Going Home* (1957): 'I long for the moment when the Africans can free themselves and can express themselves in new forms ... [a]nd yet – the stale patterns of white domination still exists ... does that mean I must go on writing about it?' (18).

But this juxtaposition can also be used to expose some of the occlusions of Lukács's theory. As Jed Esty has observed, Lukács's theory was blind to gender and did not account for the relationship between the European nation and the imperial world system, failing to extend beyond the national frame his insight about the relationship between novelistic character and the uneven development of modernity (Esty 2009). But if in Esty's account modernist fiction continues an analysis of this relationship in the imperial centre, Lessing's work models 'the problem of uneven development [and gender] in terms of the colonial world system' where the 'halting development of the youthful protagonist of *Martha Quest* throws into relief . . . the failures of late colonial development in southern Africa' (Esty 2012: 66; 209). From this perspective, Martha's 'individual conscience' must necessarily fail to reconcile with her 'collective', and her role as a character is then to show what this failure looks like within an individual for whom it also means a failure to reconcile as a self.

This juxtaposition of Lukács and Lessing in the mid-1950s gives a positive explanation for the commitment to realism in the early volumes of *Children of Violence*, a realism often dismissed – not least by Lessing herself – as a form of naivety later exposed in *The Golden Notebook* and *The Four-Gated City*. It also explains the overwhelmingly negative tone of *Children of Violence*, and why the pathologies of white settler society, and a woman's position within it, are detailed at often exhaustive length, as well as why Martha herself is treated so ironically and often cruelly by the narrative voice: presented as passive, confused, a character who in many ways repels any empathetic identification. As C. P. Snow recognised very early on in his review of *Martha Quest*: '[y]ou may not like what happens or what Martha thought: in fact, you won't, for much of it is displeasing'. Narratologically, because of this, '[i]t is possible that such a temperament is best seen at second hand . . . [d]espite the brilliant power with which Martha's feelings are entered into, the reader has to supply much for himself in order to work out what she is really like' (1952). And, finally, this juxtaposition provides a theory and practice of literary character with which Martha herself can be seen as engaging, and which is gradually dissolved out of existence as the sequence progress from the colonial periphery to the metropolitan centre, and from the eve of the Second World War to a post-apocalyptic twenty-first century.

What kind of a character is Martha Quest? If we take character as a mediation between a conception of personhood and its textual representations, then this question is one which Martha herself explores, but to which she fails to find a satisfactory answer. In *A Proper Marriage*, Martha turns to her bookshelf to find 'some pattern of words that would neatly and safely cage what she felt – isolate her emotions so she could look at them from the outside. For she was of that generation who, having found nothing in religion, had formed themselves by literature'. Martha reads for character – 'What does this say about my life?' – but an 'unsympathetic description of a character similar to her own in a novel would send her into a condition of anxious soul-searching for days'. Literature – realist literature – has failed Martha. She abandons literature for the new sciences of self-help psychology and sexology with 'the half-formulated thought that the novelists had not caught up with life', yet they provide little more than 'some such resounding and original remark as: The young husband, therefore, must be careful to be especially understanding during the difficult weeks after marriage' (83–4).

The cruelly loaded irony of the narration in this final sentence presents Martha as the kind of unsympathetic character she so fears reading about, the irony's dis-identifying effect amplified by the implication that in reading only to sympathise with characters like her, Martha is not able to see the productive effects of irony and would not able to understand this novel that is actually being written about her. It is as if the resentment Martha feels about not being able to fully formulate an explanation as to why female friendship and sexuality are missing from the novelistic tradition is transferred to the narrative voice, whose tone resents Martha's own limitations whilst at the same time illuminating them.

Martha's theory of character – that it is the locus of sympathetic identification between reader and text – is not that of *Children of Violence*; or *A Proper Marriage* at least. But Martha and the narrative technique in this passage both focus with particular attention on the emotions, and the difference between emotions felt and emotions seen from the outside. From the beginning of the series, Martha's emotions are the most powerful destabiliser of her sense of self. Her first scene of reading ends with her abandoning her book of popular science: 'Perhaps, if she could have expressed what she felt, she would have said that the calm factual air of the writing was too distant from the uncomfortable emotions that filled her; perhaps she was so resentful of her surroundings and her parents that the resentment overflowed into everything that came near her' (1952: 13). Again there is a transference of emotion from reading to character to narrative voice: Martha is resentful that she cannot locate her emotions and cannot explain herself; the narrative voice equally resentful that it cannot explain her for this reason, resorting to the subjunctive mood of 'perhaps'. Martha, we are told, is 'continuously being flooded in by emotions that came from outside, or so it seemed' (106); she 'did not understand these violent fluctuations of mood; it was as if half a dozen entirely different people inhabited her body' (189). When dancing with Perry, she becomes 'resentful because he would not accept her as *herself* – whatever that might mean, because of the different selves which insisted on claiming possession of her?'

(205). Over and over again in *Children of Violence*, Martha's negative emotions are described as coming from outside, as not being hers, a disjunction which she can only explain by ascribing herself different selves; and over and over again, this explanation becomes shared by the narrative voice.

If Martha Quest was to be given a signature emotion, it would be resentment. Or rather, a self-reflexive structure of feeling resentful about her feelings: 'Martha watched in herself the growth of an extraordinary and unpleasant emotion, a self-mockery, a self-parody, as if she both allowed herself an emotion and she did not approve of it' (1958: 264). By *Landlocked*, this self-reflexivity transforms Martha into 'the lit space onto which ... emotions would walk like actors and begin to speak without any prompting from her' (1965: 39). From being something which dissolves the self because they are 'anonymous, impersonal, formless, like water' (1952: 189), the self-reflexivity triggered by negative emotions turns Martha first into half a dozen selves, then into an empty space where emotions as selves pass through. This is a late mutation of a tendency that builds throughout the series: a 'flood of emotions' causes her to feel as if she was 'a new person' (1952: 108); Marxism fails to make her a new person because 'she had not been issued, as she vaguely expected, with a completely new set of emotions' (1958: 412) Feeling is what makes Martha a 'space' through which a series of selves pass, both within and across the sequential narrative: precisely the kind of feeling that is the opposite of identifying with a literary character.

This self-reflexivity – feeling negative about feeling negative – has been theorised as a distinctive structure of what Sianne Ngai terms 'ugly feelings'. Unlike cathartic and object-oriented feelings like anger, sympathy or shame, such 'minor and generally unprestigious' feelings like anxiety and irritation lack an object, are '*a*moral and *a*cathartic, offering no satisfactions of virtue, however oblique, nor any therapeutic release' (6). The self-reflexivity they trigger gives them a special relationship with irony, because 'the morally degraded and seemingly unjustifiable status of these feelings tends to produce an unpleasurable feeling *about* the feeling ... that significantly parallels the doubleness on which irony, as an evaluative stance hinging on a relationship between the said and the unsaid, fundamentally depends' (10). For Ngai, because of this very self-reflexivity and ironic doubleness, a 'systematic problematization of the distinction between subjective and objective enunciation' also distinguishes such 'minor affects that are far less intentional or object-directed', producing a systematic 'confusion over a feeling's subjective or objective status' (20–1). This confusion makes the presence of structures of ugly feelings diagnostic of states 'of obstructed agency with respect to other human actors or to the social as such' (3). Through this confusing self-reflexivity, they point to those moments where action is blocked because the line between subject and object, individual and collective, cannot be drawn.

As we have seen, this is the confusion which characterises Martha's emotions, one she tries to dispel by first dispersing her individual feelings into 'impersonal' flows, and then by separating herself into a collective of emotions acting on the stage that is her self. Martha's emotions are the ground upon which Lessing explores what she claimed was the goal of the series as a whole: an examination of 'the individual conscience in its relations with the collective'. The persistent inability of Martha's feelings to be located in either the individual or the collective, an oscillation which works to distance her from both rather than fusing them together, and which more than any other aspect of the series makes her the negative of the type character in which subjective and objective are reconciled, indexes the impossibly contradictory status her character represents. Committed, both diegetically and as a representation, to becoming free from the subject position of a white, bourgeois, settler female, with no literary heritage, no sustainable political structure, and blind to the racial oppression that sustains her very existence – as a person, and as a character in the realist tradition, she simply lacks the ability to do so. All Martha can do, as person and representation, is to show that this inability comes from those limitations we feel but can never quite explain.

Martha's threatened dispersion by 'violent fluctuations of mood' into 'half a dozen different people' is accentuated by her refusal to accept the one mode available to her that might bind these different people together: repetition. Before she joins the Party, this fear of 'the great bourgeois monster, the nightmare *repetition*' is a fear of genealogical determination, the 'inevitable process' where children cannot escape becoming their parents (1954: 102). Looking at her mother, she sees

> a sequence of events, unalterable, behind her, and stretching into the future
> ... [s]he saw herself sitting where her mother sat now, a woman horribly
> metamorphosed ... [a]nd beside these women, a series of shadowy men,
> broken-willed and sick with compelled disease. Thus the nightmare, the
> nightmare of a class and generation: repetition. (124)

Her struggle to avoid becoming another term in the bourgeois series becomes a struggle against literary character. In a narrative observation which characteristically points towards Martha's limitations, we are told that 'although Martha had read nothing of the great interpreters of the nightmare' – psychoanalysis, one assumes – 'she had been soaked in the minor literature of the last thirty years, which has dealt with very little else: a series of doomed individuals, carrying their doom inside them, like the seeds of a fatal disease' (124). This image of repetition as genealogy is embodied in the figure of Mrs Quest, who when thinking of her position in the sequence, between her own mother and Martha, fantasises about 'giving birth to herself' (1965: 94). If this nightmare were to come true, and repetition were to produce an eternal recurrence of the same, then Martha would be right to conclude that 'neither her nor her mother had any validity as persons' (1954: 124).

This passage in *A Proper Marriage* slightly blurs the difference between a sequence and series, although there is a distinction suggested between a sequence of events, which produces a past, present and future, and a series of repeated objects which are repetitions of the same term. But the difference does not need to be clearly stated in the novel for it to be used to show how repetition intersects with the question of how Martha is constructed as a character. Mathematically, a series is simply the sum of the terms of a sequence. But as these terms are used in narratology, a sequence connotes progression and development, a series the static repetition of the same. J. Hillis Miller, for example, opposes the 'determination of meaning based on the linear sequence of the story' (2) to the effect of repetition, which even when it produces a series of terms, tends to present these terms as 'nonprogressive variations' (23), 'virtually endless' (175), and which replaces the flow of temporality with the co-presence of all moments with each other. This latter definition of a series is what Martha fears, and she comes to fear it from reading about characters in literature. Not only in her reading have representations of autonomous bourgeois personhoods revealed themselves to be a series of repetitions, but these representations threaten to repeat themselves in her own life, and then, like the transferrable and self-reflexive feeling of resentment, to repeat themselves in the fiction being written about her.

Martha's turn to Marxism swiftly disabuses her of the 'bourgeois illusion of eternity' which explains her own 'nightmare of recurring and fated evil' (1958: 66) Yet this is only temporary, and nothing better reflects her own disillusion with Marxism's disillusions than the observation on a new group of political activists, focalised through Martha, who are 'history . . . repeating itself – and why not? If the dramatis personae were the same, presumably the plot was also' (1965: 310). Thus she rewrites her previous self as a repeated term in a series. Martha's reflections on one form of character, in which individuals are represented as terms in a series, produces a tension with the overall form of which she initially provides the centre, a series which Lessing retrospectively described as a *Bildungsroman*. As Rita Felski has written, the capacity of the *Bildungsroman* to decouple its characteristic 'depiction of identity formation as a temporal process . . . represented by means of a linear and chronological narrative' from its origins as a narration of the gendering of the bourgeois male, has been debated by female writers since the nineteenth century (135). Through Martha's reading and political education, this contested history is written into *Children of Violence*, playing out in the tension between the *Bildungsroman's* logic of sequential development, and repetitions production of a series of states without change.

Martha fears becoming a repetition of her mother, but equally her succession of selves fails to form a developing sequence, to the point in *Landlocked* where she willfully determines to keep them separate, a determination given an image in her dream of a house with rooms she 'must keep separate', to not 'try and explain, or build bridges' (25). Martha's own decision to stop explaining the causal motivations between the successive moments of her life results in the waning of her centrality, and access to her thoughts, as *The Four-Gated City* progresses. Significantly, her dream of a house of separated rooms becomes a recurring 'serial dream', whose repetitions cause a 'lack of flow' (216). Her dreams, and communions with Lynda, become conflicts between 'a series of "stills" . . . [and] a long moving dream' (84). The conflict between series and sequence, between repetition and flow, fails to resolve in the form of life that is her character, while her dreams provide no imaginary resolution to this conflict in the real, for they do not resolve the conflict but rather repeat it, over and over. Martha's last thoughts are 'silence and the birth of a repetition' (591). If *Children of Violence* is indeed a *Bildungsroman*, it is critical in Lukács's sense: both its form and its central character contradict themselves, and this contradiction is played out in the opposition between sequence and series.

Children of Violence shows us the ways in which both sequence and series are logics of bourgeois character: those relations created between concepts of personhood and their representations. The progressive sequence of the *Bildungsroman* betrays its historical determinations when it fails to transplant from centre to periphery, from unified nation to racially segregated colony, from liberal citizen to communist activist – and, in opposition to realist and pragmatic strands of feminist criticism, from male to female subject. It also fails to transplant into the work of a critical realism aiming to show decline, not development. *Children of Violence* shows that the nightmare of repetition is the nightmare of failed sequential development – the endlessly repeated series of Mrs Quest giving birth to herself over and over again. Finally, it shows how the repetitive structure of the bourgeois family and the repetition of myth and dreams are two sides of the same flight from the failure of sequentiality. As Adorno observed, 'the very fetishism of commodities which in bourgeois society brings with it inhibition, impotence, the sterility of the never-changing' raises to an absolute '[t]he concept of dynamism which is the necessary complement of bourgeois "a-historicity"' (2005: 156).

'Then silence and the birth of a repetition. *Where?* Here. Here? Here, where else, you fool, you poor fool where else has it been, ever ...?' (1993: 591). Martha, in the end, realises none of this: she is no Marcel, whose illumination as to the meaning of his life is shared at the end of the narrative whose writing is that meaning. Nor is she a mystical fool whose breakdown paves the way for transcendence. She simply remains a poor fool. Perhaps what is most displeasing about the character of Martha Quest, but which at the same time is her most important lesson, is how she fails to escape the limitations imposed upon her, the violence of history of which she is the essence, a limitation which the narration slowly reveals in its decision to leave her behind. The individual person, child of the violence of war, imperialism and totalitarianism, cannot free itself from those prisons we choose to live inside: but the work of a critical story telling can.

Works Cited

Adorno, Theodor (1974), 'Commitment', *New Left Review*, no. 87–8, pp. 75–89.

—— (2005), *Minima Moralia,* trans. Edmund Jephcott, London: Verso.

Bentley, Nick (2009), 'Doris Lessing's *The Golden Notebook*: An Experiment in Critical Fiction', in Alice Ridout and Susan Watkins (eds), *Doris Lessing: Border Crossings*, London: Bloomsbury, pp. 44–60.

Berger, John (1953), *Looking Forward,* London: The Arts Council.

Butler, Judith (2005), *Giving an Account of Oneself*, New York: Fordham University Press.

'Editorial' (1957), *The New Reasoner*, pp. 3, 2–4.

Esty, Jed (2009), 'Global Lukács', *Novel: A Forum on Fiction* 42:3, 366–72.

—— (2012), *Unseasonable Youth: Modernism, Colonialism, and the Fiction of Development*, Oxford: Oxford University Press.

Felski, Rita (1989), *Beyond Feminist Aesthetics: Feminist Literature and Social Change*, London: Hutchinson.

Frow, John (2014), *Character and Person*, Oxford: Oxford University Press.

Hirsch, Marianne (1997), *Family Frames: Photography, Narrative, and Postmemory*, Cambridge, MA: Harvard University Press.

Hughes, Linda K., and Michael Lund (1991), *The Victorian Serial*, Charlottesville: University Press of Virginia.

Iser, Wolfgang (1971), 'Indeterminacy and the Reader's Response in Prose Fiction', in *Aspects of Narrative: Selected Papers from the English Institute*, New York: Columbia University Press, pp. 1–46.

Jouve, Nicole Ward (1982), 'Of Mud and Other Matter – The Children of Violence', in Jenny Taylor (ed.), *Notebooks/Memoirs/Archives: Reading and Rereading Doris Lessing*, London: Routledge, pp. 75–134.

Lessing, Doris (1952), *Martha Quest*, London: Michael Joseph.

—— (1954), *A Proper Marriage*, London: Michael Joseph.

—— (1958), *A Ripple from the Storm*, London: Michael Joseph.

—— (1965), *Landlocked*, London: MacGibbon & Kee.

—— [1957] (1968), *Going Home*, St Albans: Panther.

—— [1969] (1993), *The Four-Gated City*, London: Flamingo.

—— (1994a), *A Small Personal Voice: Essays, Reviews, Interviews*, ed. Paul Schlueter, London: Harper Collins.

—— (1994b), *Under My Skin: Volume One of My Autobiography to 1949*, London: Harper Collins.

—— (1996), *Putting the Questions Differently: Interviews with Doris Lessing 1964–1994*, London: Flamingo.

—— (1997), *Walking in the Shade: Volume Two of My Autobiography, 1949–1962*, London: Harper Collins.

—— (2008), *Alfred and Emily*, London: Fourth Estate.

Lukács, Georg (1950), *Studies in European Realism*, trans. Edith Bone, London: Hillway.

—— (1963), *The Meaning of Contemporary Realism*, London: Merlin Press.

—— (1971), *The Theory of the Novel,* Cambridge, MA: MIT Press.

Margolin, Uri (1987), 'Introducing and Sustaining Characters in Literary Narrative: A Set of Conditions' *Style* 21:1, 107–23.

Miller, J. Hillis (1982), *Fiction and Repetition: Seven English Novels*, Cambridge, MA: Harvard University Press.

Ngai, Sianne (2005), *Ugly Feelings*, Cambridge, MA; London: Harvard University Press.

Oksenberg Rorty, Amélie (1976), 'Introduction,' in *The Identities of Persons*, ed. Amélie Oksenberg Rorty, Berkeley: University of California Press, pp. 1–16.

Romains, Jules (1932), *Les hommes de bonne volonté*, Paris: Ernest Flammarion.

Smith, Sidonie, and Julia Watson (2010), *Reading Autobiography: Interpreting Life Narratives*, 2nd edn, Minneapolis: University of Minnesota Press.

Snow, C. P. (1952), 'Frustrations on the Veld', *The Sunday Times*, 2 November.

—— [1963] (1998), *The Two Cultures*, Cambridge: Cambridge University Press.

Sprague, Claire (1987), *Rereading Doris Lessing: Narrative Patters of Doubling and Repetition*, Chapel Hill: The University of North Carolina Press.

Stimpson, Catharine R. (1983), 'Doris Lessing and the Parables of Growth' in Elizabeth Abel, Marianne Hirsch and Elizabeth Langland (eds), *The Voyage In: Fictions of Female Development*, Hanover: University Press of New England, pp. 186–205.

Taylor, Jenny (1982), 'Introduction: Situating Reading', in Jenny Taylor (ed.), *Notebooks/Memoirs/Archives: Reading and Rereading Doris Lessing*, London: Routledge, pp. 1–43.

Chapter 4

The Politics of Form:
The Golden Notebook and
Women's Radical Literary Tradition

Rowena Kennedy-Epstein

For Jane Connor Marcus

'It's a question of form.' (Lessing 1990: 454)

Jane Ellen Harrison wrote, in 1914, 'It has bothered me often – why do women never want to write poetry about Man as a sex – why is Woman a dream and a terror to men and not the other way around? . . . Is it mere convention, or propriety or something deeper?' (quoted in Rich 2002: 2). Virginia Woolf, Harrison's interlocutor and friend, went to the deepest part of that question in her writing, one that ultimately became for her and many other women writers a matter of form. In order to document if not the dream then 'the terror' of men, and to make visible that which was often invisible – the bodily acts, narrative expressions, marks of the constructions and contradictions of patriarchal power – women writers had to find new forms that were not already inscribed within that very same system, and that would not lead to the reproduction of the same kind of unequal power. Doris Lessing may have given considerable effort to distancing herself from feminists, citing their 'inflexibility' in her own perhaps misguided fear of perpetuating the binaries that produce violence (Lessing 2001). But it is also clear that the form of *The Golden Notebook* (1962) exposes a deeper meditation on and deconstruction of the terror of patriarchy – from the private terrors of sexual humiliation to the public terrors of colonialism, torture and nuclear arms. Through experimental formal strategies we are shown how these terrors reinforce each other, but also how they are, or might be, subverted. By combining fiction, documentary material, political theory and memoir in *The Golden Notebook*, Lessing offers a nuanced reading of the connections between state violence, sexual hierarchies and political crises, while at the same time interrogating the very forms in which those histories are narrated. In this sense, Lessing's complex formal strategies are intrinsic to her complex political assertions, ones that problematise fixed notions of feminism, liberation, transnational solidarity, political commitment and history. Using textual hybridity to resist closed formal and political structures that reinscribe authority, Lessing writes women as central narrators and subjects of twentieth-century politics and history, subverting the boundaries of gender and genre so inculcated in mid-century modernism. However, Lessing's radical textual and political project is not a singular one, and can be read as part of a tradition of women writers who employ similar experimental strategies to imagine beyond the violent binaries that have shaped the past.

In her Introduction to Virginia Woolf's *Three Guineas* (1938), the feminist scholar and critic Jane Connor Marcus wrote:

> keeping track of fascism and patriarchy in her own day, Virginia Woolf inspired us to do the same. It seemed that the fictional version of Woolf's ideas, her novel *The Years*, and the 'factual' (or feminist counterfactual) effort of *Three Guineas* was repeated in Doris Lessing's later experiment *The Golden Notebook* (1962). Both political writers took to the domestic staple of family life, the scrapbook, and used it for recording public events. (Woolf 2006: xxxvii)

Woolf's original intention was to write a hybrid 'essay-novel' in which fictional accounts were interwoven with factual chapters based on the documentary material collected in her reading notebooks. Woolf claimed that this experimental interweaving of fact and fiction had 'enough powder to blow up St. Paul's', and that 'there is scarcely a statement in it that cannot be verified' (Woolf 1977: 33). The notebooks, which Woolf began keeping around 1927, record women's changing position within capitalism and empire – from birth and abortion to work and education, from sports to war – but are also a catalogue of misogyny, enumerating the violent and humiliating backlashes towards women's advancement. While in *Three Guineas* Woolf writes in dialogue with this material, quoting and extending from it in order to expose the manifold interconnections of gender hierarchies, nationalism and war, in the novel version, *The Years* (1937), she fictionalises the very same evidence in order to show women's struggles for intellectual and sexual subjectivity, from the Victorian drawing room of the 1880s to the 'present day' of the 1930s. In this way she situates women's experiences around transformational political events – colonial resistance, women's suffrage, educational enfranchisement, pacifism – depicting, quoting and expanding from the documents that tangentially line the pages of her reading notebooks. If read together, Woolf's interactive 1930s texts foreshadow what *The Golden Notebook* would encompass in a single text: fact and fiction, documentary and narrative, political theory and historical record. Marcus called Woolf's project a 'radical documentary', and identified it, like Lessing's novel, as part of a larger tradition of women writers. Marcus used the term because it implies archiving, recording, witnessing, culling, collaging, photographing and filming, and can be traced in the practices of scrapbooking in the suffrage movement, left-front politics, travel narratives, war correspondences, epic poems, testimony and reportage. The term also suggests that there are in fact 'real' historical conditions that have been narrated over, while at the same time destabilising the very notion of historical narrative itself. As readers of radical documentaries, notions of which Sophia Barnes explores in this volume, we can trace the references, quotations and newspaper clippings back to their original sources, and we also become witnesses, archivists and historians. In this regard the texts are interactive: they 'create authority', Marcus notes, through quotations and documentation, and simultaneously 'teach us to dismantle it' (Woolf 2006: xlix).

The American poet Muriel Rukeyser called the experimental conjoining of fact and fiction 'extend[ing] the document' (2005: 597), and in her own hybrid Spanish Civil War novel *Savage Coast*, written in 1936 but not published until 2013, as well as in many of her experimental poems, she integrates documentary material with the poetic to show the ways in which women's sexual, political and authorial subjectivity is shaped by and shapes public political history. Included in her novel are dated newspaper clippings, a long list of the dead, radio addresses by politicians and propaganda ephemera, even a quote from a D. H. Lawrence novel, all situated in juxtaposition and in dialogue with the lyric interiority of her modernist war novel. This blurring of the boundaries between fact and fiction – the creation of the self inside history, and by extension inside text – is essential to Rukeyser's multi-decade conceit to make a cross-genre, hybrid poetry and prose where 'false barriers go down' (1996: 20). Like many of her radical and feminist contemporaries, Rukeyser engaged the potentiality of the documentary form to not only challenge and expose capitalist, patriarchal and hegemonic narratives, but to find forms that transcend the dichotomies of public and private, that undo the confinement of the traditionally female lyric and remake traditionally male genres that have historically excluded women. In Rukeyser's rendering of the conflict in Spain, in Woolf's depiction of the rise of fascism, and in Lessing's vision of the Cold War, we are given access to how women authors not only interpret their own historical moment, but shape that moment as well. Their works ultimately change how we read twentieth-century history because the factual events documented in each text become the events by which we ourselves theorise and narrate the period.

In 2007, Lessing wrote about the production of *The Golden Notebook*, 'I knew this was an extraordinary time, I was watching extraordinary events. I wanted to record them . . . What I like best is hearing that *The Golden Notebook* is on reading lists for political or history classes. The reason for its continued vitality is, I feel, not literary' (2007). Lessing's assertion that the text's value is more political and historical than literary shows how much she herself must have been inculcated into the genre norms of mid-century, even while she broke them. Interestingly, she echoes many of the first reviews, as documented by Gayle Green, that asserted that the novel's merits were not artistic but sociological, confining the text to particularly masculinist New Critical orthodoxies that often devalued women writers' desire to communicate both political, historical and aesthetic aims (Green 1995: 93–7). Of course, all forms carry political meaning, and it is usually those that insist they have no design towards that end which have proved to be the most insidious. *The Golden Notebook* is exemplary for showing the importance of how literary form and historical and political thought are structured and dependent upon each other. In the same 2007 essay, Lessing, a notorious self-revisionist, acknowledges something to this effect: 'but what I said then was that *The Golden Notebook* had a shape, a composition, that itself was a statement, a communication. If they wanted a new kind of novel, then wasn't this one? But no, "embittered", "unfair", and so on' (2007). The misreading of her formal conceit irritated Lessing perpetually, particularly in how critics wanted the text to occupy one political, subjective or even generic position when it was really about the interconnection of those things. Lessing's experience of being misread, however, was not unique for the kind of project she produced. *The Golden Notebook* becomes a central text for feminist critics at this precise moment of misreading. When Lessing opines, 'isn't this the kind of novel they wanted?', she is speaking of and to the male literary establishment, the New Critical reader and reviewer who never let her off the hook for being a woman who insisted on the relationship between form and content. Whether Lessing could fully admit it, the question of gender and genre is only a question posed to women authors. But Lessing was not alone: Woolf wrote of *Three Guineas* that 'my own friends have sent me to Coventry over it' for both the style and the political content, and many of the reviews were worse (1985: 188–9); Rukeyser's *Savage Coast* was described by the male reviewer as incoherent – neither aesthetically pleasing or politically serious – and rejected for publication (Rukeyser 2013: xxii). And this kind of gender/genre misreading has not stopped: even Arundhati Roy's recent, masterful documentary text *Walking with the Comrades* (2011) has been met with distrust from male academics and intellectuals; in a faculty/graduate student seminar that I participated in at the CUNY Graduate Center, male professors from literary, historical and political studies all found themselves in a rare moment of agreement about Roy's text – that it was 'politically and aesthetically sloppy' for both her presumption to write about a complicated revolutionary resistance movement and her insistence on formal hybridity in doing so.

Lynn Hejinian, in her landmark essay *On the Rejection of Closure*, writes:

> The "open text," by definition, is open to the world and particularly to the reader. It invites participation, rejects the authority of the writer over the reader and thus, by analogy, the authority implicit in other (social, economic, cultural) hierarchies. [. . .] The "open text" often emphasizes or foregrounds process, either the process of the original composition or of subsequent compositions by readers, and thus resists the cultural tendencies that seek to identify and fix material and turn it into a product; that is, it resists reduction and commodification. (2000: 43)

The 'closed text,' on the other hand, 'is one in which all the elements of the work are directed toward a single reading of it. Each element confirms that reading and delivers the text from any lurking ambiguity' (43). Doris Lessing's decades-long struggle against a mono-vocal reading of her novel, a reading that would close it and categorise it, speaks to her formal design in writing a text that continually subverts ideological fixity and authorial hegemony. The radical nature of the novel is in the way it challenges hierarchies by inviting participation through its 'openness'. Lessing is keenly aware of how narrative authority can become a motivation for other kinds of authority, and so on a fundamental level the text is always already about the politics of form.

How, then, can a text that resists categorisation also be a text that is explicitly radical and feminist, for lack of better words? It is through the interrupting, stuttering and juxtaposing formal strategies that the radical conceit becomes clear. Let's return to *Three Guineas* again. In it Woolf documents the violence and vitriol of men against women in context of the 'dead bodies and ruined houses' of total war. In doing so she exposes how that private violence is integral to state policies of war and empire. Written in response to a letter asking, 'how in your opinion are we to best prevent war' amidst the rising tide of European fascism, she demonstrates how war can only be understood in context of gender hierarchies, how 'the fear which forbids freedom in the private house . . . small, insignificant and private, as it is, is connected with the other fear, the fear which has led you to ask us to help you to prevent war' (2006: 168). For Woolf, ultimately, it is by refusing to participate in any of the institutions of the state, predicated as they are on gender subordination, that women can 'best prevent war'. Women, Woolf famously asserts, must find 'new forms and new methods' (170). In this way her text is self-making, for she argues this point through a series of formal disruptions: *Three Guineas* is made up of three epistolary letters (a form both public and private, as Marcus notes), is based on a series of reading notebooks full of newspaper clippings, includes photographs and descriptions of photographs, as well as quotations that can be followed outside of the text, and a polemical narrative. Here Woolf famously deploys her radical strategy:

> He is called in German and Italian Führer and Duce; in our language Tyrant and Dictator. And behind him lie ruined houses and dead bodies – men, women, and children. But we have not laid the picture before you in order to excite once more the sterile emotion of hate ... For it suggests that the public and private worlds are inseparably connected; that the servilities and tyrannies of the one are the servilities and tyrannies of the other. (168)

The documentary description of the dictator and the image of the dead bodies are placed inside a discussion about the subordination of 'the daughters of educated men', all of which is interrupted at various points by actual photographs of men, in full dress and pomp – a military man, a judge, heralds blowing trumpets, an archbishop, academics in a processional. None are identified by name; they don't need to be, for they are the architects, narrators, historians and legislators of imperial power. Through a hybridisation of image, documentary fact and narrative, Woolf is able to show how the systems that structure the history of the nation state, the wars that define its borders, and the narratives we use to tell the story of the people inside and outside of those borders are the same mechanisms that shape the servilities of the private life.

In *The Golden Notebook*, Lessing calls the private fear 'cracking up', and it is deconstructed, like Woolf's, through a process of hybridising and juxtaposing 'factual' material of political crisis, questions of narrative and authorship, and women's encounters with gendered hierarchies in the private house. As in Woolf's text, there is a kind of documentary attention paid to the terror of men's actions: their psychosis is picked apart and illuminated. Saul Green, for example, animates and embodies the insanity of Cold War American masculinity that is manifest on the public level of political policy in the newspaper clippings covering the walls of Anna's flat. Both the newspaper articles about war and Saul's sexual and intellectual violence come from the same material. Tommy extorts his power from the guilt Anna and Molly experience as failed communists nearing the end of the communist moment, and as failed mothers in a pre-feminist moment. The connection between the two is depicted through the doubling depictions of Anna/Ella as editors – 'real' and 'fictional' – of pro-communist novels written by party members, on the one hand, and the letters from housewives about disenfranchisement and depression, on the other. Read together, they connect the 'two houses'. In the Zimbabwean sections, Paul and Willi provoke and objectify women in the colonial context of the colour bar, highlighting how white and black women's bodies are defined and objectified in relation to one another, and how this dichotomy is used to support both the colonial project and women's subordination. This can be understood on the linguistic level in Willi's use of the phrase 'she needs a good hiding', which was a 'Colonial phrase, usually used by whites: "What that kaffir needs is a damned good hiding"'. It is in the colony that Anna learns how 'women liked to be bullied' (94). This expressive image is used again when Tommy, the inheritor of this same colonial legacy, takes on the didactic authority of Willi and teaches Marion about the 'poor things [Africans]' as part of her political education (384). Once blind Tommy takes on a powerful 'all seeing' role, embodying something like the listening power of the Cold War spy state, overhearing and reading Molly's and Anna's private thoughts; Lessing, we now know, was surveilled for twenty years by MI5 (Feigel 2015). Willi, Anna notes, will return to East Germany himself and work for the Stasi, an equally powerful spying operation. Tommy and Willie's doubling also brings our attention to how European powers first developed the techniques used for domestic surveillance in the colonies. Later, Anna will read Saul's diary in an equally transgressive act of surveillance. In fact, reading the novel in context of mid-century surveillance culture might not only open new approaches to how the text enacts listening as much as documenting through its experimental apparatus, but also offers new ways for analysing Lessing's complex rendering of transnational solidarity. The figure of the political dissident in the novel is the figure of the surveilled and tortured body: 'the Algerian soldier stretched on a torture bed; and I was also him, wondering how long I could hold out. I saw a communist in a communist jail' (568). These images haunt Anna throughout the text, making her question the very effectiveness of solidarity and activism in systems of power that produce the same result in either communist or colonial/capitalist countries. Importantly, this embodiment of torture is engendered by her experiences of gendered subjectivities (Saul's affairs trigger this sequence, for example, as well as her desire to read his intimate thoughts), and so she situates systems of gender hierarchy, state surveillance and biopower together. This is another textual doubling that links state power and the body at home and abroad, for which Anna acts as a kind of interpreter or record keeper. In some ways, Lessing's insistent cataloguing of the history of war and violence perpetuated by the state can be read as a response to the intricate documentary record made by the state of its own citizens.

While there has been plenty of scholarship on the potent and radical directive Lessing gives in her 1971 introduction – wherein she states that she wants to write about 'the disparity between the overwhelming problems of war, famine, poverty and the individual trying to mirror them' (1990: xvii) – the formal strategies of the text actually show that this isn't really a dichotomy at all, that the two are coexistent, mutually reinforcing systems. Thus, despite Lessing's resistance to being closed into what she believes are the ideological binds of feminism, she demonstrates through the most nuanced and factual material of the text how patriarchal power is constructed, and the detrimental effect it has for both men and women. It's not just that the individual mirrors the crisis of the greater society, but that those who make war are made of the same material, raised in the same families, educated in the same systems, and trained in the same armies as the man 'who is directing a pure stream of hatred against me, for being a woman' (601). This is not to capitulate to a reading of the text as being about 'the sex war', for that problematic bifurcation is at the centre of this argument; women are and continue to be complicit in systems of power, which Lessing demonstrates incisively in the African sections of the novel. But, as Woolf has shown, gender hierarchies are at the very centre of war culture, because women are in a forced allegiance with men, and it is only through a deconstruction of what happens in the most intimate moments of the private house that we can begin to disrupt the public crisis more fully. As Woolf writes:

> for such will be our ruin if you, in the immensity of your public abstractions forget the private figure, or if we in the intensity of our private emotions forget the public world. Both houses will be ruined, the public and private, the material and the spiritual, for they are inseparably connected. (2006: 169)

For Lessing this insistence on interconnection is a particularly radical assertion during the post-war, Cold War moment that is predicated on separation – between nations, political ideologies, academic disciplines, etc. 'The essence of the book', she writes in the 1971 Preface, 'the organising of it, everything in it says implicitly and explicitly, that we must not divide things off, must not compartmentalise' (xv). In 1974, Rukeyser writes something similar about the post-war period: 'Not to let our lives be shredded . . . anything away from anything' (1974: 370).

From the start, *The Golden Notebook* is preoccupied by form on both a generic and linguistic level. When Richard, who embodies the legacy of empire and patriarchy, asserts 'I preserve the forms', Lessing announces her dismantling project – to break the forms and, in doing so, the myths and histories which Richard represents (25). Midway through the book, during a session with Mrs Marks in the Blue Notebook, Lessing introduces a long meditation on the question of form. Anna, as the 'author' of the text we are reading, is trying to understand the totalising impulse that turns pain – both private and public – into myth, into a story or history, and the implications of this. She situates this question of form in the context of gender, literary authority and nuclear war. Anna writes against Mrs Marks's assertion that her experiences are part of a tradition, that they are not 'new'. Anna responds by saying, 'I'm living the kind of life women never lived before', both because she is a 'free woman', so to speak, as well as a person living under the hysterical threat of the H-bomb; both these experiences annihilate the separation between form and content (450). Anna says, 'I want to be able to separate myself from what is old and cyclic, the recurring history, the myth, from what is new, what I feel or think that might be new ... it's a question of form' (453). When Mrs Marks says, 'I understand that you people insist on separating form and content', Lessing is herself making visible the violence the left did to itself by shutting down the dynamic and imaginative thinking that is actually necessary for breaking with the systems of the past (454). Anna's desire for a radical formlessness is manifest in the generic experimentation of the text she is making and we are reading, one that is written in response to notions of what constitutes an appropriately politically engaged text. This is shown through the Communist Party reviews of her first novel, based on real reviews from Soviet newspapers, and through the depictions of CP editorial meetings. Importantly, *The Golden Notebook* wasn't reviewed in the *New Left Review*, despite the fact that Lessing was integrated within their milieu of 'intellectual socialism', and it is inferred that it was because she writes about gender in context of radical politics (Singer 2015). The assertion of the separation of politics and aesthetics was particularly detrimental to radical women writers, who understood that only through the interrogation of the politics of form could women be both authors and subjects of texts, because it was exactly through formal modes that gender politics were erased from politics. It was in the interstitial spaces engendered by formal experimentation that left-aligned women writers could imagine beyond the myths and traditions that had inscribed and narrated their sexual and intellectual subordination.

Because of its formal conceit, *The Golden Notebook* is being 'made' as we read it, and thus Lessing is able to assert her authority as both the narrator and subject of history, while simultaneously exposing women's lack of agency. The novel returns again and again to notions of what it means to be a 'real woman' and a 'real man', what 'real sex is', and a fear of queer contamination and the fetishisation of the colonised subject. Heteronormative mid-century roles – in which women are seen cooking, cleaning (bodies and rooms), dressing and pleasing men – are all recurrently detailed. But it is through this capitulation to those norms that the formal meaning becomes clear: there is no gender liberation inside the cultural conditions of war and empire; there is no sexual freedom when there is sexual violence, racism, torture and oppression. This connection can only be understood through Lessing's formal strategies. Earlier in the Blue Notebook, Anna tells Mrs Marks about her relationship with Michael. They discuss what constitutes real womanhood and real sex, Michael's humiliation (both verbal and sexual) of Anna for being 'an authoress' and a loving mother at the expense of his needs, and Anna's refusal to write a new novel (225). Anna interrupts this personal record with a long passage of documentary material – 'newspaper cuttings, carefully pasted in and dated' (226). The documentary materials Lessing uses are factual: they document the Korean War, the sentencing of the Rosenbergs, the Mau Mau revolt, the testing of the H-bomb. These are the real global crises in which Lessing situates fictionalised Anna's breakdown. By situating the factual documents as an extension or replacement of Anna's personal narrative of psycho-sexual exploration of both gender roles and artistic production, Lessing is creating a formal space to articulate intersections that cannot be expressed though a linear narrative practice that would be read as developmental instead of simultaneous, while at the same time showing how lived historical events are deeply implicated inside the self-created myths of private lives.

[At this point the diary stopped, as a personal document. It continued in the form of newspaper cuttings, carefully pasted in and dated.]

March, 50
The modeller call this the 'H-Bomb style,' explaining that the 'H' is for peroxide of hydrogen, used for coloring. The hair is dressed to rise in waves as from a bomb-burst, at the nape of the neck.
Daily Telegraph

April 6th, 51
WOMAN ATOM SPY TO DIE. Husband too sent to Electric Chair. Judge: You Caused Korea.

5th July, 52
Most important of all, the effect of the American witch-hunt is to produce a general level of conformity, a new orthodoxy from which man dissents at his economic peril. *Statesman*

Dec 17th, 1952
11 COMMUNIST LEADERS HANGED IN PRAGUE. Capitalist Spies Claims Czech Government.

23rd March, 1953
2,500 MAU MAU ARRESTS. *Express*

30th March
2nd H-BOMB EXPLODED. *Express*

[And now the personal entries began again.] (227–38)

Anna's newspaper collage goes on for eleven pages. Not only does it make the most public catastrophes intimate, for they are pasted into her diary – 'whenever anything happens anywhere that is terrible, I dream about it, as if I were involved in it personally' (240) – and thus make the root of Anna's personal crisis public, but it also asks the reader important questions about the material she has drawn together: why choose these public events, and why do they interrupt this particular private narrative, written in a journal? By bringing together the different material elements in this way, across the page, Lessing seems to assert that this political moment and this private catastrophe can only be understood through an intertextual and transhistorical telling. The relationship between these different generic forms, between fact and fiction, is not something that can be narrated in a traditional, linear fashion. Instead, Lessing tries to draw the kind of complex polymorphism best actualised in the graphic novel, in which the reader can engage a multiplicity of significations through the simultaneous layering of image and text. But Lessing's project can also be illuminated in the context of her modernist foremothers and contemporaries.

As Jean Tobin has pointed out, if one reads *The Years* and *The Golden Notebook* consecutively, one might find Peggy's struggle for subjectivity in the 'present day' section of *The Years* echoed in Anna's struggle for subjectivity in *The Golden Notebook* (1994: 147). Just as Peggy understands the system of patriarchy not fully articulated by her Victorian aunts, and is deeply disillusioned by the older generation, seeking 'to live differently', so Anna takes it one step further, outlining the relationships between patriarchy and the violence that eviscerates her consciousness, her subjectivity. Peggy thinks, while listening to a potential suitor:

> She had heard it all before. I, I, I – he went on. It was like a vulture's beak pecking, or a vacuum-cleaner sucking, or a telephone bell ringing. I, I, I . . . Let me shake him off then, she said to herself, feeling like a person whose blood has been sucked, leaving all the nerve-centres pale. (1969: 361)

And Anna thinks, as Saul talks to her:

> He was talking about how to bring up a small girl. He was very intelligent about it all, and very academic. He talked and talked – I found myself absent minded, then with my attention half on what he said, realised I was listening for the word *I* in what he said. I, I, I, I, I – I began to feel as if the word I was being shot at me like bullets from a machine gun. For a moment I fancied that his mouth, moving fast and mobile, was a gun of some kind. (531)

Tobin, citing these passages in particular, has, like many other critics (Saxton and Tobin 1994, Yellen 1998, Fand 1999), elucidated the profound influence Woolf's work had on Lessing's, but it is how the 'I, I, I' of the 'machine gun ejaculation' is situated in the formal conceit of each experimental textual project that is so important. It is not only that the language of patriarchy kills women – 'blood sucked', 'I was being shot' – but that this death can only be analysed in the context of how gender violence is understood as part of the larger political histories being documented simultaneously in other parts of the texts. Peggy and Anna are made invisible, are hostage to the egoist, whose 'I' takes away their own authority. They are released only when they assert their own subjectivity, as when Peggy tells her interlocutor that she's a doctor and notes that 'the fire went out of his face when she said "I"' (361). Anna, who is herself raising a daughter and thus clearly has more knowledge than Saul on the subject, is forced to demur to his hysterical assertion of knowledge about 'how to bring up a small girl', and becomes ever more diffuse and infected by his 'I'. Despite Anna's feeling that this is a topic 'chosen at random', we as readers understand that it is not. Woolf's and Lessing's response to women's authorial stripping is to catalogue and collect the history of men's hysteria in their own scrapbooks. This documentary counterhistory includes, in both novels, great attention to how the left has been unable to fully grapple with sexual hierarchies, and has thus always already failed its revolutionary aims. Both Peggy's interlocutor and Saul are writers and left-aligned or communist. Anna says, 'the structure of a Communist Party or group is a self-dividing principle' (64).

The political bifurcations that Lessing describes were manifest on an aesthetic level as well, between the various forms of political realism, avant-garde experimentation and apolitical modernism, the borders of which were heavily patrolled in mid-century by the critical and political establishment. And they still persist today – in our reading habits they define what we consider aesthetically good, and they still influence what and who we study and teach in the academy. While challenges to these systems occurred in many places, it is particularly important to consider how women writers subverted these political binaries through the transgressions of gender and genre norms, in part because these transgressions only become fully legible by reading their works in context of one another. In her 1940 lecture *The Usable Truth*, Rukeyser writes, 'we have our own tradition to retrace . . . tradition is not repetition, that is blasphemy against tradition' (1940). This impulse to break 'the nightmare of repetition', as Lessing called it, can be traced before and through Lessing's novel, from H.D., West, Hurston, Lorde, and many others to the present moment (1954: 102). The American poet Alice Notley writes in *The Descent of Alette* (1992) that the hero of her anti-war epic must 'change the forms', even 'change the forms in dreams', in order to break with the past (1996: 147). Theresa Hak Kyung Cha, in her postmodern and feminist counterhistory of the Korean War, *Dictee* (1982), which documents the lost narratives of women through a fractured and multi-genre formal process, writes, 'to name it now so as not to repeat the past into oblivion. To extract each fragment by each fragment from the word from the image another word another image the reply that will not repeat history in oblivion' (2001: 33). Like Lessing, each author posits a feminist semiotics, understanding the expressive possibilities of language to create our reality and thus to disrupt or change reality as well. That the very basis of women's material lives, the very reality of war making or empire building, begins with the formative language that becomes a narrative that we then call history, means that it is at the formal level that change or disruption might begin. 'History is preserved not in the art object, but in the tradition of *making* the art object', as Jane Marcus writes (1984: 84).

Lessing's radical formal project is a radical political one, not just for what it exposes about the relationships between power and patriarchy, relationships we would not fully understand in the first place without these kinds of texts, but in the way it repositions women's own bodies as narrators of that history. This is important because, as Anne Carson has noted, there is a 'death of meaning' for women, whose bodies are both the object and the subject, and so women writers are tasked with de-objectifying themselves in a process of authorial becoming (136). At one point, Anna asserts a Blakean idea, that if people can imagine something, there will be a time when they'll achieve it. The experimental structure of *The Golden Notebook*, read as part of the tradition of radical invention – of form and content – that women writers have undertaken, is a visionary one, for it cannot be contained or understood through any of the political theories or even formal categories that have been written already. Because of that, these texts, despite our inevitable, perhaps even provoked, misreadings of them, give us access to new material, new histories, new kinds of forms to think through.

Works Cited

Carson, Anne (1995), *Glass, Irony and God*, New York: New Directions.

Cha, Theresa Hak Kyung (2001), *Dictee*, Berkeley: University of California Press.

Fand, Roxanne (1999), *The Dialogic Self: Reconstructing Subjectivity in Woolf, Lessing and Atwood*, Selinsgrove: Susquehanna University Press.

Feigel, Lara (2015), 'Doris Lessing's MI5 File: Was She a Threat to the State?', *The Guardian,* 13 November, <http://www.theguardian.com/books/2015/nov/13/doris-lessings-mi5-file-threat-state> (last accessed 15 January 2016).

Greene, Gayle (1995), *Doris Lessing: The Poetics of Change*, Ann Arbor: University of Michigan Press.

Hejinian, Lynn (2000), 'The Rejection of Closure', in *The Language of Inquiry*, Berkeley: University of California Press, pp. 40–58.

Lessing, Doris [1962] (1990), *The Golden Notebook*, New York: Harper Collins.

—— (1954), *A Proper Marriage*, London: Michael Joseph.

—— (2001), 'I Have Nothing in Common With Feminists . . .', *The Observer*, 9 September, <http://www.theguardian.com/books/2001/sep/09/fiction.dorislessing> (last accessed 15 January 2016).

—— (2007), 'Guarded Welcome: Doris Lessing on the History of *The Golden Notebook's* Troubled Reception', *The Guardian*, 27 January, <http://www.theguardian.com/books/2007/jan/27/featuresreviews.guardianreview25> (last accessed 15 January 2016).

Marcus, Jane, (1984),'Still Practice A/Wrested Alphabet: Toward A Feminist Aesthetics', *Tulsa Studies in Women's Literature*, 3:2, 79–97.

Notley, Alice (1996), *The Descent of Alette*, Harmondsworth: Penguin.

Rich, Adrienne (2002), 'When We Dead Awaken: Writing as Re-vision', in *Arts of the Possible*, New York: Norton.

Roy, Arundhati (2011), *Walking with the Comrades*, New York: Penguin.

Rukeyser, Muriel (1941), 'The Usable Truth', Muriel Rukeyser Papers, Library of Congress, Box: 43.

—— (1974), 'We Came for Games', *Esquire* 82 (October 1974), 192–4, 368–70.

—— (1996), *The Life of Poetry*, Ashfield: Paris Press.

—— (2005), *The Collected Poems of Muriel Rukeyser*, ed. Janet Kaufman and Anne Herzog, Pittsburgh: University of Pittsburgh Press.

—— (2013), *Savage Coast (Costa Brava)*, ed. Rowena Kennedy-Epstein, New York: The Feminist Press.

Saxton, Ruth and Jean Tobin (eds) (1994), *Woolf and Lessing: Breaking the Mold*, New York: St. Martin's Press.

Singer, Sandra (2015), 'Feminist Commitment to Left-Wing Realism', in Sandra

Singer, Alice Ridout and Roberta Rubenstein (eds), *The Golden Notebook After Fifty*, New York: Palgrave.

Tobin, Jean (1994), 'On Creativity: Woolf's *The Waves* and Lessing's *The Golden Notebook*', in Saxton and Tobin, New York: St. Martin's.

Woolf, Virginia [1937] (1969), *The Years*, New York: Mariner.

—— (1977), *The Pargiters*, ed. Michael Leaska, New York: New York Public Library.

—— (1985), *The Diary of Virginia Woolf, Volume 5: 1936–41*, New York: Mariner.

—— [1938] (2006), *Three Guineas*, ed. Jane Marcus, Orlando, FL: Harcourt.

Yelin, Louise (1998), *From the Margins of Empire: Christina Stead, Doris Lessing, Nadine Gordimer*, Cornell: Cornell University Press.

Chapter 5

Readers of Fiction and Readers in Fiction: Readership and *The Golden Notebook*

Sophia Barnes

Doris Lessing's *The Golden Notebook* is peopled by fictional readers who interpret and challenge the texts of others within a layered and ontologically unstable narrative frame. While the novel's innovative portrayal of authorship and its implications for authority have long been a rich source of critical debate, the equally intriguing if less studied correlative of this portrayal is the particular pressures Lessing's depictions of readership place on her readers. *The Golden Notebook* not only includes multiple types of readers but also invites, anticipates and critiques conflicting responses. The cumulative effect of the many acts of readership which take place within the novel is to challenge its readers to question the presuppositions upon which their own reading practice rests, the modes of reading they employ, and the ways in which these modes of reading are implicated in particular beliefs about the function of literature. In the context of a recent reinvigoration of academic interest in reading practices, Lessing's exploration of various models of and motives for readership forces us to interrogate the rationale and conventions of literary criticism. This essay examines how readership is depicted in *The Golden Notebook* to ask the question: what kinds of readers does Lessing want us to be? It is a question which cannot be answered without also considering her resistance to the authority invested in professional academic criticism, her relationship to distinctive cultures of reading, and the celebration of multifarious individualistic and non-instrumental approaches to readership which is not only explicitly articulated in the 1971 Preface to *The Golden Notebook* but also made implicit in the novel's structure. Lessing is fascinated by the persistent question 'of what people see when they read a book, and why one person sees one pattern and nothing at all of another pattern'. While she may contemplate 'how odd it is to have, as author, such a clear picture of a book, that is seen so very differently by its readers', she nonetheless emphatically concludes that it is precisely this heterogeneity of reception which keeps the book 'alive and potent and fructifying' (2007: 20–1).

In her Preface to *The Golden Notebook* Lessing spoke of her desire to write a novel 'which described the intellectual and moral climate' of its time (2007: 10), responding to a historically situated crisis of faith in epistemological certainty. This desire found expression in the text's interrogation of political and creative responsibility, and its nuanced contribution to the radical scepticism of post-war and early postmodern experimentation. *The Golden Notebook* was 'an amazing ideological balancing act' between the activist and the autobiographical, in which 'the personal, the ironic, the sexual, the naïve, is part of what undermines the grand political myths; and the grand political myths are destroying Europe and the world' (Altman 1996: 20). Lessing was at one and the same time deeply invested in an inclusive and committed vision of literature's representative and communicative possibilities, and sharply aware of its inadequacies. Surveying early responses to her novel, she suggested that an author sought amongst her critics 'an alter ego, that other self more intelligent than oneself who has seen what one is reaching for, and who judges you only by whether you have matched up to your aim or not'. Needless to say – as indeed Lessing did say – this alter ego was not to be found. 'Why should there be anyone else who comprehends what [the author] is trying to do' (2007: 14)? Perhaps we come closest with the vision of an ever-growing and evolving community of readership which, in its very diversity, embodies such intelligence. From Africa to Asia to the United States, this community now spans generations, as the novel 'keeps putting its head up in new places, and often not where one would expect' (Lessing 2004: 138). Even those readings which Lessing herself lamented as being reductive nonetheless speak back to the text, and it is a wonderful and productive irony that the history of *The Golden Notebook*'s reception includes precisely those blind spots, those ideological divisions, assumptions and critical presuppositions that the novel repeatedly exposes. As John Plotz wryly notes, 'If, as a reader, you recognize that you're part of the novel's experiment, you're a step closer to the solution' (2012). In its portrayal of different kinds of readership *The Golden Notebook* probes the assumptions upon which each is premised, illuminating the tensions between them in such a way that the novel's readers are compelled into an explicitly self-reflective mode. We are challenged to 'realize (a crucial word for Lessing)' the relationship between the fictional world and our own, and thereby – if only momentarily – attain an 'external perspective' on each (2012).

Readership in *The Golden Notebook* is heterogeneous both in its motives and its outcomes. There are political readers with differing intentions – activist, utilitarian and propagandist; autodidacts and colonials, reading for self-education; people reading for self-reflection or self-discovery; tastemakers of the culture industry, and editors of journals positioning themselves as the arbiters of literary quality. The primary tension between a political or activist model of readership and the autobiographical impulse embodied in Anna's obsessive self-transcription arises in the opening section of 'Free Women', as Tommy Portmain – the son of Anna's best friend Molly – questions her reluctance to continue publishing her writing for others to read. Tommy's direct challenges to Anna constitute the novel's most explicit articulation of the particular concept of responsibility which comes with a political mode of readership. The spectre of this responsibility determines not only whether Anna writes but also what she writes, for her inability or unwillingness to publish (she is of course prolific in her private writings) stems at least partly from her conviction that what she is capable of writing – what she wants to write – is not what she should write. 'You're afraid of writing what you think about life, because you might find yourself in an exposed position, you might expose yourself, you might be alone', Tommy accuses her. He is taking her seriously – 'Why shouldn't I take you seriously?' he insists (54–5) – and in doing so places certain demands on her: that she speak seriously, and that she accord in her actions – namely her enactment of authorship – with the political principles she has professed. What complicates the relationship of author to reader which exists between them is Anna's sense that Tommy has a right to make these demands of her. Watching on as he pores over her private writings and feeling that 'she could not endure that anyone should see those notebooks', she nonetheless concedes 'that Tommy had a right to see them: but she could not have explained why' (252). Whether it is because she sees herself as a surrogate mother to him, or as a political elder, or simply as a member of one generation passing the baton to its successor, the relationship is one that demands honesty and implies responsibility.

The divergence in Tommy's fate between the novel's two central narrative threads is at least partly a consequence of the way in which he inhabits the role of Anna's reader (and antagonist). His attempted suicide in 'Free Women', which does not occur in the chronologically mirrored narrative arc of the notebooks, is at least partly provoked by his sense of disappointment in Anna, who cannot give him what he wants because she is not able to pretend a confidence in her authorial role that she does not feel. The final confrontation which takes place between them prior to the suicide attempt is fuelled by his readership of the notebooks, whose function and fragmentation confound him; he wants Anna to tell him 'what we are alive for', but this is something she cannot do (244). Tommy is a political reader challenging Anna to take on the role of political author, and her resistance to the kind of reader-ship he embodies proceeds from a dual predicament: on the one hand the weight of her responsibility to this model of readership is oppres-sive; on the other she is facing a burgeoning crisis of faith in its value. Tommy expects Anna to inhabit her authorial role in a particular way – to write, perhaps, the kind of novel whose first line she hands to Saul Green; or a novel of the Chinese peasant, the Cuban guerrilla fighter and the 'Algerian fighting in the FLN' who she imagines upbraiding her as she scribbles in her notebooks (554). Autobiography has little value for Tommy, to whom Anna's journaling is a perversion of her public status as author. 'You write and write in notebooks', he charges her, 'saying what you think about life, but you lock them up, and that's not being responsible' (55–6). In fact the text Anna does finally produce – if, like Gayle Greene, we take *The Golden Notebook* proper as the novel 'she has been writing . . . all along' (127) – is as radical as Saul's, indeed a great deal more so. As Rowena Kennedy-Epstein argues persuasively in the previous chapter, Lessing undermines and destabilises the authority inscribed in monolithic formal and political structures not only in her novel's subject but in the very radicalism of its hybrid form.

Between them Anna and Tommy play out an intergenerational politi-cal dynamic, with Tommy having grown up under the influence of com-mitted communists who have begun to question their own 'youthful certainties, slogans and battle-cries' just as he reaches adulthood and suf-frage (238). Unlike Anna and Molly – and Lessing – Tommy's formative years have come after the end of the Second World War, and for him the ethical crises with which Western Marxism is contending in the 1950s do not have the same devastating significance. In the confrontation between Anna and Tommy, Lessing conjures those same anxieties about the role of literature which inflected her own relationship to an ideologi-cally invested culture of reading at the time of the novel's composition. She was of course an active participant in 'a range of aesthetic and political debates' taking place during this time, and 'converging around the question of the role and position of the writer and intellectual, on the relationship between political commitment and realist writing, and how both might be defined' (Taylor 1982: 14). Notwithstanding her strong association with the British New Left (she was on the editorial board of the *New Reasoner* before it merged with the *Universities and Left Review* to become the *New Left Review* in 1960), by the time of *The Golden Notebook*'s publication Lessing was already in the process of moving away from the project of resuscitating and reforming com-munism in the aftermath of Stalin's death and the Khrushchev thaw.

While friends and comrades like Edward Thompson 'tried to sustain the optimism, to break with the impasse of the Cold War and to argue for a renewal of what was best in the communist tradition ... *The Golden Notebook* was denying *that* route' as well (McCrindle 1982: 49, emphasis original). In a letter to Thompson written in 1957, and published in the second volume of her autobiography, Lessing insisted: 'I don't want to make any more concepts. For myself, I mean. I want to let myself simmer into some sort of knowledge, but I don't know what it is' (Lessing 1997: 195). A recognition of the not only creatively stultifying but materially dangerous effects of monolithic ideology, and the crucial importance of individual responsibility, was at the forefront of Lessing's politics during this period. 'If anything, *The Golden Notebook* explored why people wanted to call themselves feminist, or Marxist, (not to mention Tory or Labour) – as if pinning a label on your blazer solved anything' (Plotz 2013). Hers was an ethics informed by years of Marxist activism yet one which had also moved beyond it, placing the utmost importance upon resistance to totalitarian modes of thought, insisting on the value of alterity, multiplicity, exchange and dialogue.

Saul Green is the only character besides Tommy who is described as examining Anna's notebooks (if we take Milt in Free Women as his cipher), and he is likewise antagonistic. His role as a reader of Anna, however, is by no means straightforward – he is also an author, and she is also his reader. The pairing of Anna and Saul is read by Roberta Rubenstein, in her comprehensive study of Lessing's affair with the American author Clancy Sigal, as a fictionalisation of that formative and tumultuous intellectual and sexual relationship. In the midst of their liaison Lessing began to read Sigal's private diary, upon the discovery of which trespass this diary 'evolved into an intentionally shaped record intended not simply for himself but for one particular reader' (Rubenstein 2014: 33). Sigal – or rather, appropriately enough, his 'fictional alter ego' in an unfinished novel – came finally to realise that 'he [could] no longer trust his diary as an unmediated record of his thoughts and experiences; by his own choice, it had become, at least in part, fiction' (Rubenstein 2014: 41). Compounding the experience of mediation even further, Lessing appears to have enfolded her reading of Sigal's diaries into chapters of what would become *The Golden Notebook*, leaving them, as he would later recount, 'around the house for me to stumble on, read and dash upstairs to scribble responses in my journal which she'd then creep up to examine' (39). We see this 'hall of mirrors' (to borrow the title of Rubenstein's opening chapter) transformed into fiction in the Blue Notebook, as Anna reads Saul's diaries – a fact which, like Sigal, he soon discovers (13–52). This situation has been foreshadowed in the precis for 'A Short Novel' included in the final section of the Yellow Notebook, in which 'a man and a woman, married or in a long relationship, secretly read each other's diaries'. Each soon discovers the other's intrusion and – preferring deception to confrontation – begins to write for his or her lover.

> ... for a while objectivity is maintained. Then, slowly, they begin writing falsely, first unconsciously; then consciously, so as to influence the other. The position is reached where each keeps two diaries, one for private use, and locked up; and the second for the other to read. (472)

Soon enough these secondary journals are also discovered and they too take on a deceptive function. From mutual duplicity emerges a perverse mode of performative self-transcription – one which is not only depicted within *The Golden Notebook* but appears also to have played a crucial role in its composition.

What other readers does *The Golden Notebook* depict, or presuppose? There are the multiple readings (or misreadings) undertaken by producers seeking to adapt *Frontiers of War*, whose commercial intentions conjure a romantic caricature of Anna's political drama about the colour-bar in colonial Africa. As a published author being wined and dined Anna sits uncomfortably on the fringes of a culture industry in its germinal days, finally electing to withdraw from it entirely (at least within the narrative frame of Free Women). Coterminous with the rise of this culture industry was a shift in the social, economic and political sites of literary debate and criticism, as 'the freelance intellectual was undercut by the academic, and the practice of criticism was increasingly centred in universities' (Taylor 1982: 10). This shift had implications for the culture of public intellectual and political debate, dividing readers into the knowing and the naïve: the provinces of academia and mass culture respectively. It also had implications for an understanding of a culture of reading, which was explicitly premised on class, as intellectual debate, at least in its most codified form, moved into the academy and away from the tradition of working-class self-education whose decline was then being lamented among the New Left by Richard Hoggart. It is perhaps in the context of these dual trends that literary journal editors – earnest gatekeepers of the profession – to whom Anna and her friend James Shaffer send their parodical submissions are unable to identify these for what they are. The obliviousness of these editors sits provocatively alongside Anna's own misinterpretation of an earnest paean to the Soviet motherland penned by her colleague in the British Communist Party, Comrade Ted – which she mistakenly, and cynically, reads as parody. It is an error which underscores the variety of forms political readership takes within the novel. There is for instance a marked difference between a reader like Tommy, who seeks an authentic articulation of political commitment from Anna, and the readers for whom Comrade Ted's propaganda is intended, who are expected to adhere to certain telegraphed ideological precepts. Anna misreads his text precisely because – however regretfully – she no longer adheres to these precepts, and therefore no longer reads in the necessary mode. That mode is itself differentiated from the systematic analysis and collective readership undertaken by Anna and her fellow Marxists in Mashopi, Africa, whose story she recounts in the Black Notebook. Even in that nominally most egalitarian of groups, however, we see a hierarchy of readers, from Willi Rodde, the middle-class 'refugee from sophisticated Europe stuck for the duration of the war in a backwater' to the autodidactic colonial 'roads man' George Hounslow, whose character is drawn with sympathy but redolent also of the frustrations of intellectual isolation (84; 108).

Anna Wulf is, of course, her own most critical reader – both of her published and unpublished writing. She upbraids herself for the dishonesty of the emotion by which she believes herself to have been motivated in writing *Frontiers of War*, the 'lying nostalgia' which both pervades and is engendered by it (77). Likewise she is 'disturbed' when reading over the Blue Notebook, which she has designated the closest thing to a conventional journal, by the disjunction between her remembered experience and the narrative which she has made of it. 'Matching what I had written with what I remembered it all seemed false' (418). As readers both of Anna's notebooks and of the apparently conventional narrative which frames them, we not only see Anna write herself, then read herself, and finally watch herself do so as she composes a commentary on the process; we also engage in a remarkably self-reflexive mode of readership in which we are challenged to watch ourselves reading. The splitting and multiplication of Anna through the text's many strands, and the fracturing of narrative stability which proceeds from it, encourages readers to reflect on their own multiplied, fragmentary and unstable responses to the novel. Our desire for integration; our reading choices in response to the novel's invitations and challenges; our identification with or resistance to the ethic of splitness at its centre; and the shock of retrospectively recalibrating the relationship of its individual threads, all force us to reflect on the assumptions which we have brought to the reading process and the strategies we have employed to make the text whole. That 'one text is potentially capable of several different realizations, and no reading can ever exhaust the full potential' of that text is by now a well-established precept of hermeneutics, and Wolfgang Iser reminds us that when we make our deeply individual decisions about how to fill the gaps in the texts we read, we acknowledge that very 'inexhaustibility of the text' which compels us to make these decisions. What set the texts of the twentieth century apart for Iser was their fragmentary nature, requiring readers to 'search for connections between the fragments' in order 'to make us aware of the nature of our own capacity for providing links' (285). In a manner comparable to the formal exploitation of the gaps between volumes in the *Children of Violence* series, as explored by Kevin Brazil in a previous chapter, Lessing's novel challenges its reader not only to 'search for connections' between fragments, but to consider the nature of these connections – or their absence – and their implications for one's own readership.

Readers of Lessing's novel face at least two separate temptations: one being to read around or through the structure of the novel, dismissing any inconsistencies; another to fixate on un-weaving its paradoxical form to the neglect of its thematic concerns. Critical readers are often 'unable to come to her text free of their training' and are wont to 'debate endlessly' the meaning of the text's circular authorship. Beth A. Boehm confesses to being such a reader – or at least having begun as such a reader – when she observes that:

> Lessing invites her audience of educated readers to employ the pattern-making strategies which help us make meaning of complex modernist texts; and then disdainfully creates a text for which such strategies are completely ineffective; indeed, the best such strategies do is produce a parody of meaning and intelligibility. (91–2)

In fact, Boehm argues, Lessing has far more tolerance for those who read around formal complexity to locate the relationship between text and world, and her 'antagonism toward those who privilege the text's ability to say something about the "real" world . . . is less intense than it is toward those who privilege the invitation to read the structure of the text' (96). This second set of readers who fancy themselves to have understood Lessing's project because they recognise the meta-fictional foundations of her novel, risk being complicit in enforcing the division between fiction and life, between the real and the textual. Despite the meta-fictional complexity of its 'convoluted structure' and the invitation to treat this structure as a puzzle to be solved, *The Golden Notebook*, according to Boehm, 'actually seeks to reeducate its educated readers, to make them more like the readers who . . . can "read through the structure" to seek connections between text and world' (96–7). That there can be no single, 'correct' reading of the novel is well established; perhaps one way we might negotiate the division between the two approaches described here is to recognise that the necessity of questioning our reading strategies, and the assumptions which underpin them, is precisely the novel's point.

In her 'defective or delinquent manifesto' *Uses of Literature*, Rita Felski mounts an argument for the value of naivety in reading, privileging the experiential elements of recognition, shock, enchantment and knowledge over what Ricœur called the hermeneutics of suspicion (135). In such a hermeneutics, critics 'rewrite narrative in terms of master codes, disclosing its status as ideology, as an imaginary resolution of read contradictions' (Best and Marcus 2009: 5). The literary text 'is hauled in to confirm what the critic already knows' – what, presumably, only the critic knows – begging the question: 'what is lost when we deny a work any capacity to bite back, in Ellen Rooney's phrase, to challenge or change our own beliefs and commitments' (Felski 2008: 7). As academic critics we must interrogate our own tendency, even in seeking to unpack ideological structures, to do so from a position that is itself premised on an imbalance of power, and which tends to devalue other types of reading. Published academic criticism is a kind of 'public performance subject to a host of gate-keeping practices and professional norms' which does not necessarily serve even as an 'especially reliable or comprehensive guide to the ways in which academics read' as individuals engaging with literary texts (14). Each of the critics contributing to this volume is, after all, a reader: we are readers of texts for pleasure and stimulation, for education or information, who read Lessing's fictions and non-fictions for many and varied reasons. It is doubtful any of us would be contributing to a volume devoted to her *oeuvre* if we did not experience an initial encounter with her work which engaged us precisely in our experiences of recognition, shock, enchantment or knowledge, *pace* Felski. We train ourselves to become critical readers, 'moving from attachment to detachment and indeed to disenchantment, undergoing not just an intellectual but also a sentimental education' (30). Lessing suggests that when we privilege this model of reading, we forget – and fail to communicate – 'that the point of literature is pleasure and not the dreary analysis that can be of interest only to academics who, some think, have captured literature' (Lessing 2015: 32). It is a damning, albeit hyperbolic, indictment, and one which can't be brought to bear in what is after all a collection of academic essays without a healthy dose of self-reflection. 'There is no reason', argues Felski, 'why our readings cannot combine analysis and attachment, criticism and love' (Felski 2008: 22). This is not to suggest that such readings of Lessing have not already been undertaken – we can look, for instance, to the diverse perspectives offered by the nine women critics who contributed to Claire Sprague's collection *In Pursuit of Doris Lessing: Nine Nations Reading*

– but that we must strive to be self-aware in our position as precisely those 'academics' for whose implied authority Lessing has little respect.

How might readers be guided by Lessing's own commentary on the nature of her medium and the reception of her work? Her impatience with how *The Golden Notebook* 'was instantly belittled, by friendly reviewers as well as by hostile ones, as being about the sex war', for instance, places particular pressures on anyone who identifies as a specifically feminist reader of the novel (Lessing 2007: 8). Lessing had depicted a protagonist negotiating urgent, historically situated tensions between creativity and political activism, sexual freedom and motherhood, economic pressure and intellectual independence. For many early readers *The Golden Notebook* functioned as an influential consciousness-raising novel, that kind of text which 'transformed confusion to consciousness, enabling women to understand the changes they were living through' (Greene 1992: 50). Lessing's relationship to the project of Women's Liberation and an emergent second-wave feminism cannot be decoupled from that movement's emphasis on reading as an inherently political activity, undertaken to share experience and inform action. This particular mode of feminist readership was unapologetically instrumental, as second-wave feminists 'used reading and writing to build the women's community' (Harker 2007: 155). The 'double movement of indebtedness and disappointment' (Altman 1996: 15) with which many feminist critics reread *The Golden Notebook* following Lessing's occasionally maligned move into science fiction, bears more than a passing resemblance to the demands which we see Tommy Portmain place upon Anna Wulf. In each model of readership the author is responsible to her readers in a particular way; a kind of figurehead for the collective with a specific political function. Much of Lessing's resistance to her status as a forerunner of the 'sex war' stemmed not from any objection to the project of Women's Liberation – 'I support it, of course', she reminds us in the Preface (8) – but from her frustration with the reductive nature of such a reading. She likewise resisted being read as a representative of the New Left, despite her close association with many of its leading lights and participation in many of its formative activities. *The Golden Notebook*, she insisted, was not 'a product of the milieu of the New Left' unless that milieu was 'now retrospectively to be expanded to include ideas which in fact it was impossible to discuss with any of the people I knew, most of whom were much younger that [*sic*] I was' (Lessing 1990). Notwithstanding her sympathy for its project, Lessing resisted being read as the product or the voice of a collective movement.

Both those early readings which lionised Lessing as a feminist writer and some later, revisionary approaches which located her as one of 'yesterday's heroines' (Wilson 1982: 72), tended to focus on the novel's content rather than its form. By contrast, Rowena Kennedy-Epstein's chapter in this volume places *The Golden Notebook* in a specifically female tradition of formal radicalism, subverting generic and gendered boundaries and resisting established structures, arguing that the novel became a central text for feminist critics at the precise moment it was misread by the male literary establishment who never let Lessing off the hook for being a woman who insisted on the relationship between form and content. And if Lessing resisted codification through her form, so too do the readers she depicted within her novel enact their own challenges to political and literary authority. Tommy's readership of Anna's notebooks contests what he regards as the hypocrisy of her failure to publish, while Anna herself implicitly rejects the dominant narratives of the Communist Party when she misreads Comrade Ted. She displays contempt for the authority of the literary establishment through her parodic submissions to its flagship journals, just as she refuses to participate in the culture industry through the adaptation and corruption of her first novel. Finally – if we take *The Golden Notebook* proper as the novel Anna has made of her notebook project – she resists the authority of masculinity embodied by Saul and his alter ego Milt, both of whom question the value of her autobiographical project. A reader of *The Golden Notebook* may likewise conceive of him- or herself as a 'resisting reader', challenging not only those structures which the novel interrogates but also the authority embedded in Lessing's own exhortations regarding how her novel will be read (Ridout 2011: 66). After all, the 'paradoxical position' of the novel's Preface 'is taken further by its very existence; it tries to put the record straight with the message that there is no message, no straight record' (Taylor 1982: 12). The relationship between Lessing's work and its readership is one premised on multiplicity: the proliferation of interwoven narrative threads, the layering of provocative and sometimes contradictory authorial commentary, and the diversity of us as her readers, and our interpretations. 'Should the feminist reader's response to Lessing's claim that she is not a feminist writer be to assert, "But I am a feminist reader?"' asks Alice Ridout (2011: 65–6). To which Lessing might well have replied: By all means. But don't be *only* a feminist reader.

The Golden Notebook is fuelled by a healthy scepticism towards all monolithic modes of thought and structures of authority, and likewise towards those kinds of reading which serve to buttress such structures through their refusal to let the text 'bite back'. As successive instrumental and professional modes of reading are one by one seen to be reductive, the novel asks its readers to examine the systems they are implicated in as they read, and to read as individuals, taking individual responsibility. In a letter to the *Reasoner* in November 1956 Lessing stated a principle of political organisation which could double as a description of the kind of creative and intellectual practice she valued, and by extension the kind of readers she wanted her own to be.

> There is no simple decision we can make, once and for all, that will ensure that we are doing right. There is no set of rules that can set us free from the necessity of making fresh decisions, every day ... The safeguard against tyranny, now, as it always has been, is to sharpen individuality, to strengthen individual responsibility, and not to delegate it. (1956)

Throughout her fictional and non-fictional writing Lessing insisted upon the utmost responsibility of the individual for their own education, and their own resistance to totalitarian or doctrinaire modes of thought or action. 'People who love literature have at least a part of their minds immune from indoctrination', she observed, forty years after *The Golden Notebook* was published. 'If you read, you can learn how to think for yourself' (Lessing 2015: 3). The response of a reader or community of readers in a given historical moment to the authorial invitations and challenges extended by *The Golden Notebook* is necessarily contingent. We experience 'recognition', for instance, in our encounter with a text not because literary works 'are repositories for unchanging truths about the human condition', but as a manifestation of the 'interplay between texts and the fluctuating beliefs, hopes, and fears of readers, such that the insights gleaned from literary works will vary dramatically across space and time' (Felski 2008: 46). Lessing wants her readers to approach all texts for what they can offer to us, putting aside those for which we are not ready and returning to them when we are – 'and never, never reading anything because you feel you ought, or because it is part of a trend or movement' (2007: 17–18). *The Golden Notebook* continues to engage diverse readers from Zimbabwe to China, Europe to Vermont – a community which already spanned 'three generations' more than twenty years ago (2004: 141). While this diversity flourishes it seems doubtful that we will have cause 'to throw the book aside, as having had its day, and start again on something new' any time soon (Lessing 2007: 21).

Works Cited

Altman, Meryl (1996), 'Before we said 'we' (and after): bad sex and personal politics in Doris Lessing and Simone de Beauvoir', *Critical Inquiry* 38:3, 14–29.

Best, Steven and Sharon Marcus (2009), 'Surface Reading: An Introduction', *Representations* 108:1, 1–21.

Boehm, Beth A. (1997), 'Reeducating Readers: Creating New Expectations for *The Golden Notebook*', *Narrative* 5:1, 88–98.

Felski, Rita (2008), *Uses of Literature*, New York: Wiley Blackwell.

Greene, Gayle (1992), *Changing the Story: Feminist Fiction and the Tradition*, Indianapolis: Indiana University Press.

Harker, Jaime (2007), *America the Middlebrow: Women's Novels, Progressivism, and Middlebrow Authorship Between the Wars*, Boston: University of Massachusetts Press.

Iser, Wolfgang (1972), 'The Reading Process: A Phenomenological Approach', *New Literary History* 3:2, 279–99.

Lessing, Doris (1956), Letter, *The Reasoner*, 3 (November 1956).

—— (1990), Letter, *London Review of Books*, 12:7 (5 April 1990).

—— (1997), *Walking in the Shade: Volume Two of My Autobiography, 1949– 1962*, New York: Harper Collins.

—— (2004), *Time Bites: Views and Reviews*, New York: Harper Collins.

—— [1962] (2007), *The Golden Notebook*, London: Harper Perennial.

—— (2015), 'Doris Lessing', in Antonia Fraser (ed.), *The Pleasure of Reading: 43 Writers on the Discovery of Reading and the Books that Inspired Them*, London: Bloomsbury, pp. 28–37.

McCrindle, Jean (1982), 'Reading *The Golden Notebook* in 1962', in Jenny Taylor (ed.), *Notebooks/Memoirs/Archives*, London: Routledge, pp. 43–56.

Plotz, John (2012), 'Feeling Like a Stoic: Doris Lessing's Experimental Fiction', *Public Books*, 7 August 2012, <http://www.publicbooks.org/fiction/feeling-like-a-stoic-doris-lessings-experimental-fiction> (last accessed 23 December 2015).

—— (2013), 'Lessing Is More', *Slate Magazine*, 18 November 2013, <http:// www.slate.com/articles/double_x/doublex/2013/11/doris_lessing_the_ golden_notebook_is_more_than_feminist_rage.html> (last accessed 29 December 2015).

Ridout, Alice (2011), *Contemporary Women Writers Look Back: From Irony to Nostalgia*, London: Continuum.

Rubenstein, Roberta (2014), *Literary Half-Lives: Doris Lessing, Clancy Sigal, and* Roman à Clef, New York: Palgrave Macmillan.

Sprague, Claire (ed.) (1990), *In Pursuit of Doris Lessing: Nine Nations Reading*, New York: Palgrave Macmillan.

Taylor, Jenny (ed.) (1982), *Notebooks/memoirs/archives: Reading and Rereading Doris Lessing*, London: Routledge.

Wilson, Elizabeth (1982), 'Yesterday's Heroines: On Reading and Rereading Doris Lessing', in Jenny Taylor (ed.), *Notebooks/memoirs/archives: Reading and Rereading Doris Lessing*, London: Routledge, pp. 57–74.

Chapter 6

From *The Grass is Singing* to *The Golden Notebook*: Film, Literature and Psychoanalysis

Laura Marcus

The relationships between writers and the cinema in the twentieth century have received significant critical attention, but the work of Doris Lessing has not, to date, played a central role in explorations of this topic. Yet in a number of her works we can locate the multiple influences of cinema. As with many of her contemporaries, there is at times a perception of the threat which cinema represented to authors, competing for their readers as it turned them into spectators and, more dangerously, with the Hollywood machine imposing a restrictive set of narrative norms on authors. The cinema was, however, also a promise. The work of many writers, novelists and dramatists found new life on the screen through adaptation. The art of writing itself was, moreover, undoubtedly shaped and altered by the modes of representation which developed in the film medium, in ways which could be creative as well as restrictive.

In addition to questions of narrative in fiction and film, we find Lessing's complex representations of what I would term 'the cinema mind'. This is connected, as in the work of many film theorists, to representations of collective and individual dreaming, an analysis underwritten by psychoanalytic theory's own engagements with the technologies of vision and models of perception. This chapter explores the meanings and representations of the cinema in these particular contexts, with a focus on two of Lessing's novels; *The Grass is Singing* (1950) and *The Golden Notebook* (1962).

Film and cinema play a significant role in *The Grass is Singing*, Lessing's first novel. This was begun in the mid-1940s, during the period of her marriage to Gottfried Lessing, when she was living and working in Salisbury, Southern Rhodesia, and was finally published in 1950, in a much shortened and revised form, after she had arrived in London. The novel tells the story of the ill-fated marriage of Mary, a woman in her thirties living and working in the city, who is impelled towards marriage to the farmer Dick Turner by her discomfort with her single status: he, in turn, is driven by loneliness and need. The narrative opens with a news report of Mary's murder by a black farm-servant: borrowing the model of the detective novel, *The Grass is Singing* begins with a corpse and a police investigation, and then retraces the events that have led to the crime. In a context, however, in which any concept of justice is utterly skewed by the racial dynamics of a settler society, there can be no compensatory restoration, such as the traditional detective story provides, of a 'proper' order to the world. Moreover, we see, in the final stages of the narrative, Mary walking towards her murder, as 'something she could not visualize, but which waited for her inexorably, inescapably' (167). For Mary, and not just for the reader, this is a death foretold.

Mary is no heroine for her author, although the novel is sensitive to the limited options available to her as a woman, and to her fears of repeating her mother's impoverished life. Arriving on the farm after her marriage, dismayed at its meanness and discomfort, and feeling no desire for her new husband, she embarks on domesticity by behaving abusively towards the black servants who work for her. She first encounters Moses, who will become her murderer, when she briefly takes over running the struggling farm from Dick when he is ill: enraged by what she perceives as Moses's insubordination, she strikes him across the face with a whip. When he becomes the Turner's house-servant, she becomes locked into an increasingly tortured relationship to him, compounded of hatred, fear, guilt and desire – 'though this she did not know, would have died rather than acknowledge – of some dark attraction' (154) – a desire she has never felt towards the white men in her life. In the last chapters of the novel, Lessing represents Mary's total mental and physical breakdown into an existence of bad dreams, distorted mirror reflections, split vision and dystopian images of the future ruination of her habitus, overrun and overtaken by the wildness of the African landscape and the life forms it supports.

There is much of the Gothic, as Sheila Roberts has noted, in *The Grass is Singing* (130). It emerges in many forms, and merges with Lessing's representations of colonial society and its vicissitudes. It is also embodied in the very figure of Mary herself, who appears, towards the novel's close, to a visitor to the farm (the brutal colonialist Charlie Slatter) as 'a dried stick of a woman, her hair that had been bleached by the sun into a streaky mass falling round a scrawny face and tied on the top of her head with a blue ribbon. Her thin, yellowish neck protruded out of a dress that she had apparently just put on. It was a frilled raspberry-coloured cotton . . . She laughed, twisting her shoulder in a horrible parody of coquetry' (175). A version of this scene is replayed a

little later, as witnessed by the young Englishman, Tony Marston, who
has come to help on the farm:

> Mary was sitting on an upended candle-box before the square of mirror
> nailed on the wall. She was in a garish pink petticoat, and her bony yellow
> shoulder stuck sharply out of it. Beside her stood Moses, and, as Tony
> watched, she stood up and held out her arms while the native slipped her
> dress over them from behind. When she sat down again she shook out her
> hair from her neck with both hands, with the gesture of a beautiful woman
> adoring her beauty. Moses was buttoning up the dress; she was looking in
> the mirror. The attitude of the native was of an indulgent uxoriousness.
> (185)

Madness, as in a number of Hollywood films of the period, thus takes
as one of its forms the no-longer desirable woman who still sees herself
as a charming or seductive girl: here the pathos and repulsiveness of this
figure is overdetermined by the absolute taboo of the racial encounter.
The scene of Mary and Moses together (their images presumably held
together in the mirror, though this is not made explicit) is focalised
through both the novel's third-person narrative and the eyes of the naïve
and shocked Tony, who was, in the novel's early, satirical, version, its
central consciousness. Not yet absorbed into colony culture, he retains
some empathy, but with a limited understanding of the world in which
he finds himself.

The novel's representations of bad faith and false consciousness, in
their many varieties, are deeply intertwined with concepts of self-image
and of double and 'cracked vision', and while film more or less disappears as a topic from the novel after Mary's marriage and her move to
the farm, associated as it is with her single, city life, it retains a penum-
bral presence through the rest of the work. In the novel's opening chapters we are told that, as a young woman, Mary Turner 'modelled herself
on the more childish-looking film stars', and that 'sometimes she went
to the pictures five nights a week' (Lessing 1950: 38). In many ways,
Lessing repeats, in this early text, familiar tropes of the cinema as a
dream-factory, creating unrealistic desires in its (largely female) spectators. Of Mary, Lessing writes: 'If a man kissed her . . . she was revolted:
on the other hand she went to the pictures even more frequently than
before and came out feverish and unsettled. There seemed no mirror
between the distorted mirror of the screen and her own life; it was
impossible to fit together what she wanted for herself, and what she was
offered' (Lessing 1950: 45). In this formulation, 'what she wanted for
herself' becomes a creation of 'the distorted mirror of the screen'.

Mary's marriage to Dick Turner comes about through the medium
or mediation of the cinema. On coming to town from his remote farm,

Dick who, we are told, 'loathed the cinema', reluctantly agrees to go to a picture-house:

> He could not keep his eyes on the screen. The long-limbed, smooth-faced women bored him; the story seemed meaningless. And it was hot and stuffy. After a while he ignored the screen altogether, and looked round the audience. In front of him, around him, behind him, rows and rows of people staring and leaning away from each other up at the screen – hundreds of people flown out of their bodies and living in the lives of those stupid people posturing there. It made him feel uneasy.
>
> He fidgeted, lit a cigarette, gazed at the dark plush curtains that marked the exits. And then, looking along the row he was sitting in, he saw a shaft of light fall from somewhere above, showing the curve of a cheek and a sheaf of fairish glinting hair. The face seemed to float, yearning upwards, ruddily gold in the queer greenish light. He poked the man next to him, and said, 'Who is that?' 'Mary', was the grunted reply, after a brief look. But 'Mary' did not help Dick much. He stared at that lovely floating face and the falling hair, and after the show was over, he looked for her hurriedly in the crush outside the door. But he could not see her. He supposed, vaguely, that she had gone with someone else. He was given a girl to take home whom he hardly glanced at. She was dressed in what seemed to him a ridiculous way, and he wanted to laugh at her high heels, in which she tiptapped beside him across the street.
>
> But he dreamed about the girl with the young uptilted face and the wave of loose gleaming hair. It was a luxury, dreaming about a woman, for he had forbidden himself such things. (Lessing 1950: 45–6)

Here the focus is not on the screen, which fails to capture Dick's attention, but on the cinema auditorium. Lessing's image of 'the rows and rows of people staring and leaning away from each other up at the screen' could be a description of any number of images and cartoons of the cinema space and cinema spectatorship from the early and middle decades of the century. It also recalls early accounts of film spectatorship which attempted to negotiate the paradoxes of association and of solitude in modernity, condensed into the cinematic arena but referring more broadly to urban experience. The cinema audience is a collectivity of sorts, possibly a crowd, but film viewing is defined as akin to a dream-state, with the isolated response that this implies: this is collective provision unaccompanied by communal feeling.

Despite Dick's alienation from the screen-world, the shaft of light from somewhere above – that of the projector – turns the auditorium itself into a form of dream-screen or dream-arena, creating the auratic image of a woman's face, 'floating' as it might in a filmic close-up. This 'Mary' – a creation of the projector's beam of light – is so radically other to the 'real' woman to whom the face belongs that Dick fails to recognise her as the uninteresting woman whom he subsequently escorts home. Meeting Mary again, he attempts to re-enchant her image and to 'find in her the girl who had haunted him': 'glancing at her sideways as they passed street lamps . . . he could see how a trick of light had created something beautiful and strange from an ordinary and not very attractive girl' (Lessing 1950: 48). The knowledge that is 'a trick of light' (the street lamps are an extension of the light-beam of the cinema projector) does not prevent him from, eventually, finding in her image that of the girl about whom he had dreamed: he wills the illusion and, for a time at least, makes it stay.

As I have suggested, the cinema has little direct role in the novel after Dick and Mary's marriage, and is invoked directly only once to represent the unreality of Mary's former existence, as she comes to perceive it. But, as the film-world had extended, for Dick, beyond the screen into the space of auditorium and city street, modes of mirroring, daydreaming and dreaming, projection, vision and (mis)recognition permeate the rest of the text as it moves towards the violence of its end. Mary's face – initially doubled as the real and the auratic 'face' of the cinematic arena – remains twofold, but in a very different guise, as the life of farm and veldt take their toll: 'it was if she wore two masks, one contradicting the other . . . Sometimes she would present the worn visage of an indomitable old woman who has learnt to expect the worst from life, and sometimes the face of defenceless hysteria' (90).

This doubling then intersects with the distorted and divided lenses of racial consciousness: 'when a white man in Africa by accident looks into the eyes of a native and sees the human being (which it is his chief preoccupation to avoid), his sense of guilt, which he denies, fumes up in resentment and he brings down the whip' (144). There are important connections here with the structures of oppression explored in Frantz Fanon's *Black Skin, White Masks* (1952, English translation 1967), in which he writes of the 'third-person consciousness' brought into being by the white world's image of him: 'And then the occasion arose when I had to meet the white man's eyes' (Fanon 1986: 110). The difference is that in Lessing's novel the focus is on the psychology of the coloniser rather than, as for Fanon, the colonised.

In *The Grass is Singing* Mary descends into a state in which her nightmares 'become more real than her waking':

> And time taking on the attributes of space, she stood balanced in mid-air, and while she saw Mary Turner rocking in the corner of the sofa, moaning, her fists in her eyes, she saw, too, Mary Turner as she had been, that foolish girl travelling unknowingly to this end . . . The conflict between her judgment on herself, and her feeling of innocence, of having been propelled by something she did not understand, cracked the wholeness of her vision. (195)

The novel opens up a number of the themes that *The Golden Notebook* would more fully develop, and in particular those of self-division, break-down and 'cracked vision'. Both the early and the later novel represent the arena of dream-world and film-world, with cinema variously linked to the spheres of desire, illusion and delusion, projection, and individual and collective daydreams.

Dreaming in *The Grass is Singing* becomes caught up in a realm of nightmare sexual imaginings which are at once Oedipalised and racial-ised: Mary dreams (in a way that recalls Freud's understanding of the work of 'condensation' in the dream-work) that Moses 'approached slowly, obscene and powerful, and it was not only he, but her father who was threatening her. They advanced together, one person, and she could smell, not the native smell, but the unwashed smell of her father' (165). Dream-states are also central to *The Golden Notebook*, and to the novel's depictions of the psychoanalytic process, and they remain vital to Lessing's later work, as Tom Sperlinger shows in his chapter in this volume. In the first volume of her autobiography, *Under My Skin*, Lessing writes of the domination of her childhood by 'the world of dreams, where I have always been at home' (119). In her childhood, her dreams were frequently nightmares (with seemingly close connec-tions to the nightmares described in *The Grass is Singing*), which she learned to 'sanitize': 'Every night before going to sleep I went over the incidents of the day, those that seemed to have the stuff of potential nightmares . . . till they seemed tame, harmless' (119). The 'interminable day' is thus reduced 'to something like a picture storybook whose pages you flick through faster and faster' (120). Lessing suggests a connection between this process and the clear perception of discrete 'moments' in her childhood, which endure, unchanged, in memory: it is cognate with, we might say, the relationship between the moving and the still image, cinema (and flicker-book) and photograph. Lessing's 'moments' have the quality of scenes, recalling Virginia Woolf's assertion, in her autobiographical work 'A Sketch of the Past', that 'scene-making' was her way of 'marking the past': her 'moments of being' always included, photographically, 'a circle of the scene which they cut out' (Woolf 2002: 91). They are taken up in *The Golden Notebook*, a novel absorbed by the question of the relationship between experience and narrated time. At points in the text, Lessing (through her fictional writer-protagonist Anna Wulf) represents an event as 'Scene', as if in a play or film, and as if the self were observing itself from the outside. As Rowena Kennedy-Epstein shows elsewhere in the volume, both this continuation of Woolf's hybridisation of image and literary narrative, and the interroga-tion of the relationship between experience and narrated time, places

Lessing within a broader tradition of twentieth-century radical women's writing.

Published twelve years after *The Grass is Singing*, *The Golden Notebook* extends and elaborates representations of dreams, film and experience or consciousness. Anna brings her dreams, which she describes in the diary sections of the novel, to her Jungian analyst, Mrs Marks (or 'Mother Sugar', as she calls her): 'They all had the same quality of false art, caricature, illustration, parody. All the dreams were in marvellous fresh vivid colour, that gave me great pleasure' (238). Central questions of authenticity and art emerge in Anna Wulf's fragmentation of the different aspects of her experience, and her different ways of representing that experience (autobiography and fiction, first and third person narrative), in a series of notebooks. The contested terrain of 'realism' is central to the later novel – as its Preface makes clear – bringing with it questions of immediacy versus retrospection. The writer seeks to create a literature which comes as near as possible to the lived experience it describes, a project doomed to fail because 'literature is analysis after the event'. Film, Anna feels, comes closer to 'the physical quality of life, that's living, and not the analysis afterwards, or the moments of discord or premonition. A shot in a film: Ella slowly peeling an orange, handing Paul yellow segments of the fruit, which he takes, one after another, thoughtfully, frowning: he is thinking of something else' (231). The presentness of film gives it this advantage over literature – it is truer to our 'living through something'. As Iris Murdoch, writing in 1956, argued, there is a close connection between 'the film' and 'the moment-to-moment vagaries of the human consciousness . . . From a painting we can stand back, with a novel we can pause and ponder, but a film is as near to us as our own self-awareness, and comes over us with the inevitability of time itself' (Murdoch 1956: 198, 187). In the passage from *The Golden Notebook*, Lessing identifies human intimacy, narrative contingency and the inescapability of temporal succession with the cinema: the yellow segments of the orange, given and received 'one after another', are like the sequencing of the film medium and film movement, which are as inevitable, in Murdoch's formulation, as 'time itself'.

On a different level, daydreaming (as a form of visionary consciousness), dreaming (in a novel in which psychoanalysis is central) and films share a mode of representation:

> An image kept coming into my mind; it was like a shot from a film, then it
> was as if I was seeing a sequence from above. A man and a woman, on a
> roof-top above a busy city, but the noise and the movement of the city are far
> beneath them. They wander aimlessly on the roof-top, sometimes embracing,

but almost experimentally . . . Then the man goes to the woman and says:
I love you. And she says, in terror: What do you mean? . . . When I slept I
dreamed this film sequence – in colour. (479)

The blurring of the division between waking life, dreaming and film
spectatorship is one aspect of the dissolution of Anna's protective
compartmentalisations of her life. The aesthetic of her film-dream is
indeed 'experimental', a sequence that might well be found in a film of
the European avant-garde – that of Michelangelo Antonioni, Jean-Luc
Godard or Chris Marker.

Yet these dimensions of cinematic authenticity are, Lessing appears to
suggest, nowhere to be found in the Hollywood machine, and the novel
contains numerous encounters with 'Americans to do with television or
films', whose relationships to the film and televisual media are driven by
entirely commercial considerations. Throughout *The Golden Notebook*,
Lessing represents her author-figure defending, or failing to defend, her
successful first novel, *Frontiers of War*, from the simplifications and cru-
dities of its studio-adapters. In the notebooks:

> Had lunch with film man. Discussed cast for *Frontiers*. So incredible wanted
> to laugh. I said no. Found myself being persuaded into it. Got up quickly and
> cut it short, even caught myself seeing the words *Frontiers of War* up outside
> a cinema. Though of course he wanted to call it *Forbidden Love*. (76)

The disgust felt by Anna after this meeting indicates the perceived contamination of literature by film, or rather by the film industry, which
is one prominent strand of the novel. Lessing would address this again
in the second volume of her autobiography, *Walking in the Shade*, in
which she describes the ways in which the film industry attempts to buy
'that firefly, creative excellence':

> Anyone coming from the sober world of literature into films will be astounded
> by the crises, the tears, the threats, the hysterics, the telephone calls at three in
> the morning, all the unreal melodramas that accompany film-making. What
> is it all about? They are manufacturing their own fuel, that's all. They don't
> understand, either, how wastefully they use it. (102)

In the final sections of the novel, Anna has an affair with the volatile,
troubled Saul, a Hollywood screenwriter who has been blacklisted for
his communist sympathies. The relationship sends Anna into a breakdown, in which her vivid dreams are experienced as projected films:
'these people appeared briefly, distorted with speed, and vanished again,
and then the film broke off, or rather ran down, with a jarring dislocation. And the projectionist, in the silence that followed, remarked: "And
what makes you think that the emphasis you have put on it is the correct

emphasis?"' (596). The 'films' relate to the characters about whom we have been reading in the earlier parts of the novel:

> They were all, so I saw now, conventionally, well-made films, as if they had been done in a studio; then I saw the titles: these films, which were everything I hated most, had been directed by me. The projectionist kept running these films very fast, and then pausing on the credits, and I could hear his jeering laugh at *Directed by Anna Wulf*. (596)

A little later, Anna enters a further dream-state:

> As soon as the dream came on, the projectionist said, in Saul's voice, very practical: 'And now we'll just run through them again.' I was embarrassed, because I was afraid I'd see the same set of films I had seen before – glossy and unreal. But this time, while they were the same films, they had another quality, which in the dream I named 'realistic'; they had a rough, crude, rather jerky quality of an early Russian or German film. Patches of the film slowed down for long, long stretches while I watched, absorbed, details I had not had time to notice in life . . . I realized that all the things to which I had given emphasis, or to which the patterns of my life had given emphasis, were now slipping past, fast and unimportant . . . Then the film went very fast, it flicked fast, like a dream, on faces I've seen once in the street, and have forgotten, on the slow movement of an arm, on the movement of a pair of eyes, all saying the same thing – the film was now beyond my experience, beyond Ella's [Anna's fictional alter ego], beyond the notebooks, because there was a fusion, and instead of seeing separate scenes, people, faces, movements, glances, they were all together, the film became immensely slow again, it became a series of moments where a peasant's hand bent to drop seed into the earth, or a rock stood glistening while water slowly wore it down, or a man stood on a dry hillside in the moonlight, stood eternally, his rifle ready on his arm. Or a woman lay awake in darkness, saying, No, I won't kill myself, I won't, I won't. (610–11)

Lessing's representations of a 'film-mind', and her correlation between film and dream, is part of a longer conceptual tradition, to which she adds the representation of mental states which would become the preoccupations of existential psychoanalysis, including the concept of the dissociated personality and the split self. The film-dream equation, in the history of psychoanalytic thought, has its origins in earlier correlations made between mind or consciousness and visual technologies (the phantasmagoria, the magic lantern, the kaleidoscope and, at the turn of the nineteenth and twentieth centuries, the cinematograph), and was extended in the writings of psychoanalysts such as Hanns Sachs, Ella Freeman Sharpe, Bertram Lewin and Didier Anzieu.

These analysts and theorists took up the cinematic dimensions of such concepts as 'projection', 'scene' and 'screening', as in Sharpe's and Lewin's accounts of the 'dream screen' and Anzieu's formulations of 'the skin ego'. As Sharpe wrote, in her account of the dream mechanisms of 'dramatization' and 'secondary elaboration' (whereby dream images are transmuted into narrative form): 'A film of moving pictures is projected on the screen of our private inner cinema' (Sharpe 1937: 39). For Freud, the dream is a 'projection' – an externalisation of an internal process – and the concept brings together 'projection' as 'prosthesis' (whereby the body is extended into the world) and as a 'screening' (Freud 1957: 223; Freud 1961: 26). In this latter idea, not only the subject's body, but his or her relationship to the 'skin' – the screen/surface of the other (the mother) is projected or imaged. This is central to Bertram Lewin's model of the 'dream screen', which becomes the hallucinatory representation of the mother's breast, which once acted as a prelude to sleep: he draws a distinction between the screen (the blank screen of sleep) and dream images (the play and projection of visual images on that screen) (Lewin 1946: 419–34).

There is no evidence that Lessing was aware of these dimensions of psychoanalytic thought, nor of the film theory (such as that of Siegfried Kracauer (1965) and Christian Metz (1982), for whom film spectatorship is a mode of dreaming/daydreaming) in which films and dreams (or daydreams) are so fully connected. Yet there are intriguing connections between the network of ideas represented by these thinkers and Lessing's representations of the film-dream world. In one of Anna's narrated dreams:

> I dreamed there was an enormous web of beautiful fabric stretched out. It was incredibly beautiful, covered all over with embroidered pictures. The pictures were illustrations of the myths of mankind but they were not just pictures, they were the myths themselves, so that the soft glittering web was alive . . . In my dream I handled and felt this material and wept with joy. (297)

As with so many of the dreams depicted in *The Golden Notebook*, the dream is self-reflexive, bearing on questions of representation (the imagining of a 'realism' so unmediated that the 'pictures' would be the 'myths themselves') as well as on its own 'material'. The 'web of fabric' is a version of Sharpe's and Lewin's 'dream-screen', on which the mythic pictures move. To this we should add, however, the Jungian dimensions of the dream (with its images of the 'myths of mankind'): as Lessing suggested in her autobiography, and as much psychoanalysis endorses, the analysand's dreams are dreamed for the analyst, as a form of confirmatory gift (Lessing 1998: 40). Beyond this, Anna's dream extends from the mythic fabric of the dream-space into the world: the material reveals itself as a map, the beauty of the fabric's 'redness' becoming the marking of the communist countries, with Africa as 'a deep, luminous, exciting black' (297). Then, as the dreamer watches from a high place (as in the dream discussed earlier, in which it was 'as if I was seeing a sequence from above'), a form of 'hovering' which Didier Anzieu, in a discussion of Proust, associates with authorship (Anzieu 1981: 17), the colours merge, there is an explosion, and 'very clear in my ear a small voice said: Somebody pulled the thread of the fabric and it all dissolved' (298). Dream becomes apocalyptic vision. As Frantz Fanon suggests, in a discussion of dream interpretation: 'What must be done is to restore [the] dream *to its proper time*' (Fanon 1986: 104, italics original). Dreams speak of culture as well as the individual subject.

While 'film' plays a somewhat abstract and allegorical role in the passages quoted earlier, it is nonetheless significant that Lessing invokes different aspects of film history in a novel struggling to finds its proper form, with the 'inauthentic' dimensions of her experience and her writing becoming framed and projected in the mode of 'Hollywood cinema'. An 'authentic' way of being, to which the projectionist and the dream point the way, is, by contrast, imaged as an early Soviet or German cinema, in which the details of gesture, faces and movements in close-up and the passing of time, variously slowed down and speeded up, enact an overturning of habitual emphases and values. Within the framework of the novel, the represented dream-work as film-work is (like the different notebooks) a way of rupturing the linearity and causality of conventional narrative form from within. While Lessing does not offer a strongly gendered model of the distinctions between 'Hollywood style' and 'experimental' film, there are nonetheless resonances here with the film theorist Laura Mulvey's highly influential essay/manifesto 'Visual Pleasure and Narrative Cinema'. Here Mulvey argued, polemically, for an 'attack' on 'the ease and plenitude of the narrative fiction film', which 'coded the erotic into the language of the dominant patriarchal order' (16): 'the unconscious of patriarchal society has structured film form', rendering 'woman . . . still tied to her place as bearer, not maker, of meaning' (14–15). 'The first blow' against traditional film conventions and the associated representation of 'woman' as passive recipient of 'the male gaze', in Mulvey's account, 'is to free the look of the camera into its materiality in time and space and the look of the audience into dialectics and passionate detachment' (26).

These concerns are by no means absent from the novels of Lessing discussed in this chapter, in which gender, vision and narrative form, inflected by psychoanalytic understandings of unconscious life, are central. A fuller account of Lessing's engagements with cinema also necessitates, however, a recognition of questions of authorship and authority. Her figure of the Projectionist has a counterpart in the person of the Director or Producer, which features, explicitly or implicitly, in the work of a number of contemporaries, as they explored the relationship between the director's construction of a film and the novelist's control over his or her fictional characters and the plots in which they are inscribed. At a time of intense debate about 'the future of the novel', the question of the particularities and potentialities of novel and film respectively had also become a central question, often revolving round concepts of 'realism' and 'experimentalism'.

Among Lessing's writer contemporaries, there were many commenting, in ambivalent terms, on the impact of film on the writer's creative processes. For John Fowles, to take one prominent example:

> to write a novel in 1964 is to be neurotically aware of trespassing, especially on the domain of the cinema ... So over the novel today hangs a *faute de mieux*. All of us under forty write cinematically; our imaginations, constantly fed on films, shoot scenes, and we write descriptions of what has been shot. So for us a lot of novel writing is, or seems like, the tedious translating of an unmade and never-to-be-made film into words. (Fowles 1998: 7)

Film images enter the writer's mind to shape what he or she describes. Fowles's response to this anxiety of influence was to suggest that writers are in fact more powerful visualisers than screenwriters or film-makers: he also argued that 'the necessary co-operation between writer and reader, the one to suggest, the other to make concrete, is a privilege of *verbal* form; and the cinema can never usurp it' (Fowles 1998: 21).

'For all its faults', Fowles wrote of the genre of the novel, 'it is a statement by one person. In my novels I am the producer, director, and all the actors; I photograph it' (Fowles 1998: 20). The concurrent activities of writing a novel and participating in the film adaptations of his work led Fowles to postulate 'the legitimate and the illegitimate influence of the cinema on the novel': he wrote that a lifetime's weekly film-viewing has made it inevitable that the experience has 'indelibly stamped itself on the *mode* of imagination', while his dreams revealed 'purely cinematic effects: panning shots, close shots, tracking, jump cuts and the rest. In short, this mode of imagining is far too deep in me to eradicate – and not only in me, but in all my generation' (1998: 21). Yet (and as he had argued in the earlier essay), the novel is in possession of 'a still-vast domain' not available to the cinema.

Fowles's arguments and concerns here are also to be found in Lessing's writings, and in particular in *The Golden Notebook*. In the work and thought of Lessing, however, they fit into broader contexts: the nature of realism; the workings of dream-life; time and narrative; gender and experience; power and politics. In *The Golden Notebook* Lessing opened up the form of the novel from within, creating a Chinese box of stories within stories. She simultaneously represents and interrogates the dynamics which Fowles sees as intrinsic to the modern novel, turning them inside out for our viewing and analysis. In Anna's record of her film-dream, she writes of the quality of the projected films 'which in the dream I named "realistic"': the dream thus tests the nature of the 'cinematic' and comments on its own form and aesthetic, as if 'realistic' were a dream-neologism, rather than a settled and known quantity or category. Nothing is to be assumed: everything is to be explored and examined.

Works Cited

Anzieu, Didier (1981), *Le Corps de l'oeuvre*, Paris: Gallimard.

Fanon, Frantz (1986), *Black Skin, White Masks*, trans. Charles Lam Markmann, London: Pluto.

Fowles, John (1998), *Wormholes: Essays and Occasional Writings*, ed. Jan Relf, London: Jonathan Cape.

Freud, Sigmund (1957), 'A Metapsychological Supplement to the Theory of Dreams', in James Strachey (ed.), *Standard Edition of the Complete Works of Sigmund Freud* (1956–74), vol. 14, London: Hogarth Press, pp. 217–35.

—— (1961), 'The Ego and the Id', in James Strachey (ed.), *Standard Edition of the Complete Works of Sigmund Freud* (1956–74), vol. 19, London: Hogarth Press, pp. 3–66.

Kracauer, Siegfried (1965), *Theory of Film: The Redemption of Physical Reality*, New York: Oxford University Press.

Lessing, Doris (1950), *The Grass is Singing*, London: Fourth Estate.

—— (1962), *The Golden Notebook*, London: Granada Publishing.

—— (1994), *Under My Skin*, London: HarperCollins.

—— (1998), *Walking in the Shade, Volume Two of My Autobiography 1949–1962*, London: Flamingo.

Lewin, Bertram (1946), 'Sleep, the Mouth and the Dream Screen', *Psychoanalytic Quarterly*, 15, 419–34.

Metz, Christian (1982), *The Imaginary Signifier: Psychoanalysis and the Cinema*, trans. Celia Britton, Annwyl Williams, Ben Brewster and Alfred Guzzetti, Bloomington: Indiana University Press.

Mulvey, Laura [1975] (1989), 'Visual Pleasure and Narrative Cinema', in *Visual and Other Pleasures*, London: Macmillan, pp. 14–26.

Murdoch, Iris [1956] (1986), 'What I See in Cinema' in Josephine Ross (ed.), *The Vogue Bedside Book II*, London: Hutchinson, pp. 187–8.

Roberts, Sheila (2003), 'Sites of Paranoia and Taboo: Lessing's *The Grass is Singing* and Gordimer's *July's People*', in Harold Bloom (ed.) *Doris Lessing: Bloom's Modern Critical Views*, Philadelphia: Chelsea House, pp. 127–44.

Sharpe, Ella Freeman (1937), *Dream Analysis*, London: Hogarth Press.

Woolf, Virginia (2002), 'A Sketch of the Past', in Jeanne Schulkind (ed.), *Moments of Being: Autobiographical Writings*, London: Random House, pp. 78–160.

Chapter 7

'A funny thing laughter, what's it for?': Humour and Form in Lessing's Fiction

Cornelius Collins

It's safe to say that humour is rarely considered one of Doris Lessing's strong suits. Indeed, her writing is more typically noted for its serious intent, with a 'hectoring' tone and a quality of 'unrelenting analysis' that make for uncommonly demanding reading (Watkins 2010: 164; Singer 2010: 106). This aura of seriousness can be attributed to the sweeping developments in twentieth-century history she wrote about, addressing her life's experience of colonialism and decolonisation, imperialism and global communism, class and gender, and youth and ageing, and developing advance perspectives on such new topics as ecology, posthumanism, and the Anthropocene. This is the side of Lessing's work the selection committee highlighted when awarding the author the Nobel Prize in Literature for 2007, citing her 'visionary power' and her 'scrutiny' of 'a divided civilization'; her sense of humour was not mentioned ('Nobel Prize').

But perceptions of literary seriousness are based not just on the content of a writer's work, but on its style and form. And rather than being interested in play, Lessing is routinely described as a 'didactic' writer, concerned to instruct. Among the first critics to apply this word was Joan Didion, who judged in 1971 that Lessing comes off as a 'missionary devoid of any but the most didactic irony' (1990: 119). Didion herself is hardly known to leave readers in stitches, but her renown as a stylist connects her opinion that Lessing cannot manage shades of irony – the rhetorical basis of most literary humour – to the wider sense of her writing as deficient in style. To never be funny is not 'to "write well"', if we invoke, with Didion, the jargon of the workshop (119). But one needn't be as condescending as Didion, nor so unfamiliar with the full range of Lessing's thought, to share the view that her writing is not well crafted (a judgement reassessed by Tom Sperlinger elsewhere in this volume). Claire Sprague, for example, cites Roger Sale's comment, echoing Didion, that 'she has no wit, and only a very serious kind of humor' (Sprague 1987: 14). A rare defence comes from Gayle Greene, who argues that while Lessing is 'assumed to have no sense of humor', in fact her sentences 'bristle with irony', the humour 'understated' but 'potent' – 'dark comedy, admittedly', perhaps not for everyone, but still 'wonderful' (1994: 31–2).

Current studies now have the benefit (and burden) of viewing Lessing's career in full and therefore of coming to terms with the many significant shifts that occurred not only in her perspective on her times but also in her approaches to literary form. Her use of humour is no exception here, and therefore in this chapter I want to identify and analyse its shifting styles, especially in the crucial passage of her work from the 1960s to the mid-1970s, when humour becomes an object as well as a tool of her 'unrelenting analysis', a vehicle and a ground for her experiments in form. Didion wasn't wrong to highlight irony, rather than wit or wordplay, as the leading mode of humour in Lessing's work before 1971. But since she wasn't alert to the way Lessing was at that moment reconsidering humour's function in human sociality, nor sympathetic to what she discerns, but dismisses, as Lessing's programme for 'immediate cosmic reform', she couldn't notice the different kinds of humour Lessing's formal experiments were already allowing her to develop (Didion 1990: 120). From the start, a means for Lessing to speak truths otherwise unrecognised or denied in class-based societies, humour becomes in her work a crucial modality for representing the emergence of new perspectives and stimulating their development in her readers. Humour thus appears crucial to Lessing's didactic purpose as a writer, since as Simon Critchley has put it, humour has the rhetorical potential to 'change the situation in which we find ourselves' (2002: 11). But over the years Lessing made modifications to her humorous technique, which unexpectedly became subtler as her vision grew more radical and her analysis of global conditions more severe. From an early facility with the traditional realist weapons of irony and satire, after a period of questioning she turned ultimately to the Sufi teaching story as a formal resource for developing a mode of humour more therapeutic and, hence, better suited to address her readers' situation amid a darkened forecast for humanity.

Defensive humour: satirical realism in the early fiction

Early in *Martha Quest* (1952), Martha happens to be in town when the region's Afrikaners come in from their farms to run errands and pick up mail. Martha is still brooding over an encounter with Joss Cohen, her would-be political mentor: when she giggled at his attempt to 'catechize' her regarding socialism, he grew angry, then tried to smooth things over with an awkward remark and a laugh. Feeling condescended to, Martha exits to the street and watches the evolving scene. At this point, the authorial narrator intrudes to comment:

> Now, it is quite easy to remark the absurdities and contradictions of a country's social systems from outside its borders, but very difficult if one has been brought up in it; and for Martha . . . it was a moment of illumination. (Lessing 2001: 57)

Already put off by the failure of humour with Joss, Martha observes the Dutch-derived small farmers as never before, as a subjugated minority. She recalls that settlers from various parts of Britain seem to coexist in the colony, at least at this stage of its settlement, 'without any consciousness of degree' (58). But the Afrikaners, she sees, form a more cohesive community, bound by resentment at having been supplanted by the British. Thus Martha recognises the historical absurdity of class difference.

This passage illustrates some important points about humour in this early phase of Lessing's work. The first is that laughter is more often represented in the text than humour is actually realised from it. For a writer assumed to have no sense of humour, Lessing has her characters laugh surprisingly often – but usually as an ineffectual response to their situations' uncomfortable ironies. Even when nothing is funny, however, the modality of humour stands as a potential means for promoting a critical perspective; hence Lessing's special interest in representing moments when laughter occurs but the humour, for characters and readers alike, is thin. In this way the adolescent Martha soon comes to assume her role as 'a silent and critical figure', directing scorn and sarcasm first at her parents' absurd delusions, then her society's contradictions (33). She performs, in other words, the mode of humour Critchley terms its '*critical* function with respect to society' (2002: 10). This kind of humour, through its play upon recognisable social forms, criticises the established order, laughing at power. At sufficient depth, humour in Critchley's critical phase can reveal the contingency and illogic of 'shared practices, the background meanings implicit in a culture', and thereby indicate 'how those practices might be transformed or perfected' (16). Thus radical potential stems from recognising the gap between conditions as they are and as they could be, and the unease resulting from this rhetorical disjunction, like irony, often produces humour.

Or, at least, laughter – as in Martha's strained exchange with Joss, or later, when she visits Mr Van Rensberg, seen earlier at the station carrying 'rabid' nationalist pamphlets from South Africa (62). Encountering him again at a party at their home, Martha gets flustered by his allusions to English 'arrogance' and falls into 'the defensive humour which she could not prevent, though she knew he found it insulting' (97). She deflects his aggrieved questions with laughs and smiles made in the light of her earlier 'illumination' as to the higher class status she enjoys in the colony, even though the Quests' finances are precarious. She hopes her laughter will underscore the contingency of their situation, but without sufficient common ground with Mr Van Rensberg, the humour fails, and the disparity is only reinforced. Lessing's unwillingness to play the Afrikaner for a country fool shows her ambivalence toward the class-rooted style of humour especially prevalent in British literary tradition. Instead, Martha's reflexive attempt at humour as a social solvent is itself made a target of the text's 'critical attack', or satire (Knight 2004: 203). Laughter as a means for sublimating conflict is a device Lessing exposes in various contexts during her career. But the tendency of humour to fail across social groups is featured in the early fiction, which uses the novel's historical kinship with satire to dramatise the development of a critical perspective on the absurdities that produce such tensions.

When, on the other hand, Lessing aims to achieve critical laughter, she models her deft satirical portrayals on the style of Charles Dickens. According to James Kincaid, Dickens innovated humour in fiction by placing 'tremendous importance on his characters' language rather than their actions or gestures', thus separating his more realistic characters from the stock figures of low comedy (Kincaid 1968: 320). Lessing does likewise with Mr Quest, an armchair philosopher humorously incapable of articulating his insights into Being: prone to observation of the African skies, 'he would emerge after hours of silence, remarking, "Well, I don't know, I suppose it all means something" or "Life is a strange business, say what you like"' (26). The nascent mysticism of Martha's father represents a potential alternative to the bourgeois affectations of her mother (whose pathos is developed later in the series), but his entrapment in the past and susceptibility to psychosomatic illnesses render him a figure of mockery. Lessing's 'catch-phrase' for him, following Dickens's technique (Kincaid 1968: 322), is 'the Great Unmentionable', his summation of how the sacrifices made by his generation are not recognised by British society. Throughout the early volumes, his face takes on 'that look of baffled anger' as he issues the generalised complaint, 'It's all very well for you . . . We came out of the trenches, and then suddenly the war was bad form. The Great Unmentionable, that's what you called it' (34). As the story of Martha Quest develops into the *Children of Violence* series, the psychic wounding behind, and emanating from, such repetitions assumes greater salience. At this stage, however, it is played – skilfully – for critical laughs, in order to emphasise Martha's developing satirical stance.

The bitter grimace: satirical surrealism in *The Golden Notebook*

As with many of the practices and convictions that define her early fiction, Lessing puts satirical realism under intense analytical pressure in *The Golden Notebook* (1962). In this way she searches for the limits of critical humour's capacity for indicating how 'the situation' might be changed in the manner Critchley outlines, and she discovers that these limits are determined by the historically new conditions of discourse in Western society after the Second World War. In this novel, therefore, satire becomes so extreme as to render a humorous '*surrealization* of the real', with 'the familiar defamiliarized, the ordinary made extraordinary and the real rendered surreal' (Critchley 2002: 10).

But as much as surreality defines the experience of this novel for its many readers, they may not find themselves smiling as they work through the text, which overflows with paradoxically pained laughter and smiles worn by characters on the edge of madness. Nearly every page features a version of the 'small bitter grimace' made in response to nervous joking (Lessing 2008: 192). This is what the writer-protagonist Anna Wulf recognises as 'bad laughter, the laughter of helplessness', but, like Martha Quest, she cannot help reproducing it (54). According to Critchley, 'true' humour's forceful articulation of the falsity of such socially conditioned laughter should expose it and, on recognition, produce conditions for a more genuine, communal relation. The near total absence of such efficacious humour from *The Golden Notebook*, for all its laughter, does not owe, however, to Lessing's failure to be funny, but to her use of writing the text to work out her sense that novelistic satire no longer provides adequate means for promoting critical consciousness in her readers.

Many of the satirical performances in the novel are funny, particularly the passages concerning Anna's writing and her dealings with the industries of publishing and media, which seize every opportunity to try to capitalise on her talent. A strong example is the sequence of letters Anna receives from a television producer with the Dickensian name 'Mr Reginald Tarbrucke', interested in acquiring her novel for development by his company, 'Amalgamated Vision' (269). He writes breezily to Anna, having read her 'delightful book', *Frontiers of War*

'– by chance, I must confess! –', and invites her to meet for a drink at a pub, 'the Black Bull' (270). When Anna replies, categorically denying interest in television, he responds immediately to flatter her principles with a better offer, still seeking her 'charming' text: 'Will you meet me for lunch next Friday at the Red Baron? It's a small unpretentious place, but they do a very good steak' (270). Anna again rejects him; he again replies, this time upping the class of the restaurant: 'Please join me for lunch next Monday at the White Tower. I think we need time for a really long, quiet talk' (270). The close repetition of the letters, with key points replaced and intensified, produces a play on 'duration' – what Critchley calls, following the influential formulation of Henri Bergson, the 'deliberate distention of time' – that typifies the expert telling of a joke (2002: 7). Here, in fact, the humour arises from how the time between Tarbrucke's letters is sped up in the text, as in a silent comedy film, while Anna's deferrals distend the socially expected exchange of invitation and acceptance. Anna, though, subverts the punchline by arriving dressed as 'herself' and not the type of 'the lady writer' she assumes he expects (270). At lunch, she responds to his questions sarcastically, and within a few lines he is forcing 'the now automatic humorous grimace'; the scene turns awkward, most of its humour evaporating (271).

Notwithstanding the dispiriting conclusion to the joke, Anna's refusal to play a 'role' is a hopeful early sign that she may preserve an authentic 'self' against the pressures of fragmentation evidenced everywhere else in the novel. When she returns to writing, however, Anna produces not her next novel, but humorously parodic versions of her authorial self – as if, in the absence of other options, she were deliberately trying on Tarbrucke's unconscious mimicry of a TV executive. She 'concocts' many entries for an 'imaginary journal', written to match 'the right tone for a literary review in a colony or the Dominions' (like the absurdly titled '*Pomegranate Review*, New Zealand'), and they are hilarious (415). One example purports to be the self-indulgent jottings of a young American expatriate writer:

> April 17th. *The Gare de Lyon.* Thought of Lise. My God, and that was two years ago! What have I done with my life? Paris has stolen it . . . must re-read Proust. (416)

This time there is a punchline – the specious text is accepted for publication. So she begins again: in response to an editor's breathless request for 'something of *yours* – at last!', Anna writes as 'a lady author of early middle age, who had spent some years in an African colony' (419). The editor accepts the florid mock-diary as hers, thereby endorsing the same indulgent, 'lying nostalgia' that has disgusted Anna when she attempts serious fiction (61). A similarly confused response occurs earlier in the novel when a naïvely Stalinist (and very funny) short story is read aloud at a Communist Party meeting: it is well received until Anna mocks it, to 'a roar of uncomfortable laughter' from the group, and a member reflects, 'I thought it was a parody at first – makes you think, doesn't it' (291).

These performances are all funny, but distressingly so; there is ultimately no stable target for the satirical effect, no end to the joking, and this compromises the opportunity for true humour. According to Lisa Colletta, 'traditionally, satire has demanded at least an implicit moral standard' to be effective, and the knowability of this norm is called into question in modern culture (2003: 5). This is also Lessing's statement about reality at this stage: Anna and her writing partner call off their experiments in pastiche when editors only request more of it. When the worst conceivable representations are accepted as truth, history has passed the limits of satire: 'It was at this point that James and Anna decided they were defeated; that something had happened in the world which made parody impossible' (421). The 'something' is multiply determined – the 'cracking up' of 'everything' announced on the novel's first page, a perceived loss of coherence of the discourses holding society and culture together before the threats of nuclear war and a rising global capitalism. Thus *The Golden Notebook* involves readers in its bad laughter, relentlessly parodying novelistic satire in the absence of any other means for changing a hopeless situation.

Laughing at, laughing with: toward a posthuman perspective

One occurrence of laughter in *The Golden Notebook* is different from the rest. In 'The Shadow of the Third', Anna Wulf's draft novel, Ella, its writer-protagonist, is asked by her new lover, Paul, what her father is 'like'. Unexpectedly, Ella laughs, and Anna writes, 'the sound held affection which was spontaneous and genuine, and a bitterness which she did not know was there' (181). A startling question, rather than any joke or parody, induces the one example in the text of what Critchley calls the 'highest laugh', which is the 'mirthless laugh', evoking 'pure' laughter: 'laughter that opens us up and causes our defences to drop momentarily' and rebounds dialogically, so that 'the object of laughter is the subject who laughs' (49–50). Critchley draws his typology from a passage in Samuel Beckett's *Watt*, where the bitter laugh – 'at that which is not good' – and the hollow laugh – 'at that which is not true'

– are distinguished from the mirthless laugh – 'at that which is unhappy' (Beckett 2009: 38–9). Beckett's 'bitter laugh' responds to an ethical force (the 'good'); therefore, Ella's bitterness properly belongs to the 'mirthless' type, since it represents an authentic reflection upon her own unhappiness concerning her emotional distance from her father. While so much of the laughter in the text is of the fruitlessly ironic, 'hollow' kind – what Beckett also terms 'the intellectual laugh' (39) – Ella's outburst offers an unbidden glance at the potential for humour's more productive function, to spark laughter at unhappiness.

It's significant that it is Ella's relation to her father that points the way toward the alternative mode of humour Lessing develops in her later work, since in rough outline, Ella's father strongly recalls Mr Quest: 'a military man turned some sort of mystic', now 'absorbed in his garden, his books', and given to expressing deep alienation from human fellowship (442). As he expounds upon the 'unreality' of familial feeling, to Ella his face resembles 'an insect's', with 'protuberant' blue eyes and dried, 'yellowish' face the correlatives of his ascetic mindset (443). Compared with the earlier, satirical portrayals of Mr Quest, this is a more interesting presentation of the father-figure with his head in the clouds. Correspondingly, when Mr Quest returns near the conclusion of the *Children of Violence* series, in *The Four-Gated City* (1969), he is cast in a similar light. Glimpsed on his deathbed, 'in a moment of extra lucidity' he sees 'the creatures fussing around his bed' as 'animals with clothes who made strange noises with their mouths and noses to communicate and to express feelings' (Lessing 1969: 394–5). To them, he offers a sublimely detached comment: 'A funny thing laughter, what's it for?' (395). This remark – perhaps the only pun in all of Lessing's work – circles upon itself, like Ella's mirthless laugh. Such a laugh – 'at that which is unhappy' – is particularly apposite to this scene, since Mr Quest's dying question is hardly a joke, yet it elicits laughter. Seeming at first daft, then profound, it causes readers to laugh at themselves for having laughed at him. The fact that it's not quite clear whether he grasps the import of his comment only makes it funnier, in an unresolved way. The line perfectly expresses what Critchley holds to be at 'the heart of humour': humans' unique recognition of 'the fact of our solitude' in nature, which implies 'a basic ineradicable loneliness', to be consoled by humour and philosophy (2002: 52).

For Lessing too, humour here has become a crucial index of the human: Mr Quest's cosmic removal from human affairs leads him directly, if unexpectedly, to the question of humour, much as Lessing focuses on humour as she begins to consider humanity from a wider, planetary perspective. Thus in several texts in the period from *The*

Four-Gated City to *The Memoirs of a Survivor* (1974) she engages in the conventionally humorous trope that Critchley identifies as 'moving back and forth across the frontier that separates humanity from animality' (2002: 29). People as animals is the stock-in-trade of the harsher, Juvenalian form of satire. Lessing's portrayals, however – whether of Ella's father, Mr Quest's attendants, or the alien animal societies of *Briefing for a Descent into Hell* (1971) – do not disgust nor amuse so much as fascinate by repelling. They are a vehicle for a productive alienation, not a wholesale condemnation of the target species, the human.

This concern to put humanity in position to see itself critically is creatively objectified in 'Report on the Threatened City' (1972), Lessing's first foray into the space fiction she would take up again in the late 1970s. In this story, an alien ship's crew attempts to warn the inhabitants of San Francisco of the inevitability of catastrophe in their location. The aliens, possessing advanced seismic forecasts, are shocked to learn that the city has already seen a major earthquake, and yet people are still living there. The 'report' adduces numerous factors for the human species' irrational behaviour, but several sections focus on the harmful role of laughter. As 'a possible device for release of tension to ward off or relieve fear', laughter is suspected to be 'therefore, possibly one of the mechanisms to keep these animals passive in the face of possible extinction' (Lessing 1972: 95). This function of laughter as an organic social control appears yet more problematic when the aliens stage a televised debate as a stratagem for communicating their thesis that 'this society is indifferent to death and to suffering' (111). Hearing laughter in the audience at the event, they interpret it as the type they hold, counter-intuitively, to be dangerous: 'laughing with', the 'sympathetic laughter' that 'arouses feelings of anxiety in those watching, if the ideas put forward are challenging to norms accepted by them' (111). Although the opposite type, 'laughing at', is 'aggressive and hostile' in tone, it is by contrast the more dialogic form; 'because it reassures onlookers that a balance is being kept', it allows more views to be openly expressed (111). The aliens' propositions are poorly received and they soon depart, convinced that 'the present society is too inflexible to adapt' in time to avoid disaster but having evidently found willing ears among the area's youth cultures (114).

'Report on the Threatened City' extends Lessing's search in this phase of her work for a way that laughter might function in society besides as a tool for supressing change, a concern that has here been transposed from the arena of class consciousness onto the scale of planetary ecology. This search goes hand in hand with her formal experimentation in this period, as the 'report' follows on the documentary interpolations that make up the 'appendix' of *The Four-Gated City*. These meta-fictional forms allow Lessing a more striking and urgent presentation of her alarms about the imminent future. The story is not told in such a way as to be funny, but in light of the text's criticisms of reflexive laughter, that is the point. Instead, it is a serious exemplification of the capacity for estrangement found in true humour, which, as Critchley describes it, gives us 'an alien perspective on our own practices . . . as if we had just landed from another planet' (66). While this metaphor parallels the 'dispassionate eye' of the 'detached observer' worn earlier by Martha Quest (2001: 11–12), here the interest is not so much in representing laughter critically in order to expose its role in sustaining oppression, but in embodying new, stranger, more progressive modes of humour through experiments in narrative form. Lessing's way out of the critical impasse discovered in *The Golden Notebook* is through this salutary dislocation of her and her readers' perspective toward the planetary, which is realised in large part by reflecting, and reflecting on, the posthuman implications of humour.

The silent smile and the teaching story

Another striking aspect of Mr Quest's reflection on humour is its connection to its narrative context. His deathbed scene, a single paragraph, is inserted without transition into the Aldermaston episode of *The Four-Gated City*. The previous paragraph concludes with a description of Martha and the Coldridges at home between demonstrations, wondering:

> if perhaps the spirit of the march, the wry gaiety, its gentle self-mockery, was perhaps a salute to the knowledge that no one wished to own; and despair being its own antidote, it was breeding from its nucleus something like a laugh. (1969: 394)

The multiple pronoun references in this sentence make it difficult to parse (and the mixed metaphors don't help, either.) But in the resemblance of 'gentle self-mockery' to Critchley's 'pure laughter', where 'the object of laughter is the subject who laughs', as well as in despair's healing operation upon itself, what Critchley calls the 'therapeutic' value of true humour comes into view (2002: 50, 13). This mode is a superior alternative to merely critical humour because it not only reveals absurdities but offers a path toward correcting them, bringing 'human beings back from what they might become to what they might be' (13). Because correction and healing are Lessing's overriding concerns in this phase of her work, therapeutic humour is the kind she cultivates in the texts that follow her pause to re-examine humour's function at the turn of the 1970s.

The greater remove of the posthuman perspective affords Lessing a freer approach to narrative structure and point of view in her fiction in this period, and this unpredictability leads to fresh humorous effects. One example occurs in *The Summer Before the Dark* when the protagonist Kate Brown begins working at Global Food, a prestigious non-governmental organisation. Describing the delegates there, the narrator does not simply intrude, as in the satirical realism of *Martha Quest*, but irrupts into the text to lampoon their class's cosmopolitan privilege. What has up to this point been a sober 'inner-space' exploration of the main character's passage into life's next phase swings to an unhinged commentary on the vanity of 'these indispensable fortunates' (1973: 31). 'What an extraordinarily attractive lot they were!' (29). Tied to no specific incident or character, the commentary is nonetheless extensive: 'How harmonious! How consoling it all was: this was certainly how the future would be, assemblies of highly civilised beings all friendly and non-combative' (46). These passages are certainly ironic; they can be read as didactic, even 'hectoring'. But the whimsical excess of the critique, made heedless of the conventions of realist description, amuses as well as jolts the reader, inviting laughter and reflection upon the larger truths contained in the blistering tirade.

These sometimes puzzling narrative disjunctions likely owe some structural debt to the form of the Sufi teaching story. This distinctive genre, which Lessing studied and promoted as early as the mid-1960s, consists of brief, often humorous narratives, akin to folk tales, intended to communicate in vivid but enigmatic form the principles of Sufi thought, with layers of meaning that offer up gradual interpretation over the course of many retellings. As explained by Nancy Shields Hardin, 'the value of the Sufi tale is to be found in the unexpected juxtaposition of ideas', which jars readers from their habitual patterns of mind (1977: 315). Lessing herself highlighted the irregular and dialogic qualities of the teaching story, saying that 'each tale . . . will appeal to the people who, for that time, are right for it, as it is right for them' (quoted in Galin 1997: 103–4). The emphasis on structural incongruity accounts for the role of humour in many teaching tales as well as the wider interest in humour evidenced by Idries Shah, Sufism's twentieth-century populariser and Lessing's mentor, who published a short book on the subject, *Special Illumination*, in 1977. There he acclaims the didactic purpose of jokes as 'correctives' against 'single-minded attitudes which prevent . . . further understanding' (53). Didactic does not, however, mean simplistic: 'Sufi jokes', according to Dee Seligman, 'mock the ultimate inadequacy of logic' and thus can be usefully compared to the unpredictable structures and plots in Lessing's work of the early 1970s (quoted in Galin 1997: 105).

Readers of these texts find therapeutic humour in rarely knowing what will happen next and in sensing that more is going on beneath the surface of the narrative than they can easily explain. Later in *The Summer Before the Dark*, Kate arrives at a London hotel, dishevelled and ill after a long journey, and in the foyer encounters a peculiar couple. They are 'very attractive and obviously rich', speaking German and turning to stare at her with 'a steady, quite friendly, but attentive gaze' (1973: 150–1). Their attraction seems genuine, magnetic but benign, 'radiating a harmony of sensual fulfilment' (151). Yet the narrator's final comparison is so wild as to provoke laughter: 'They looked as if all their lives they had been licked all over by invisible tongues dipped in honey . . .' (151, ellipsis original). Kate next wakes up in bed in a room at the hotel, attended by a maid; her unfolding vision of the splendid couple has functioned therapeutically, as her entrée into a restorative place.

What makes this encounter humorous is not only its mystery, but also its air of calm. The couple is accustomed to being stared at; there is the sense that they are waiting to be recognised. And then, at the height of her curiosity, Kate faints. The entire episode seems unaccountable, but the disjunctive movement from one moment to the next is not explosive, as critical humour would have it. Whether or not the reader laughs, a smile results. And the smile, for Critchley, is what laughter ideally moves toward, ultimately to 'take its place': the smile is 'silent and subdued', speaking with an 'eloquence' that is 'reticent' as to meaning (2002: 108). Seeing the 'gentle play' of a smile on the face – as opposed to the many grimaces across Lessing's work – is a therapeutic event, often produced by unanticipated shifts in narrative such as this one (Critchley 2002: 108). This is what is funny, too, about the widely decried ending of *The Memoirs of a Survivor*, when the unnamed narrator finally glimpses the 'person whose presence' she has been seeking in a parallel dimension for much of the story, and declines to identify or describe her (1988: 158). On the last page, when the zones of the narrative merge around the iron egg at the centre of the inner world, this 'person' appears, and all the narrator will say is, 'there she was', and 'she was beautiful' (213). Since 'she' turns her face 'just once' and satisfies the narrator's yearning, it is easy to imagine she smiles, as the narrator's charges Emily and Gerald are seen doing as they leave the 'collapsed little world' they came from – an analogue for crisis-ridden 1970s Britain – for another (213).

These intriguing, even confounding turns in *The Summer Before the Dark* and *The Memoirs of a Survivor* realise humour in a manner structurally equivalent to the workings of the baffling but instructive Sufi joke. The episodes are not themselves attempts at recreating such texts, since they are woven into much lengthier, more exploratory narratives than the compactness of the modernised Sufi tale would support. Instead, their disjunctions in narrative form, perspective, and plot mirror the uncategorisable qualities of Sufi literature. This therapeutic mode moves beyond the explosive defensive laughter and the pained 'bitter grimace' that typify earlier stages of Lessing's work. The calm, silent smile, finally, offers a remedy to mere laughter's 'emotionalism', which defeats the function of true humour by acting as a barrier to understanding situations so that they might be changed (Lessing 1994).

Ten years after arriving at this form of humour, Lessing's tone was drier, but her method similar. To open her 1985 essay series written for Canadian radio, *Prisons We Choose to Live Inside*, she tells the story of a white farmer in colonial Southern Rhodesia who executes his prize bull for killing its keeper, a young black boy. 'An eye for an eye, a tooth for a tooth', the farmer tells those pleading for mercy for the unknowing, 'magnificent beast' (1987: 2). Lessing lays out, but does not explain, the humorous incongruity of applying biblical code to punish an animal with the intention of restoring justice to a community organised by white supremacy. Like a Sufi teaching story, this understated anecdote is, as Lessing remarks, one of 'those happenings that seem to give up more meanings as time goes on' (3). To contemplate a superseded ruling class that could proclaim, against all evidence, 'I know how to tell right from wrong, thank you very much' (3) – what is it but to laugh?

Works Cited

Beckett, Samuel (2009), *Watt*, New York: Grove.
Colletta, Lisa (2003), *Dark Humor and Social Satire in the Modern British Novel*, New York: Palgrave Macmillan.
Critchley, Simon (2002), *On Humour*, New York: Routledge.
Didion, Joan (1990), *The White Album*, New York: Farrar, Straus and Giroux.
Galin, Müge (1997), *Between East and West: Sufism in the Novels of Doris Lessing*, Albany: State University of New York Press.
Greene, Gayle (1994), *Doris Lessing: The Poetics of Change*, Ann Arbor: University of Michigan Press.
Hardin, Nancy Shields (1977), 'The Sufi Teaching Story and Doris Lessing', *Twentieth-Century Literature*, 23:3, 314–26.
Kincaid, James R. (1968), 'Dickens's Subversive Humour: *David Copperfield*', *Nineteenth-Century Fiction*, 22:4, 313–29.

Knight, Charles A. (2004), *The Literature of Satire*, New York: Cambridge University Press.

Lessing, Doris (1969), *The Four-Gated City*, New York: Knopf.

—— (1971), *Briefing for a Descent into Hell*, New York: Knopf.

—— (1972), 'Report on the Threatened City', in *The Temptation of Jack Orkney and Other Stories*, New York: Knopf, pp. 79–116.

—— (1973), *The Summer Before the Dark*, New York: Knopf.

—— (1987), *Prisons We Choose to Live Inside*, New York: Harper Perennial.

—— [1974] (1988), *The Memoirs of a Survivor*, New York: Vintage.

—— (1994), 'On Sufism and Idries Shah's *The Commanding Self*', *Sufis. org*, <http://ishk.net/sufis/lessing_commandingself.html> (last accessed 29 December 2015).

—— [1952] (2001), *Martha Quest*, New York: Harper Perennial.

—— 'Nobel Prize in Literature 2007 – Press Release', *Nobelprize.org*, <http://www.nobelprize.org/nobel_prizes/literature/laureates/2007/press.html> (last accessed 29 December 2015).

—— [1962] (2008), *The Golden Notebook*, New York: Harper Perennial.

Sale, Roger (1974), 'Doris Lessing – Mostly Throwaways', *New York Times Book Review*, 22 September 1974, <https://www.nytimes.com/books/97/09/14/reviews/lessing-voice.html> (last accessed 29 December 2015).

Shah, Idries (1977), *Special Illumination: The Sufi Use of Humour*, London: Octagon Press.

Singer, Sandra (2010), 'London and Kabul: Assessing the Politics of Terrorist Violence', in Debra Raschke, Phyllis Sternberg Perrakis and Sandra Singer (eds), *Doris Lessing: Interrogating the Times*, Columbus: Ohio State University Press, pp. 92–112.

Sprague, Claire (1987), *Rereading Doris Lessing: Narrative Patterns of Doubling and Repetition*, Chapel Hill: University of North Carolina Press.

Watkins, Susan (2010), *Doris Lessing*, New York: Manchester University Press.

Chapter 8

Lessing and the Scale of Environmental Crisis

David Sergeant

As Timothy Clark recently noted, 'the intellectual challenges of the Anthropocene and its unreadability' raise 'the inevitable question of scale': it 'enacts the demand to think of human life at much broader scales of space and time' (2015a: 13). Lessing's writing was essentially concerned with questions of scale from the very beginning, as Adam Guy's chapter earlier in this volume has shown: tracing how Lessing's attempts to use number to render the scale of political commitment in the 1950s were ultimately doomed. This chapter will follow Lessing's concern with scale through a later period, starting with *The Four-Gated City* (1969), the novel which marked both her turn to a science-fiction inflected non-realism, and the first full impact of the Sufism related by Idries Shah.[1] A split response to the problem of scale determines how Lessing's fiction develops from this point, in novels such as *Shikasta* (1979) and *Mara and Dann: An Adventure* (1999). It also makes her work an unusually eloquent intervention in debates about the relationship between criticism, literature and environmental crisis, as it encapsulates two divergent paths which emerge from this meeting.

Despite the breadths of time and space that this topic immediately invites, we start with the start of *The Four-Gated City*, and a teacup:

> She sat by a rectangle of pinkish oilcloth where sugar had spilled, and on to it, orange tea, making a gritty smear in which someone had doddled part of a name: Daisy Flet . . . Her cup was thick whitey-grey, cracked. The teaspoon was a whitish plastic, so much used that the elastic brittleness natural to it had gone into an erosion of hair lines, so that it was like a kind of sponge. When she had drunk half the tea, a smear of grease appeared half-way down the inside of the cup: a thumb mark. How hard had some hand – attached to Iris, to Jimmy? – gripped the cup to leave a smear which even after immersion in strong orange tea was a thumbprint good enough for the police? (11, ellipsis in original)

The passage anticipates environmentally engaged theorising by Donna Haraway and others in which categories such as natural and cultural, human and non-human are blurred.[2] For instance, the 'orange' of the tea groups it with the 'whitish' plastic and 'pinkish' oilcloth, as an 'unnatural' – man-made, non-organic – object. Yet tea can be drunk, becomes bodily – and thus surely pulls away from a category that might also contain plastic? Similarly, the teaspoon is like 'a kind of sponge', suggesting the marine organism as much as the modern cleaning object: the epigraph a page earlier is from Rachel Carson's *The Edge of the Sea*, and society will later be compared to a 'sea creature' (471). This also implies that the spoon as absorbing sponge – animal or not – might take the tea into itself: and so human and plastic merge as ingesters of this liquid. A reciprocal transference is also implied as the humans imprint themselves into what they might have been expected to ingest, via the thumbprint which not only connects this organic-inorganic palimpsest to an unseen psychological dimension (the hard grip indicating tension?), but also to the societal structures that surround it, which in turn merge abstraction (the police as Law) and embodied existence (who might attend to a print).

Such a reading might be elaborated by tracing other complications of the nature/culture divide in *The Four-Gated City*: for instance, how its insidious circulation of nuclear and chemical pollution anticipates Stacy Alaimo's theorising of 'transcorporeality'. However, attending to the novel's own logic means tracking instead the intensity of observation which is key to the passage above, into the next paragraph:

> Although both were now 'resting' [. . .] both observed Martha. Or rather, their interest, what was alert of it, was focused on what she would do next, but they were too good mannered to let this appear [. . .] From time to time the two exchanged remarks with each other, as thickly indifferent as words coming out of sleep, sleep-mutters; but yet it was open to Martha to join in if she wished, to comment on weather and the state of Jimmy's health, neither very good. Today he had a pain in his stomach. Really they wanted to be told, or to find out, why the telephone call was so important that Martha could not make it and be done. The air of the small steamy box which was the café vibrated with interest, tact, curiosity, sympathy – friendship, in short; all the pressures which for a blissful few weeks since Martha had been in England, rather, London, she had been freed from. (11–12; my ellipses in square brackets)

The attentive observation – more attentive than the somnambulist 'interest' it faces – is as much empathetic as visual. Martha's combination of a concentrated alertness with the ability to feel accurately allows her to go beyond a lazily habitual reading of the scene – an indifference in the couple, a pain in the stomach – to a more complex reality: one that allows for another redefinition, only this time of a nebulously immaterial and predominantly human category, 'friendship'. A positive thing, of course: only here Martha discerns how it can also be self-serving, as 'interest, tact, curiosity, sympathy' become synonymous manifestations of the social energies needed to sustain the self and its groupings. If the first paragraph interrogated material reality in a way that invites comparison with recent environmentally engaged criticism, it is nevertheless of a piece with an interrogation of the social and cultural reality in which Martha exists, which possesses a less immediately obvious environmental relevance.

This observatory mode then evolves once again, as we learn that one of the freedoms Martha has gained is a release from the 'false' personality she has labelled 'Matty'. We are still on the level of personal scale, in one sense; but in another, not:

> 'Matty' gained freedom [. . .] in an act of deliberate clumsiness – like a parody, paying homage as a parody does to its parent-action. An obsequiousness in fact, an obeisance. Exactly so, she understood, had the jester gained exemption with his bladder and his bells; just so, the slave humiliated himself to flatter his master: as she had seen a frightened African labourer clown before her father. And so, it seems, certain occupants of recent concentration camps, valuing life above dignity, had made themselves mock those points of honour, self-respect, which had previously been the focus-points of their beings, to buy exemption from the camp commanders. (12–13)

Rather than relying on visuality and empathy alone, Martha now observes more accurately by branching out – first to an emblematic example (jester); and then to an example halfway between the emblematic and the historical (slave); before these gain a pressing historical acuteness through her own biographical witnessing and the traumatic witnessing of recent times. The self – psychological, personal, individual – becomes fractal, gains a hold on every rung of the ladder of historical scale: the individual through to the communal, the present through to the past.

Always implicit in this multifaceted observation – where not explicit as rhetorical questions – has been an interrogatory mode, a feedback-loop of question and answer: as if each observation prompts, too, a questioning of itself, thereby generating the next observation as a possible route to an answer, with the process then repeating. However, the process of seeking that answer can entail apparent leaps and meanders in scale – as in the continuation of the paragraph above into the next:

> But here [Matty] was [. . .] In this house. With Jimmy and Iris. (Not with Stella down the river, not at all.) Here. Why? For some days now Martha had been shut inside this person, it was 'Martha' who intruded, walked into

'Matty', not the other way about. Why? She was also, today, shut inside clothes that dressed, she felt, someone neither Martha, nor 'Matty'.

For the weeks of her being in London the sun had shone. Strange enough that she could now see it like this. In a country where the sun is always so evident, forceful, present; clouds, storms, rain, briefly disguise the dominating, controlling presence of the sun; one does not say: 'Today the sun shone,' for it always does. But after a few weeks in England, she could say 'The sun shone today' and only by putting herself back on that other soil felt the truth that the sun never stopped shining. Even in the middle of the night, the sun blazed out, held in its blaze all planets and the earth and the moon, the earth having merely turned away its face, on its journey around away from light and back. (13)

The transition from 'why?' might seem disjunctive: from Martha's monad self and the split within it, to differences in weather between England and the Africa she recently left, and then to the constant presence of the sun. However, it resembles the extrapolation from Matty to the concentration camps and a universal record of human self-preservation through abasement before power. A single instance contains within it aspects of a larger history in which it is enmeshed: in this case the concatenation of events both large (British colonialism, the First World War) and small (personal love, damage, hope) that sent Martha's parents to Africa. However, the expansion here is even more vertiginous for climbing beyond Martha's contingent biography to the source of all life on earth – which is, of course, a part of anyone's life, but not in a way that often or easily seems as relevant as recent actions. But the sinuously organic expansion of Martha's empathetic and interrogative observation of herself and the world around her bridges such gulfs in scale to make them a whole, micro and macro joined. Vast extremes and various points between them are strung like beads along the thread of Martha's perception.

In such expansions and returns *The Four-Gated City* might be read as anticipating Clark's account of how an environmentally chastened 'scale framing' reading practice might progress: with the three scales of personal, national/historical and the 'larger, hypothetical' (2015a: 100) in space and time simultaneously brought into play. However, where Clark anticipates a creative derangement of the text from such a reading, Martha's observation makes it potentially concordant; particularly given that here it puts into perspective – as the scale-aware idiom has it – the fragmentation of Martha, Matty and 'someone', as they seem momentarily aligned in their distance from the constant sun. Given this divergence from Clark's perspective, it is no surprise that Lessing's narrative practice at the start of *The Four-Gated City* also recalls aspects of phenomenology, that philosophical movement which played an important role in early ecocriticism, but which has more recently been criticised by Clark (2015b) and others for being of limited relevance to the Anthropocene.[3] The resemblance is particularly compelling if phenomenology is considered via the work of Henri Bortoft, who combined it with Goethean science.

There is good reason for viewing any connection between Lessing's work and phenomenology through this filter. Shah had become the formative influence on Lessing by the time of *The Four-Gated City*, following her disillusionment with politics and other movements such as Subud; Bortoft, similarly, moved away from an association with J. G. Bennett to 'attach' himself to Shah.[4] Both later gave papers at the Institute of Cultural Research (ICR), founded by Shah in 1965. More to the point, Bortoft's reading of phenomenology emphasises the kind of dynamic observation of a holistic world which has characterised Martha's observation, and which constituted one facet of Shah's stories – which Bortoft used as exemplary material in his first book. The way each act of observation entails both a distinguishing from and a connecting with the contingent world – from a teaspoon to a sponge, from clothes to the sun – recalls Bortoft's description of how 'any entity is what it is only within a network of relations' (2012: 27); an idea he links with Heidegger's referential totality, the tracing of the context of significance which makes a world. Or the way in which Martha's refusing customarily available interpretations (friendship, the sun shines) to try and catch the world in its appearance resonates with Bortoft's account of how meaning and understanding are a 'unitary event . . . prior to the subject-object separation' (2012: 100), with the subject becoming 'receptive' rather than 'active' in the 'event of understanding' (2012: 105–6). Similarly, the intensively multidimensional nature of Martha's observations and their recursively unfolding progress, whereby each step arises from but also transforms the one before it, suggests Bortoft's account of Goethe's '"exact sensorial imagination"' in his studies of plants and colour: 'active seeing', as a way of experiencing 'the wholeness of the phenomenon', its '"unity without unification"' (1996: 42, 59).[5]

Key to all these phenomenological correspondences is the concept of the whole, a dynamic concordance between the one and the many. However, there is a disjunction at the heart of *The Four-Gated City* between two versions of this holism: a disjunction which both determines how Lessing's work develops from this point, and also makes it a powerful intervention in contemporary debates about the relationship between criticism, literature and environmental crisis. The first holism is the fallen one in which the realist *The Four-Gated City* takes place, constituted of the kinds of connections seen thus far: it is, ultimately, degraded and destructive, a complex system bound up with human behaviours but passed beyond human understanding. The second holism is fulfilling and balanced: the organic non-human world provides one exemplary – if assailed – model for it, though it is also anthropic and utopian. These two holisms encapsulate divergent paths in environmental criticism. For instance, they reflect the split between a phenomenological approach emphasising human reciprocity with the environment, and a deconstructionist approach set on recalibrating concepts such as human identity. The split also mirrors the divergence Clark identifies between two possible images for the new human collectivity entailed by planetary environmental crisis – between a 'new universal history of humans' redolent of hope (Chakrabarty, quoted in Clark 2015a: 14); and a schizoid Leviathan composed of 'the often unforeseen consequences of the plans and acts of its constituents' (2015a: 15).

We can observe this split cohering around the hunk of wood that Martha observes on a bomb site early in the novel. At first it is treated similarly to the other phenomena seen thus far: registered in a variety of ways, in rapid succession, such that its existence comes into a networked and multidimensional view. First we see it *in situ*, how it looks and smells, an existence redolent of pollution and corruption. It is 'almost spongy' (17) with damp: like the sponge-teaspoon, a thing one would expect to be inviolate but which is now susceptible to a helpless intake of its surroundings, with disturbing implications for the people around it. Lessing's 'active seeing' shows another facet of itself here as she also sees the wood through the viewpoint of a long-term resident, Iris, whose historically informed speculation mingles with Martha's visual examination. Martha's observation thus becomes 'other in order to remain itself', to borrow Ronald Brady's description of the multiplicity in unity of plant forms, as perceived by Goethe (quoted in Bortoft 1996: 358 n29): an organicism Bortoft also identifies in Gadamer's phenomenological hermeneutics, thus confirming its congruence with texts as much as plants. Extending this multi-perspectival observation allows Martha to posit the real existence of London in the loving minds of its long-term female observers, 'a sort of six-dimensional map which included the histories and lives and loves of people. London – a section map in depth' (18).

Such a richness might seem positive; however, within the context of the novel as a whole this 'love' is at best misplaced, and the wood exists like the individuals within it, as connective nodes in a system deranged at every level. They are part of a holism, but it is a bad holism: one that must be tracked and observed only so as to be placated and eluded. It is, as such, the world in which we currently live, a complex system in many ways alien to us, that we have impacted in ways we struggle to grasp, and which now threatens us in an equally baffling fashion. This bad holism is exemplified by the room in which Mark draws colour-coded lines connecting 'facts objective and subjective' and 'statements' (454) in an attempt to map reality: such that 'a rocket failing to get itself off the launching pad' connects to 'the breakdown of an electric iron the first time it is used' (456). The bad holism is incomplete and must remain so, partly because so much of it remains beyond comprehension – as the characters' groping after it shows – and partly because its yokings are so wildly disjunctive. In this sense it corresponds to the hyperobjects described by Morton (2013a), amongst which Clark brackets climate change (2015a: 8–9): phenomena that terminally undermine phenomenology, with its reliance on sensory perception.

Within this broil of insanity, however, the text occasionally reaches out to a more phenomenologically authentic holism for which the organic 'natural' world is an exemplary model. Martha later passes the 'more-stone-than-wood' timber and sees that 'a minute yellow flower' (86) has emerged from it. This could be read as a metaphoric promise of a similar renewal in Martha, but the link is actual, related to Martha's authentic existence, just as her malfunctioning as a self was related 'in degree' to other incidents obeying the same functional pattern on a different historical scale. Later in the novel Martha sees a tree anew, deploying the sort of 'exact sensorial imagination' that Bortoft describes as characteristic of Goethe's holistic phenomenological perception:

> Nothing was more extraordinary and marvellous than that tree, a being waving its green limbs from a grey surface. Beneath the surface was a structure of roots whose shape had a correspondence with the shape and spread of its branches. This curious being that stood opposite the window, was a kind of conduit for the underground rivers of London, which rushed up its trunk, diffusing outwards through a hundred branches to disperse into the air and stream upwards, to join the damp cloud cover of the London sky. She felt she had never seen a tree before. The word 'tree' was alien to the being on the pavement. Tree, tree, she kept saying, as she said Martha, Martha, feeling the irrelevance of these syllables, which usurped the reality of the living structure. And, as if she had not lived in this room now, for four years, everything in it seemed extraordinary, and new, and when the old black cat rose, arching its back, from the white spread, the delight of that movement was felt in Martha's back. (239)

This leads into a similarly fresh and sensorially exact recovery of Martha's own past a few pages later, in which she discovers herself to be an essence that precedes and exceeds the realist biography that attaches to her: just as the existence of the tree precedes the naming of it as 'tree' which also cancels its appearance. 'Who are you then? Why, me, of course, who else, horse, woman, man, or tree, a glittering faceted individuality of breathing green, here is the sense of me, nameless, recognizable only to me' (245). As Kevin Brazil describes in his chapter, Martha both fears and risks becoming a stagnant repetition of selves across the *Children of Violence* sequence; but here, at its latter end, that self finally glimpses a phenomenologically rooted continuity. The 'living structure' of Martha is commensurate with the tree, which as an organism in harmony with its ecosystem is also harmonious across gulfs of scale, from underground rivers to the sky: only Martha's harmony extends first through her own life, in that the recognition of this 'individuality of breathing green' arises from the recollection of her past. Just as in the bad holism personal and environmental malfunction were parts of the same whole, so they are, too, in the good holism. This allows us to reread Martha's earlier expansion from a contemplation of her false self to the foundational sun as a momentary connection to an extreme limit of the organic scale, whose permanency underwrites the obscuring moment-by-moment chaos in which she lives.

This modelling of tree and individual as fluent in scale, staging posts in a congruent whole that reaches out from them in both directions, is concordant with both a phenomenological sense of the natural environment as an interdependent whole, and with Lessing's Sufi-influenced belief in a concordant pattern underlying creation. The epigraphs to *The Four-Gated City* encapsulate how it merges these two perspectives. Part One's epigraph, from Rachel Carson's *The Edge of the Sea*, emphasises how a seemingly permanent macro world is built from the conglomeration of countless smaller, constantly changing processes. Part Four then carries three epigraphs: one from 'a schools broadcast' about how a 'cell' in a toad is 'encoded' with the potential to be something different ('a head cell') to that which it originally finds itself to be ('a gut cell', 467); one from Rumi via a translation by Shah, in which human spiritual evolution is seen as congruent with planetary organic evolution; and one from Shah himself, making a similar point. This congruence is even clearer in the epigraphs to Lessing's next novel, *Briefing for a Descent into Hell* (1971). The first, from the Sufi Master Shabistari, describes how a raindrop might contain a hundred seas – a passage Lessing followed Shah in reading as anticipating nuclear energy[6] – just as 'the gnat in limbs doth match the elephant', while 'Upon one little spot within the heart / Resteth the Lord and Master of the worlds. / Therein two worlds commingled may be seen' (1). The second is again from Carson, describing how 'the miniscule world of the sand grains is also the world of inconceivably minute beings ... so small that our human senses cannot grasp its scale, a world in which the microdroplet of water separating one grain of sand from another is like a vast, dark sea' (1). As Clare Hanson observes later in this volume, Lessing's ideas of evolutionary continuity might have been encouraged by the transhumanism of Julian Huxley and his circle: though as Martha's phenomenological exploration shows, Lessing's emphasis is far less upon the human capacity for instrumental reasoning.

This scalar fluency between organic existence and human spiritual existence emerges as foundational to both *The Four-Gated City* and the fiction which succeeds it. Thus the city described in Mark's story, which gives the novel its name, consists of a perfect harmony between individuals, community and environment; while in *Shikasta* the cosmic alignment of planets parallels the patterning of organic life on Earth. This vision provides an implicit answer to the scepticism Clark and others have expressed about the human ability to cope with forces acting at scales of time and space incomprehensible to individuals: because if you take care of the scale available to you – yourself – then this will scale both down and up, from atom to cosmos. In being both predicated on action and enabling it, this model breaks through the impasse that often ensues when literary and cultural criticism engages with environmental crisis. Clark takes a crucial step further than most such criticism to ask: '*how far does a change in* [cultural] *knowledge and imagination entail a change in environmentally destructive modes of life?*' (18, italics original). As he notes, a positive answer to that question 'touches the heart of ecocriticism'; but Lessing's answer to it would be, if not flatly negative, then scornful. What needs to change is not just 'the imaginary' of the culture, 'the interpretation of cultural artefacts' (19) as Clark puts it, but the individuals doing this imagining, through an empirical self-development that simultaneously and paradoxically entails an engagement in the collective, in ways that vary from the humdrum to the ineffable. A change in the cultural imaginary might be required, but this can only take place if accompanied by meaningful work on oneself, in and through the world, of the sort that Martha attempts in *The Four-Gated City*.

Lessing's work therefore also poses questions to those critics whose analysis of literature in a time of environmental crisis often seems to fall back on the conflation of a more mimetically adequate representation with utility: a conflation that risks effacing action. For instance, Ursula Heise's praise of fictions that 'develop a narrative form commensurate with the complexities and heterogeneities of cultures joined in global crisis' (208) moves unquestioningly into the assertion that this is to 'address' (208) humanity's environmental situation – the verb eliding action and rhetoric a little too conveniently. Similarly, Morton's celebration of artwork that 'in its very form' (2013b: 39) corresponds to hyperobjects, coincides with confident assertions about how such 'Nature art ... change[s] attitudes ... upgrade[s] human consciousness' (2013a: 184). However, representation appropriates change in familiar ways: as, for instance, when a piece of installation art 'forces us to confront the rainforest' (185) in a new manner. Elsewhere, a well-worn language of consumption and didacticism contrasts strangely with Morton's celebration of the radical novelty of this art: as each piece 'captures' (185) and 'contains' (188), 'conveys' (186) and 'demonstrates' (188) new insights. Even Clark's masterly account reads at times as if it is stuck in the mimetic cul-de-sac, exploring at length 'the literary representation of environmental issues' (2015a: 73), while scarcely considering the utility or otherwise of such representation, and the kinds of action that both environmental crisis and the literature of it might demand. However, Clark's mentioning decisive and/or collective action as a brief aside to or unelaborated qualification of our current helplessness and the efficacy of environmental criticism (e.g. 109, 143, 165), as well as his turning to it at greater length only in the last few pages, suggests an unnecessary truncation in his account. In this sense, Fredric Jameson's reading of utopian fictions as inevitable failures that might nevertheless catalyse change has more to say to fiction in an age of environmental crisis.[7]

However, although Lessing knows the solution requires individual action, and although she is even able to represent the harmony which lies on the other side of decisive change, there is nevertheless a breach in her scalar fluency, in that she is unable to imagine the kind of communal action which is the necessary hinge between individual work and its envisaged global result. The crisis lurking in the negative answer to Clark's question – about how far a change in imagination might equate to a change in our mode of life – is thus also realised in Lessing's work. From *The Four-Gated City* onwards Lessing struggles with this dilemma, which can remain instructive even if we do not follow her in any or all of her details: for instance, in the idea – seemingly serious and following Shah again – that the mechanism for human communality is telepathy.[8] However, a comparable sense of impossibility attaches to more secular and realist attempts to address the scalar gap between individuals, communality and biosphere: of the sort encountered in the novels of Kim Stanley Robinson, for instance, or the political writings of Murray Bookchin.[9]

It has become almost a commonplace to observe that it is easier to imagine the end of the world than the end of the global capitalism which has driven the degradation of the biosphere. Nevertheless, Lessing's writing seems to bear this out, as in *The Four-Gated City*, where her answer to the scalar deadlock is to nuke the world: a fatal version of the 'interruptions' described by Tom Sperlinger in this volume. Dipesh Chakrabarty has distinguished between the anxieties engendered by climate change and nuclear war on the basis that while the former 'would have been a conscious decision on the part of the powers that be', the latter is 'an unintended consequence of human actions' (221). However, in *The Four-Gated City* they are doppelgänger children of the bad holism: because the cause of the nuclear event is as simultaneously known (human stupidity) and unknown (its exact mechanisms and extent) as climate change. Rather than being the result of conscious decision, it is the tipping point in a wider accumulation of myopic human actions, of the sort the novel has traced in detail. In *Shikasta* (1979) a few individuals might struggle into alignment with the universal harmony of Canopus, but Lessing cannot write, in the realism via which the bulk of the novel proceeds, a wholesale conversion to that harmony: and so another nuclear apocalypse ensues, followed by more non-realist cities embodying the alignment of individual, community and environment. Because Lessing's solutions are so outrageously utopian they also advertise their non-realism: thus Mark's story in *The Four-Gated City* is a 'fable', and the harmonious community at its end is built from science-fiction tropes. Indeed, this catch-22 of mutual unintelligibility between genre and reality – that the most 'realistic' genre, in terms of the good holism, is also the non-realist genre in the bad holism in which we exist – is foregrounded, as Martha finds science fiction to be the contemporary literature most relevant to her own development.

Thus the harmony of scale is inextricably linked to genre – though not genre pegged to subject matter, whether a fictional world is 'made-up' or not. Realism in Lessing is commensurate with the scalar breach that is humanity's planetary disaster, because it cannot help but replay the bad holism engendered by wilful ignorance and the inflationary destruction arising from it; while the posited solution can only be achieved via some kind of fabular abstraction, whose overtness advertises the fact that Lessing cannot represent it in the terms of our customary reality. This abstraction might involve the foregrounding of a fiction's fabular nature, or an obviously schematic spatial and structural modelling, as with the ideal cities, or the map of the Canopean system. This split – which is simultaneously generic and ecocritical – can be used as a heuristic for reading much of Lessing's work in the period after *The Four-Gated City*. For example, we can now see how the realistically notated strife – individual and social – in *The Memoirs of a Survivor* (1974) is resolved by a flagrantly non-realist structural figuring: as in the division between the worlds behind and before the patterned wallpaper, or the symbolic egg at the climax, around which the characters become emblems that can join in a holistic unity, though only after the realist world in which they formerly existed has been subjected to a slow-motion apocalypse. Similarly, *The Making of the Representative for Planet 8* (1982) proceeds from a relatively realistic notation of human behaviour and thought – for instance, of surviving in ice-age conditions – into a merging across scales both atomic and planetary, figured via suddenly perceived 'intricate structures and shapes', the planet seen as 'a fine frail web or lattice' and its individuals become 'patterns of matter, matter of a kind' in 'a tenuous though strict dance' (157–8).

This recourse to abstraction could be read as a desperate positivity: the failure of realist representation emphasising the need to move instead to action. This would accord both with Shah's assertion that meaningful self-development cannot be described (or merely read about) but be lived, and Jameson's proposition that the failure of utopian fictions might catalyse change. However, the absoluteness of the split in Lessing's work, as well as the comprehensive failure in it of all communal endeavour, presses hard on such positivity. A comparison with Ursula Le Guin's *The Dispossessed* (1974) – subtitled 'An Ambiguous Utopia' – is instructive in this regard. While there is a comparable mysticism, informed by Le Guin's commitment to the *Tao Te Ching*, and an emphasis on personal transformation via the protagonist, this is embedded in the verisimilar imagining of an anarchist society, and of communal action within an unjust capitalist society that mirrors our own. Comparable utopian or semi-utopian societies in Lessing (e.g. *The Marriage of Zones Three, Four and Five,* 1980; 'The Reason for It', 2003) are, in contrast, overtly fantastic, while any realist treatments of society and politics are invariably pessimistic, with all utopian endeavour doomed to undermining by age-old human weakness: see *The Good Terrorist* (1985) or *The Sweetest Dream* (2001). This is, doubtless, a legacy of Lessing's total disillusionment with her early communism. Indeed, the two holisms – bad and good – map to Marxism and mysticism, the first a broken version of the second precisely because it tried to fulfil itself in the (realistic) world.[10] 'I personally think we were round the bend', Lessing later said of the utopian beliefs of her youth ('Sunday').

This is where Lessing had ended up, even by the early 1970s; and where, perhaps, we currently remain. A newly harmonious human collectivity within a nurtured biosphere exists as a utopian concept but cannot be realistically conceived of: the generic impasse equivalent to the political. Some form of apocalyptic civilisational collapse seems to be the unavoidable outcome of this failure. Therefore a grim but doughty fidelity to the human potential that might survive disaster is the only valid form of optimism. Indeed, while in *Mara and Dann* the imagining of a future ice age might be read as a chastening correction to the idealisation of stable and balanced ecologies that was current in the early waves of ecocriticism, it is as much concerned with removing any prospect of coping with environmental crisis, as it vanishes the kinds of technology and global community that might take reparatory action commensurate with the destruction already caused. In this sense *Mara and Dann* remains very much a contemporary climate change novel, and one that partakes of the apocalyptic fatalism often attendant on the field – notwithstanding Lessing's identification of herself in 2004 as 'an optimist', on the grounds that she 'think[s] that the human race will survive because we are good survivors' (Lev-Ari).

However, the good holism has not vanished from this later work, and its new form is entwined with the importance of storytelling in Lessing's later career. In earlier novels she posited a harmonious outward expansion from the self: into the ideal city, or the Canopean Lock. However, her conception of stories involves a contraction, as they become carrying agents for a harmony that cannot yet be achieved at that larger scale: they are arks or seed banks in which the essence of the good holism can survive. The chief influence on this conception was, unsurprisingly, Shah, who celebrated the importance of stories to humanity, as well as their ability to adapt across civilisational difference and huge expanses of time.[11] In her 1988 *Paris Review* interview Lessing stated that 'we value narrative because the pattern is in our brain. Our brains are patterned for storytelling, for the consecutive' ('Art'). This recalls the various 'patterns' detected in *The Four-Gated City*, from the universal patterns of global politics (307) and adolescent development (409), to the schematically patterned cities in which the scalar harmony is embodied; only now the emphasis is on the holistic link between story and brain, rather than between individual and larger (human and non-human) environment. This scaling down comes with an emphasis on movement through time, 'the consecutive', as highlighted by Lessing's remarks in 2003:

> The human race has been telling stories since it began [. . .] Humanity's legacy of stories and storytelling is the most precious we have. All wisdom is in our stories and songs. A story is how we construct our experiences. At the very simplest it can be: He/she was born, lived, died. Probably that is the template of our stories — a beginning, middle, and end. This structure is in our minds. (2003)[12]

Implicit in the spatialised perfection of the ideal cities was a utopian or mystic conclusion of historical time, but now the emphasis is on narrative temporality: as is only appropriate, given the new focus on survival rather than a resolving transformation.

This explains the recuperation in *Mara and Dann* of the recursive observational practice we saw at the beginning of *The Four-Gated City* – formalised now in the 'game' by which Mahondi children are educated:

> It was called, What Did You See? [. . .] At first she chattered: 'I played with my cousin . . . I was out with Shera in the garden . . . I made a stone house.' And then he had said, 'Tell me about the house.' And she said, 'I made a house of the stones that come from the river bed.' And he said, 'Now tell me about the stones.' And she said, 'They were mostly smooth stones, but some were sharp and had different shapes.' 'Tell me what the stones looked like, what colour they were, what did they feel like.'
>
> And by the time the game ended she knew why some stones were smooth and some sharp and why they were different colours, some cracked, some so small they were almost sand. She knew how rivers rolled stones along and how some of them came from far away. She knew that the river had once been twice as wide as it was now. (23–4)

As with *The Four-Gated City*, this active seeing extends to less materially evident realms, as the questions expand to 'What were you thinking? What made you think that? Are you sure that thought is true?' (24). However, where in the earlier novel this narrative practice was stuck in the bad holism, haunted by its inability to make the eponymous city real, here it is rehabilitated as a microcosmic 'pattern' of the good holism, realisable in both 'realism' and linear narrative in a way the city was not. This is seen in the symbiotic extension of 'What Did You See?' to the novel itself, as if the creation of the storyworld is simultaneous with the author playing the game:

> Soon they were walking through the rock houses. Some were bigger than Daima's, some smaller, some not more than a room with a roof of rough grass. The stone roofs of some houses had fallen in. There were heaps of rock that had been houses. Outside every house was a big tank made of rock. There was one outside Daima's. All kinds of little pipes and channels led from the different roofs to the tank. (43)

The storyworld pieces together like Mara's childhood movement from stones to river: a referential tissue, a constantly unveiling whole. The novel possesses the largely paratactic style characteristic of Lessing's work, with its propulsive effect heightened by the frequent employment of 'and' and 'now' at or near the start of sentences. This acts as a textual approximation of the immediacy of oral storytelling, as if the moment of reading is coterminous with the moment of fictional creation. The seed-bank thinking implicit in Lessing's conception of stories is thus substantiated: add the water of reading to text, and what might have seemed dead comes to life.

In this heightening of the hermeneutic relationship between text (or 'story') and reader, Lessing enacts a form of holism whose realisation and survival she can believe in. Individual, community and environment cannot be brought into a scalar fluency, though individual and text can be, in a manner that recalls – even if it cannot actually intervene in – that larger harmony. Lessing's storytelling thus constitutes a peculiar *Ding an sich* version of the miniaturisation Clark describes in critical readings, where texts are seen 'as enacting in fictional miniature a cultural politics that could be usefully held to apply, scaled-up again, to innumerable people and situations in actual life' (2015a: 77); only Lessing's miniaturisations are essential rather than representational, a DNA coding rather than description. They can thus be read as a strange variation of the generation starship genre, in which mankind escapes earth's exhausted biosphere by taking to space in a craft that replicates in miniature the conditions for life on the home planet. In Lessing's final estimation, we cannot change our environmentally destructive forms of life, but the stories that are us can – like those spaceships – pass beyond it. Is this enough? In Kim Stanley Robinson's recent novel, *Aurora* (2015), a generation starship returns to earth and all its problems having discovered that such dreams of escape are consoling fantasies, magical thinking. What would it mean for Lessing's stories to return to a dwelling in the present? It is no coincidence that where Lessing cannot write of transformative communal action, Robinson excels in it; and that as 'hard SF' his writing cleaves closer to a realist mode. Such action is the missing link in Lessing's scalar writing, just as it is in environmental criticism's sense of itself, and what it can and might – and cannot – do.

Notes

1. Sufism: a mystic tradition often associated with Islam but claiming, in Idries Shah's relating of it, a universal relevance and lineage. *The Sufis* was published in 1964; while *Landlocked* (1965) uses Shah's work as an epigraph, its full impact is first felt in *The Four-Gated City*. Shah published six other works between 1966 and 1969; Lessing was also in personal contact with him.
2. See for instance Haraway (2003); Alaimo (2010); Morton (2010).
3. For other environmentally minded criticisms of the phenomenological tradition, particularly as it derives from Heidegger, see Plumwood (2008), Garrard (2010), Morton (2010). For more positive re-evaluations see Clark (2013) and (with relation to Merleau-Ponty) Toadvine (2009).
4. The word choice is Ken Blake's (Blake, n.p.).

5. Lessing's monograph for the ICR cites Goethe as a model of how to read, in a way that recalls Bortoft's Goethean account of seeing as meaning: 'passively, but alertly, without interposing our own agendas between the prose and ourselves' (1999b: 17).
6. See Shah (1968: 22); Lessing (1994a).
7. See for instance Jameson (2005: 288–9).
8. See for instance Shah (1978: 42–3).
9. However, it is worth noting that Robinson's utopias often blend an Eastern spiritual outlook with a more secular Western one: Sufism in *The Mars Trilogy*, Tibetan Buddhism in the *Science in the Capitol Trilogy*, and both in *The Years of Rice and Salt*. It thus lies closer to Lessing's more scandalously non-secular work than might immediately seem the case.
10. See Lessing's preface to *The Golden Notebook* (1962), where the failure of Marxism is framed in terms of an unsuccessful holism.
11. See for instance Shah (1979).
12. cf. 'But our experience, it seems to me, when you're actually living, is: and, and, and. It's not either/or at all' (*Shadows*: 7).

Works Cited

Alaimo, Stacey (2010), *Bodily Natures: Science, Environment, and the Material Self*, Bloomington: Indiana University Press.
Blake, Tony, 'The Rascoorano of Ken Pledge', <http://campcaravan.org/d_other/Pledge.html> (last accessed 31 October 2015).
Bortoft, Henri (1996), *The Wholeness of Nature: Goethe's Way of Science*, Floris Books: Edinburgh.
—— (2012), *Taking Appearance Seriously: The Dynamic Way of Seeing in Goethe and European Thought*, Edinburgh: Floris Books.
Chakrabarty, Dipesh (2009), 'The Climate of History: Four Theses', *Critical Inquiry*, 35:2, 197–222.
Clark, Samantha (2013), 'Strange Strangers and Uncanny Hammers: Morton's *The Ecological Thought* and the Phenomenological Tradition', *Green Letters: Studies in Ecocriticism* 17:2, 98–108.
Clark, Timothy (2015a), *Ecocriticism on the Edge: the Anthropocene as a Threshold Concept*, London: Bloomsbury.
—— (2015b), 'Phenomenology', in Greg Garrard (ed.), *The Oxford Handbook of Ecocriticism*, Oxford: Oxford University Press, pp. 276–90.
Garrard, Greg (2010), 'Heidegger Nazism Ecocriticism', *Interdisciplinary Studies in Literature and Environment*, 17:2, 251–71.
Haraway, Donna (2003), *The Companion Species Manifesto: Dogs, People, and Significant Otherness*, Chicago: Prickly Paradigm Press.
Heise, Ursula K. (2008), *Sense of Place and Sense of Planet: the Environmental Imagination of the Global*, Oxford: Oxford University Press.
Jameson, Fredric (2005), *Archaeologies of the Future: The Desire Called Utopia and Other Science Fictions*, London: Verso.
Lessing, Doris [1971] (1972), *Briefing for a Descent into Hell*, New York: Bantam.
—— (1974), *The Memoirs of a Survivor*, London: Octagon Press.

—— [1979] (1981), *Shikasta*, London: Grafton Books.

—— [1982] (1983), *The Making of the Representative for Planet 8*, London: Granada Publishing.

—— (1988), 'The Art of Fiction No. 102', Thomas Frick, <http://www.theparisreview.org/interviews/2537/the-art-of-fiction-no-102-doris-lessing> (last accessed 31 October 2015).

—— [1969] (1990), *The Four-Gated City*, London: Paladin.

—— (1994a), 'On *The Commanding Self*', <http://ishk.net/sufis/lessing.html>, (last accessed 31 October 2015).

—— (1994b), *Shadows on the Wall of the Cave: A Talk*, London: The British Library, Centre for the Book.

—— (1999a), *Mara and Dann: An Adventure*, London: Flamingo.

—— (1999b), *Problems, Myths and Stories,* London: The Institute for Cultural Research.

—— (2003), 'Book interview; *The Grandmothers*', <http://645e533e2058e72 657e9-f9758a43fb7c33cc8adda0fd36101899.r45.cf2.rackcdn.com/book-inte rviews/BI-9780060530112.pdf> (last accessed 31 October 2015).

—— (2007), 'Sunday Profile', <http://www.abc.net.au/sundayprofile/stories/ s2065058.htm> (last accessed 31 October 2015).

Lev-Ari, Shiri (2004), 'Doris Lessing, 1919–2013: Brave Woman, Brave Writing', <http://www.haaretz.com/world-news/1.558587> (last accessed 31 October 2015).

Morton, Timothy (2010), *The Ecological Thought*, Cambridge, MA: Harvard University Press.

—— (2013a), *Hyperobjects: Philosophy and Ecology After the End of the World*, Minneapolis: University of Minnesota Press.

—— (2013b), 'Poisoned Ground: Art and Philosophy in the Time of Hyperobjects', *Symplokē* 21, 37–50.

Plumwood, Val (2008), 'Shadow Places and the Politics of Dwelling', *Australian Humanities Review* 44, 139–50.

Shah, Idries (1968), *The Way of the Sufi*, London: The Octagon Press.

—— (1978), *Learning How to Learn*, London: The Octagon Press.

—— (1979), *World Tales*, London: The Octagon Press.

Toadvine, Ted (2009), *Merleau-Ponty's Philosophy of Nature*, Evanston: Northwestern University Press.

Chapter 9

Lessing and Time Travel

David Punter

To speak of time travel is immediately to become involved in conundrums and paradoxes. I won't attempt to list them here, but one is perhaps particularly important. What could it possibly mean, we might ask, *not* to be travelling through time? Time travel is what we all do, and most usually we do it – or we think we do it – lineally. We regard yesterday as the past, tomorrow as the future. Under strange circumstances, this might not be what happens at all. Under conditions of trauma, for example, it might seem that the past is constantly revisited. In the realm of dream, we may encounter different arrangements of time. Freud (to whom I will briefly return) established his difference from conventional theories of dream – of which there have been many, spanning millennia – by suggesting, indeed, insisting, that dreams were not omens; in other words, they did not predict the future. In a strict sense, he may have been right; in other ways, he may have been wrong. 'I have a dream', said Martin Luther King in 1963, and it seems at least arguable that he was prophetic. 'I had this dream', says a person in the grip of psychosis; and lo and behold, he or she goes forth and proceeds to act on this dream. Are these omens? Well, perhaps not *sensu stricto*, but they play a part in organising the future. Whatever the notion of 'future' means; and I shall come back to that. 'Back', one might say, 'to the future'; what might that really mean?

Doris Lessing's work, although this may at first seem counter-intuitive, can be understood as centrally concerned with time travel. As other chapters in this volume show, Lessing was profoundly interested in questions of scale, from narrating personal history to the histories of civilisations. I propose to follow the theme of time travel, as an expansion of those questions, by looking, first and mainly, at *The Memoirs of a Survivor* (1974), and then, more briefly, at *Shikasta* (1979) and *The Marriages between Zones Three, Four and Five* (1980) – although something about time travel could no doubt be demonstrated in other

Lessing texts, for example *The Fifth Child* (1988) and *The Cleft* (2007).

There may be a general misapprehension that time travel pertains to the future. It is easy to see how this error occurs: after all (whatever that strange phrase might mean), we want, do we not, to know what happens in the future, to know what happens next, which may itself be a reflection on the omnipresence of death. But that is itself to put the issue in a peculiar 'present' tense; perhaps it would be better to say that we want to know what is 'going to happen' in the future – but even there, are we sure? Is it not more that we want to know what 'will have happened' in the future – the future perfect; or the future imperfect? What tense are we talking about here? We can find these questions addressed in general terms in Frank Kermode's *The Sense of an Ending* (1967), but here we need to be more specific.

For time travel is not always about the future; sometimes it is about the past. Here is Lessing's protagonist in *Memoirs of a Survivor*:

> I had gazed down and fancied myself back in time: all of us did this a great deal, matching and comparing, balancing facts in our minds to make them fit, to orient ourselves against them. The present was so remarkable and dream-like that to accommodate it meant this process had to be used: *It was like that, was it? Yes, it was like that, but now* . . . (114, italics original)

This last thought, in fact, recapitulates the opening paragraph of the novel. So what the speaker is doing is attempting to measure the 'present' against the 'past': striving to make some sense of the conditions among which she finds herself by 'matching and comparing' – but of course this is an attempt which is doomed to failure. We cannot – can we? – imagine the past with the same degree of colour, vividness, as is possessed by the present.

But then, as Lessing goes on to ask, what is this texture, this vividness which we imagine to be the present? For her protagonist, this apparently transparent question becomes increasingly opaque, as her 'present' divides into two, or probably three, realms of experience.

> I've said, I think, that when I was in one world – the region behind the flowery wall of my living-room – the ordinary logical time-dominated world of everyday did not exist; that when in my 'ordinary' life I forgot, and sometimes for days at a time, that the wall could open, had opened, would open again, and then I would simply move through into that other space. But now began a period when something of the flavour of the place behind the wall did continuously invade my real life. (131)

And so there is this possibility, it would seem, of access to another world which is not 'time-dominated', although aspects of this realm of apparent freedom from time become deeply constricting, even suffocating. Let us think for a moment about the 'forgetting' – 'sometimes for days at a time': there is an incompatibility here which is typical of Lessing's concern for different timescales, a possibility of forgetting what – just a moment ago – one was sure one had on the tip of the tongue, as it might be. And from here one could move towards Freud, particularly towards parapraxis, towards the 'slip of the tongue' which reveals that the past is not, after all, absent; that it is there ready to spring out unbidden and thwart the apparent logicalities of the chain of discourse (Freud 1898).

This process of forgetting – amnesia, as one might call it – has, perhaps, its joyous side, an aspect turned towards jouissance. Provided one can keep realms separate, then there is always the possibility of escape from one to another; although when one thinks of H. G. Wells's terrifying and tragic short story 'The Door in the Wall' (1911), one might feel that the agony of nostalgia, the pain of being readmitted for even a single moment to the jouissance of childhood, is not worth the candle. For memory may indeed end in terror. As the narrator says of the protagonist, Lionel Wallace, after his death, which resulted from walking through the door in the wall which he believed would permit him to return to a childhood paradise:

> I am more than half convinced that he had, in truth, an abnormal gift, and a sense, something – I know not what – that in the guise of wall and door offered him an outlet, a secret and peculiar passage of escape into another and altogether more beautiful world. At any rate, you will say it betrayed him in the end. But did it betray him? . . . By our daylight standard he walked out of security into darkness, danger, and death.
>   But did he see it like that? (161)

Let us try a hypothesis: without memory, there is no possibility of imagining a future – and that is all we do with the future, is it not – imagine it? And with what rhetoric, with what arrangements of form, can we imagine the future except with those drawn from experience, in other words from the past? In *Memoirs of a Survivor*, Lessing illustrates this conundrum perfectly in her title; how can we write a 'memoir', remember, unless we have survived? But, therefore, how can we re-imagine a past except from the position of a future which we have made our own, even if, as in this text, under conditions of considerable deprivation? We have outlasted the present; we have even outlasted the immediate future (whatever that might mean); now we are 'writing back' to the present – in the hope, perhaps, that the 'present' is still there. It may not be.

But then again, perhaps there are different styles of future.

In general, I try and distinguish between what one calls the Future and 'l'avenir' (the 'to come'). The future is that which – tomorrow, later, next century – will be. There is a future which is predictable, programmed, scheduled, foreseeable. But there is a future, 'l'avenir', which refers to someone who comes whose arrival is totally unexpected.

For me, that is the real future. That which is totally unpredictable. The Other who comes without my being able to anticipate their arrival. So if there is a real future, beyond the other known future, it is 'l'avenir;' in that it is the coming of the Other when I am completely unable to foresee their arrival. (Derrida, Kirby and Kofman 2005: 53)

This passage from Jacques Derrida seems precisely to encapsulate the 'originary moment' of *Memoirs of a Survivor*, when the young girl Emily arrives on the doorstep accompanied by her unprepossessing pet, Hugo, and a strange man who then immediately disappears, leaving Emily as our protagonist's responsibility. This is an event which is entirely unpredicted and indeed unexplained. 'L'avenir' pure and simple perhaps; outside that other realm of the future signified by diaries and calendars, those tools we use to plan our lives. This would seem consonant with a refrain which occurs throughout Lessing: that we cannot see what is awaiting us, what is 'coming for us', in several senses – what gifts the future might bring, for example, but more usually what apocalyptic fate may be just around the corner.

There is perhaps a little too much of Peter Pan about the ending of *Memoirs of a Survivor*. Nonetheless, here is how part of it goes:

Emily took Gerald by the hand, and with Hugo walked through the screen of the forest into . . . and now it is hard to say exactly what happened. We were in that place which might present us with anything – rooms furnished this way or that and spanning the tastes and customs of millennia; walls broken, falling, growing again; a house roof like a forest floor sprouting grasses and birds' nests; rooms smashed, littered, robbed; a bright green lawn under thunderous and glaring clouds and on the lawn a giant black egg of pockmarked iron, [. . .] that world, presenting itself in a thousand little flashes, a jumble of little scenes, was folding up as we stepped into it, was parcelling itself up, was vanishing, dwindling and going – all of it, trees and streams, grasses and rooms and people. (189–90)

There are two things here of particular interest. The first is the gesture towards, or rather in the face of, the inexplicable – 'it is hard to say exactly what happened' – an admission, almost perhaps a proclamation, of the inadequacy of language to describe crucial moments of experience. The second is the mention of a place 'which might present us with anything'; in other words, a space of the 'present', but the 'present' is of course the most fleeting, the most evanescent of moments: it may appear substantial, but it is already predicated upon, and intelligible only in terms of, the past; and it is also already fleeting under the sign of the future; the present is 'that which disappears'. 'Time itself', Derrida says, 'cannot be sent. The uniqueness of the moment is that which one cannot explain to a third party, it cannot be put in an envelope, it cannot be sent very quickly' (1995: 388); for, after all, it cannot be put into words, there can only be a gesture towards it, a gesture which is simultaneously one of acceptance and one of denial.

Shikasta is a book in which Lessing's previous concern with what we might call the micro-scale of *Memoirs* mutates into the macro-scale of cosmic speculation. She remarks in the introduction:

> What a phenomenon it has been – science fiction, space fiction – exploding out of nowhere, unexpectedly of course, as always happens when the human mind is being forced to expand: this time starwards, galaxy-wise, and who knows where next. These dazzlers have mapped our world, or worlds, for us, have told us what is going on and in ways no one else has done, have described our nasty present long ago, when it was still the future and the official scientific spokesmen were saying that all manner of things now happening were impossible... (93)

What can be 'expected'? – one might reasonably ask, following from Derrida and Lessing, those improbable companions on the route towards the future – both of them, perhaps we need to remind ourselves, now no longer living. What can we know of what is possible or impossible, how can we proceed except by following the vanishing trail, attempting to see what shapes are emerging among the stars, within the tracks on the trail, in the footprints of genders and races whose divisions will always be things of the past, things of the present, things of the future? As Lessing, in my opinion, always seemed concerned to do.

In *Shikasta*, amid impossible manipulations of time in the macro-sense, Lessing recapitulates those times which we Europeans ignorant of the Islamic world seem to like to call the 'Dark Ages':

> Whereas, in the early days of the post-disaster time, it had sometimes been enough for one of us to enter a village, a settlement, and sit down and talk to them of their past, of what they had been, of what they would one day become, but only through their own efforts and diligence – that they had dues to pay to Canopus [...] – told this, it was often enough, and they would set themselves to adapt to the current necessities. But this became less and less what we could expect. Towards the end one of our agents would begin work knowing that it might take not a day, or a month, or a year, but perhaps all his life to stabilise a few individuals, so that they could listen. (146–7)

It would be impossible in this space to explain the complexities of Shikasta, Canopus and Shammat; suffice to say that here there are problems of time travel at work. Are the Canopean agents returning from a future – and if so, which one? What does it mean to suggest that the Shikastans have a destiny already worked out for them, albeit one which, it appears, may not come to pass? How can that be possible – is time made up of thwarted possibilities, of events that have never taken place, of paths which have not been taken? And what are the relations here between personal destiny and the workings of larger cosmic fate?

Notice, before the next quotation, the word 'expect' – what, indeed, do we 'expect'? Here is another quotation from Derrida.

> If there is anamnesis, it is not just a movement of memory to find again what has been forgotten, to restore finally an origin, a moment or a past that will have been present. One would naturally have to distinguish between several kinds of anamnesis. The Platonic discourse is essentially anabasis or anamnesis, that is, a going back toward the intelligible place of ideas. [. . .] if there is anamnesis, it is because the memory in question is not turned toward the past, so to speak, it is not a memory that, at the end of a return across all the other anamneses, would finally a reach an originary place of philosophy that would have been forgotten. The relation between forgetting and memory is much more disturbing. Memory is not just the opposite of forgetting. (1995: 382–3)

'Anamnesis': the opposite of 'amnesia'. But memory is not just the opposite of forgetting. Here is Canopus at its Renaissance work again, ensuring, or attempting to ensure, a type of survival:

> They were prepared [. . .] to learn anything I could teach them in the realm of the practical arts, which they were in danger of forgetting. I taught them – or retaught them – gardening and husbandry. I taught them to tame a goatlike creature, which could give them milk, and I demonstrated butter- and cheese-making [. . .] All these crafts I was teaching to creatures who had known them for thousands of years and had forgotten them a few months ago. (93)

Time travel: in this case, travel from a putative future back into the remnants of the past so that – what? So that the past can catch up with the future, so that it can be considered as a suitable progenitor, so that the butterfly effect may be countered – or, perhaps, so that one can be certain of one's own parenting, that one's progenitors are indeed one's own – perhaps *Homo sapiens* rather than *Homo habilis*. Who knows.

Freud (1922) again addresses the crucial issue in Lessing's fiction of time travel, namely, how do we know? How do we know what is going on? Or, to put it in a different rhetoric, what are our verification techniques – and this, of course, touches on the whole vexed issue of Lessing as a realist writer and as a writer of fantasy. For time travel, seen from one point of view, and perhaps most interestingly in Marge Piercy's

Woman on the Edge of Time (1976), is a matter of telepathy; of how we might receive messages from the future – and what is most interesting to me about this passage is that it seems as though Freud is assuming that telepathy has a certain 'reality', whatever that means. We might think here too of Nicholas Royle's comments on Salman Rushdie's *Midnight's Children* (1981) in *The Uncanny* (269–71). Freud writes:

> It is perfectly conceivable that a telepathic message might arrive contemporaneously with the event and yet only penetrate to consciousness the following night during sleep (or even in waking life only after a while, during some pause in the activity of the mind). (219–20)

Time travel and telepathy – after all, 'telepathy' only means 'feeling from a distance', and why should that be a distance in space rather than in time? In fact, the whole issue of the telepathic has historically been bound up with messages from the dead, with intimations of an afterlife, or afterlives; with communications with those who, somehow and in some shape or form, 'live on'. The question of 'penetration to consciousness' may also be important, if vertiginous – what would it mean to receive a message at all, whether or not within an 'envelope', if its effect can only be felt after a period of delay, of *Nachträglichkeit* which could, of course, mean that, for example, whether one had a premonition or not would be thrown into flux – when exactly was the moment of 'reception', and indeed by what receptors, if some of those receptors are less, or other, than conscious?

This question of the transmission of knowledge through time – call it telepathy, or *Nachträglichkeit* – is one of Lessing's perennial concerns, and is taken up in this passage from *The Marriages between Zones Three, Four and Five*. How, she asks, does understanding travel – and in this case she appears to suggest that such understanding travels in the form of myth and legend, types of narrative, for what other means of transmission have we when we have no tools with which to dissect the 'origins' of time's constant travelling? How shall we transmit our own messages to the survivor? Or return our own messages, as survivors, to those who may learn from them? Only, it would appear, stories remain – which is, in one sense, obviously true: we all tell stories about our origins, whether these be personal, familial, national, or, increasingly, intergalactic, which would be greatly to Lessing's taste. Her interest in time travel in the 1970s and 1980s is clearly connected to the fascination with storytelling which comes increasingly to the fore in her later work.

Yet at the same time, we are also *told* stories. There are two messages encapsulated there: the pleasure of being narrated to as a child; the continuing disaster of being imprinted, implanted, with untruths – all that

Marx summarised in his continuing descriptions of ideology. And the stories we tell cannot be fully distinguished from the stories we are, or have been, told: thus myths continue down the line, constantly embellished, constantly threatened, but surviving against all the odds in forms which are, from one perspective, ever-changing, from the other, the custodians of something apparently immutable. 'This is a scene', Lessing resonantly says,

> particularly loved by our artists who embellish it with a vast yellow moon positioned so that it is close to, or behind, Al·Ith's head. Or there is a delightful crescent set off by a star or two. And they often add a large peacock, whose shimmering tail fills the orchard with reflected lights.
>
> But it is on the whole a realistic depiction, and I am saying this because it is the last of the truthful scenes. For there is something in the tale of Al·Ith that goes beyond popular taste. [. . .] Another figure that never achieved realism is Dabeeb, who is shown most often as a singer, as if this was her profession. (1980: 277–8)

In this passage, Lessing appears to summarise some of the major factors, problems, achievements of her own literary career. 'Another figure', she says, 'that has never achieved realism'; perhaps Lessing herself is such a one, but there is a complex irony here. Why would it be necessary to 'achieve' realism? Why would realism, whatever that contested term might mean, not be the bedrock of fiction? Might it be because reality – again whatever that might be – is too complex to be represented by any obvious form of 'realism', it is constantly invaded by telepathy, by time travel, by disruptions of all kinds which menace linear time and space; and thus we need, of course, to have recourse to myths and legends – indeed, we have no choice – and we need also to realise that time is not something we have to accept as a given, we are all, after all – or before all – time travellers.

Works Cited

Derrida, Jacques, Dick, Kirby and Kofman, Amy Ziering (2005), *Derrida: Screenplay and Essays on the Film*, Manchester: Manchester University Press.
—— (1995), 'Passages – From Traumatism to Promise', in *Points . . . Interviews, 1974–1994*, ed. Elisabeth Weber, Stanford: Stanford University Press, pp. 372–98.
Freud, Sigmund (1898), 'The Psychical Mechanism of Forgetfulness', in *The Standard Edition of the Complete Works of Sigmund Freud*, ed. James Strachey, London: Hogarth Press, vol. 3, pp. 288–97.
—— (1922), 'Dreams and Telepathy', in *The Standard Edition of the Complete*

Works of Sigmund Freud (1956–74), ed. James Strachey, London: Hogarth Press, vol. 18, pp. 196–220.

Lessing, Doris (1974), *The Memoirs of a Survivor*, London: Octagon Press.

—— (1979), *Shikasta*, London: Jonathan Cape.

—— (1980), *The Marriages Between Zones Three, Four and Five*, London: Jonathan Cape.

Marx, Karl and Engels, Friedrich (1970), *The German Ideology*, ed. C. J. Arthur, London: Lawrence & Wishart.

Royle, Nicholas (2003), *The Uncanny*, Manchester: Manchester University Press.

Wells, H. G. (1927), *The Short Stories of H. G. Wells*, London: E. Benn Limited.

Chapter 10

Lessing's Interruptions

Tom Sperlinger

'When I start I can write easily', Doris Lessing once noted in an interview: 'I've got a terrific, great facility' (1996: 93). Jenny Diski has recalled how while she lived with Lessing in the 1960s: 'The shotgun sound of typing went on continuously for hours. She typed incredibly fast and only infrequently paused, perhaps for a sip of tea or to light a cigarette [. . .] She thought as she typed' (2014). There has been a tendency to judge Lessing's prose unfavourably, partly because of the speed of its composition and to suggest that she did not omit enough material. Lessing conceded in the same interview that Anthony Burgess was 'probably' right to suggest that she wrote 'too much, too many words' and that she did not edit sufficiently (93). J. M. Coetzee asserts that Lessing was 'never much of a stylist – she writes too fast and prunes too lightly for that' (2002: 291).

The evidence in Lessing's typescripts complicates these claims.[1] Lessing's draft material supports the idea that she wrote quickly and its sheer volume is daunting: a novel such as *Shikasta* exists in multiple full-length drafts. But the typescripts show that Lessing revised heavily too, if not in the manner Burgess and Coetzee advise. Indeed, Lessing's draft material, examined here for the first time, poses challenges to received notions of literary style. Hannah Sullivan has shown that it is a modernist view of the creative process to assume that it is always beneficial to cut drastically, citing Marianne Moore's statement: 'Anything is improved by omissions' (2008: 502). Sullivan argues that this emphasis suited the environment of modernism, which favoured 'making' art (rather than inspiration) and utilised emerging technologies that made revision easier, including the typewriter.

Lessing's mode of composition is similarly intertwined with use of a typewriter. But whereas, as Sullivan shows, modernist writers often typed up their work from a handwritten draft, none of Lessing's drafts that I have examined exist in a handwritten form; each begins as a typescript. Thus we may take Diski's memories literally. Lessing 'thought as she typed'; typing was an integral element of composition rather than a way in which the work was edited or presented for publication. Typing had also been a means of employment for Lessing who, before she was a published novelist, worked as both a Hansard and a shorthand typist in Southern Rhodesia. In *Under My Skin* she recalls:

> The requisite in the [Hansard] typists was speed and the ability to use words reduced sometimes to no more than a letter. Min of Agric: T H M is ooo, t sbjt o cattle food w b o t agen tmrw. This ruined my typing for ever. Extreme speed, yes. (1994c: 325)

Speed is not the only characteristic of her approach. While she was training to be a Hansard typist, Lessing notes: 'I was also writing *The Grass is Singing*, which is now a tidy little book on a shelf. It began three times the length it is now, and was a satire.' (1994c: 325) Not many of Lessing's works qualify as a 'tidy little book on a shelf'. She did not edit most of her subsequent books as heavily as her first. But she did revise. An early version of the typescripts is often overlaid with frequent small changes by hand and contains numerous inserted passages, usually also typewritten. Lessing wrote of D. H. Lawrence, in her introduction to *Lady Chatterley's Lover*: 'It was his way to completely rewrite, not so much a revision as a fresh vision. He valued the liveliness of the new more than a rewriting' (2006: xi). Most of Lessing's novels also exist in multiple versions, as if she too rethought a work by typing it out again from start to finish.

In this chapter, I argue that 'interruptions' provide a useful framework for thinking about Lessing's creative process. Rather than excluding and omitting as she edits, Lessing (often) continues to write so that the work of revision is evident in the work itself.[2] In her typescripts, in the midst of a draft or a setting copy, she sometimes inserts a new section into the narrative or a radically rewritten version of an existing one. Often this insertion will appear in a passage of the novel that is otherwise unchanged, so that it interrupts an existing narrative sequence. At other times, the insertion alters subsequent aspects of the work. This helps to explain why her novels sometimes get longer rather than shorter as she edits. It also produces striking episodes in her fiction, in which the narrator may speak directly to the reader or in which the course of the action is reinterpreted.

Diski's remark that Lessing 'thought as she typed' has two further implications. Firstly, it gives an indication of the speed of Lessing's thought. Her novels can sound as if they have urgent news to impart. Philip Hensher has written: 'From the first page, there is the sense of someone saying "You see? You see?" in a state of high righteousness. In general, yes, one does see, but it is strange that one doesn't quickly start to resent the tone' (2001: 33). Hensher does not speak for all readers; as Cornelius Collins has discussed in an earlier chapter, Joan Didion and others have found Lessing uncomfortably didactic. Secondly, it suggests that she understood books as something one *thinks with*, rather than as objects one might stand back from and admire. Lessing's self-education may be relevant. Lessing wrote that 'autodidact' is 'an ugly blocky little word for a free-ranging unhedged condition':

> If you have taught yourself through books then every one has been chosen by you, as part of a personal Odyssey, has been absorbed and becomes part of your substance. But later you keep unearthing areas of ignorance, and have to spend time catching up on information every schoolchild has. (Fraser 2015: 43)

Lessing tended to 'absorb' all she could from a book, whether she was reading or writing it, and then move on. A reading of Lessing's creative process needs to be responsive to her particular relationship to literary culture. Lessing's writing offers the reader a similar experience: to *think* as we read and to see or understand. Rather than didactic, it may be more useful to see Lessing's style as 'pedagogic', since dialogue is key. Her books are things one might range freely among and discard; they can prove revelatory or provide the reader with much-needed information.

The dialogue that Lessing maintains in her work is also with herself. One might see Lessing's whole career as a series of interruptions. Josna Rege notes: 'At a talk in Boston [. . .] someone asked Doris Lessing which one of her books was her personal favorite. She looked bewildered for a moment, then replied that she saw her work as "a process, a development," as "just one book," not in terms of individual books' (1999: 122). It is almost as if each book interrupts the one before it, so that no book is 'finished'. Lessing noted: 'Nearly all my books have weak patches but that is because I'm the kind of writer I am, which means I'm always trying things out and I'm very seldom interested in a perfect book' (1996: 93). She thus tends to disappoint anyone seeking intellectual or stylistic unity in her writings. Her work is also interrupted by events. One can see this in the Martha Quest novels, published over seventeen years, in which Lessing tries in sequence to make sense of the past, to accommodate events that happen as she writes and to predict the future.

This chapter focuses on 'interruptions' in two of Lessing's novels: *The Summer Before the Dark* (1973) and *The Marriages Between Zones Three, Four and Five* (1980). These books were composed relatively close to one another chronologically but they are radically different in their use of the novel form and in their conception of the reality described. The former is broadly realist, although it integrates aspects of dreams and shows a conventional middle-class life under the assault of new ideas. *Marriages*, by contrast, is the second of Lessing's 'space fiction' novels, although one that she notes in a preface to *Shikasta* is 'oddly . . . more realistic' than its predecessor (1979: ix). In light of Lessing's remark in Boston, I treat the two novels as parts of a development in which *The Memoirs of a Survivor* (1975) and *Shikasta* also play a part, although it is beyond the scope of this chapter to consider all four books.

The formal 'interruptions' in these two novels foreground thematic preoccupations. In previous chapters in this volume, Kevin Brazil and David Punter consider repetitions and 'time travel' in Lessing's novels. An interruption is a disruption to an existing continuity, such as linear time. One function of the 'interruptions' in Lessing's work is to insist on the repeated urgency of the present. (I wonder whether any other writer uses the word 'now' as frequently.) Lessing often writes about unexpected events that rupture the patterns of everyday life. Such events happen on various scales in her fiction, including through the arrival of a person (in *Memoirs of a Survivor*), an arranged marriage (*Marriages*), a nuclear war (*The Four-Gated City* (1969)), an ice age (*Mara and Dann* (1999)) or a change in the balance of power on a galactic level (*Shikasta*). Lessing's work is thus peculiarly attentive to the way in which the present continually interrupts the process of entering what was assumed to be the future. *Marriages* further eschews a conventional understanding of linear time. The narrator speaks to the reader from a much later time in Zone Three than that of the events he describes. Yet the novel shows different epochs coexisting across the zones and interrupting one another, so that the linear time in each zone coexists with another conception of time (and space).

Lessing's much-discussed interest in the relationship between the individual and collective, explored by Adam Guy, Kevin Brazil and David Sergeant in this volume, is also relevant. Derrida suggests that he distrusts the word 'we' because we are all individuals with 'an interrupted connection', going on to state: 'To say "we" is a mad gesture in a certain way, mad with hope, with fear, with promise' (2001). Lessing, in contrast, ultimately sees us as individuals who have an 'interrupted' connection that must be recovered. As Phyllis Sternberg Perrakis argues: 'In her early realistic novels Lessing presents individuals trying to relate themselves to a fragmented social reality [. . .] whereas in her space-fiction *Canopus in Argos* series she places fragmented individuals and societies in a galactic context which reveals their egoism and disunity as aberrations' (2003: 61). A character's attempt to recover such unity can be interpreted as a 'mad' gesture, as Kate Brown's actions sometimes appear to others in *The Summer Before the Dark*. It can also be taken as 'mad with hope, with fear, with promise'; that is to say, as utopian. In Zone Three, *Marriages* offers and critiques a utopian mode in which, for example, individuals have a strong sense of communion with the non-human world.

In *The Summer Before the Dark*, Kate Brown visits the theatre for a production of Turgenev's *A Month in the Country* (1855). Kate and her husband 'often went to the theatre' (1995: 148) and this play offers Kate the sort of 'confirmation' she relishes: 'the sort of play where one observed people like oneself in their recognizable predicaments'. In the section that follows, the narrative switches between two third-person narrators. The first is the narrator of *The Summer Before the Dark* who observes Kate from the outside: 'And, indeed, Kate was thinking.' But Kate also observes herself as if impersonally: 'A woman sat prominently in the front row of the stalls.' This technique echoes how the novel opens – 'A woman stood on her back step, arms folded, waiting' (5) – but adds a hallucinatory quality. Kate is no longer able to establish with confidence what is internal or external to her. As a consequence, she loses a sense of the usual formal relationship between the actors on stage and the audience:

> Natalia Petrovna said: *And what, pray, am I hoping for? Oh, God, don't let me despise myself!* – and this distressing creature, who must nevertheless be rich, to be able to afford such a price for her ticket, said out loud, speaking direct to the players in an urgent, and even intimate, way: 'Oh, nonsense, nonsense, why do you say that?'
>
> She was thinking that there must be something wrong with the way she was seeing things. For although she was so close in to the stage, she seemed a very long way off; and she kept trying to shake herself into a different kind of attention or participation, for she could remember her usual mood at the theatre, and knew her present condition was far from that. (149)

Kate interrupts the performance, responding directly to the words that the actress playing Natalia Petrovna speaks on stage. She also disrupts her usual 'kind of attention or participation' at the theatre. Rather than 'observing' people who provide 'confirmation' of her own situation, Kate feels 'a very long way off' from the stage and yet speaks to the actors in an 'intimate way'. She has lost hold of the fixed categories upon which a 'usual mood' at the theatre depend: actors/audience, fiction/ reality and self/other. She is also a spectator to herself: her own situation is seen as if in a fiction. Ironically, Kate's state of mind is only rendered comprehensible because of this play upon the authority of the actual third-person narrator (whose point of view remains intact).

Kate has an urgent sense that the usual mode of attention to this play is wrong:

> But no matter how she called out, 'Wonderful!' – or felt that she ought and refrained, for people were glaring at her and telling her to shush – there was no doubt that what she was paying money to sit here and look at seemed (it was the mood she was in, that must be it) as if a parcel of well-born maniacs were conducting a private game, or ritual, and no one had yet told them they were mad. It was a farce, and not at all a high-class and sensitive comedy filled with truths about human nature. The fact was that the things happening in the world, the collapse of everything, was tugging at the shape of events in this play and those like them, and making them farcical. (150)

Kate's reception of the play has three aspects. Firstly she is aware that the theatre is an elite pastime ('she was paying money [to] look at [. . .] well-born maniacs') that involves make-believe ('a private game, or ritual') and which is akin to madness. The second is an insight that the play is being received in the wrong genre, that far from being a 'high-class and sensitive comedy' it should be perceived as Kate sees it: as 'a farce'. This observation relies on a third aspect of what Kate senses: that present-day reality ('the things happening in the world, the collapse of everything') has radically altered 'the shape of events in this play *and those like them*' (my italics). The individuals in the play no longer seem like characters that are explicable because of their social and political situation and to whom Kate can relate. Rather than the present being shaped by historical forces, in ways that are explicable, at this moment it seems as if the present has erupted into history and altered it: 'the things happening in the world, the collapse of everything, was tugging at the shape of events'. It is as if the genre and meaning of reality itself has changed.

Part of what Kate fears in the theatre scene is repetition, a recurrent nightmare for Lessing's heroines (and for the author). Looking at the actors on stage, Kate thinks: 'That lot on the stage had been swept off the boards by a revolution, and what of it, there they were still at it, and nothing had changed, and the same thoughts went revolving and revolving in their grooves in people's heads' (153). The 'revolution' has happened, although a particular revolution is not specified: the upper classes, symbolised by the actors, were 'swept off the boards' but 'nothing [. . .] changed'. Thus the 'revolution' comes to seem like a circular motion ('revolving') rather than a change; both meanings are available in the word as Raymond Williams has shown (1983: 270–4). In *On Revolution*, Hannah Arendt writes:

> It is in the very nature of a beginning to carry with itself a measure of com-
> plete arbitrariness. Not only is it not bound into a reliable chain of cause and
> effect, a chain in which each effect immediately turns into the cause for future
> developments, the beginning has, as it were, nothing whatsoever to hold
> on to; it is as though it came out of nowhere in either time or space. For a
> moment, the moment of beginning, it is as though the beginner had abolished
> the sequence of temporality itself, or as though the actors were thrown out of
> the temporal order and its continuity. (2009: 198)

Such a 'beginning' is not available to Kate in the theatre. This partly
reflects that this is a novel about being in the middle of one's life. Kate's
life appears to be settled and she reflects at the start of the book that
'nothing had "happened" to her for a long time' (9). Yet in Lessing's
novel, as for Arendt, the critical realisation is that action is possible: that
an individual 'actor' may act outside the existing temporal order and its
continuity. Kate's visit to the theatre dramatises this through her interruptions to the play, but it has implications in her own life too. During
the novel, Kate has been trying on roles that she has played for a long
time (wife, mother) or that are new to her such as her position within
the Global Food organisation, although this feels like a repetition of her
position as a mother. But Kate slowly discovers that it is possible for
'things to happen' to her. Arendt wrote in *The Human Condition* that
action is related specifically to plurality; indeed, she states that action
would be 'an unnecessary luxury' if all people were the same (1998: 8).
Kate Brown discovers plurality in herself. This in turn creates the possibility of a different kind of remembrance, of plural versions of her own
history, as figured in her dreams (a form which often disrupts temporality). Kate is thrown out of the temporal order and sense of continuity
that her life had relied upon prior to the action of the novel.

Kate is developing a theory of historical process with which the literary
forms she enjoys cannot keep pace. She begins to see art as something that
can be shaped by events and thus radically altered, so that even an apparently 'fixed' text will change its meaning. An influence on Lessing here
may be the Sufi belief that stories must be re-told with different emphases
and in different ways depending on the circumstances. As Lessing writes
in an essay about Idries Shah collected in *Time Bites* (2005): '[It is] essential to the Sufi way of thinking that books and teachings are for a time
and a stage in culture, and must be superseded' (357). This Sufi mode of
relating to texts echoes a pre-existing impatience in Lessing's work with
notions of literary posterity, as if it undermines the purpose of a book to
worry only about its particular relevance for the future.

The play-within-the-novel in *The Summer in the Dark* thus enacts a
search for a relationship to literary form that can accommodate more

permeable boundaries between fiction/reality, past/present and self/ world. This search is also evident in the typescript for this section of the novel. *The Summer Before the Dark* exists in four versions, which are held in six folders in one administrative box at the Harry Ransom Center (box 31, folders 1–6). The first (in folder 31.1) appears to be a relatively early draft and includes a large number of insertions, many of them handwritten notes on the typescript. Some of these are revealing. For example, the dream sequences which permeate the novel in its published version appear as insertions, suggesting they were not part of the first conception of the novel. The sequence at the theatre appears in a very different version in the draft in 31.1; is then substantially revised in the next draft in folder 31.3; is repeated in a similar version in 31.6; but is then again heavily revised in the setting copy of the book, in which word-processed pages (presumably from the publisher) are interrupted with the version of the theatre sequence that would be published, in Lessing's recognisable typescript.

In the version in 31.3, Lessing initially gives the title of a different play, which is struck out, and then *Uncle Vanya* (1897) with *A Month in the Country* appearing alongside it. This is an extract from the typescript of this version, presented (as near as possible) as it appears in the original:

> It was all of utter insignificance, unimportance..
> [the] To do this so well, to protray [*sic*] this ridiculous stupid
> neurotic behaviour, in front of a crowd that found it interesting,
> men and women spent years of aspiration, hard work, study,
> sweating in the [deleted, unreadable] provincial rep, living on twopence
> haplpenny [*sic*]
> beteen [*sic*] parts – just for this, for the moment when Madame
>   could sweep those languid skirt[s] across dirty boards and
> and say to a girl
>   – no, this was all no use, ~~it was very bad, she~~ Katie could have laughed
> out loud, could have shouted out:
> Absolute bloody nonsense, all of it . . . except, of course, that the
> audience would have lynched her.

It is hard not to see parallels with Lessing's memory of Hansard typing from *Under My Skin*: misspellings, quick changes of mind, and most of all evidence of speed, as if Lessing has continued typing to get the section written, rather than stopping and reworking individual sentences. In this version, 'Katie' is able to maintain the boundary between herself and the actors on stage. She restrains herself from calling out during the performance: '[she] could have shouted out . . . except of course, that the audience would have lynched her'. At the same time, the critique of the play – and the whole notion of the performance – stays within recognisable bounds. Katie maintains her privacy. It sounds like the critique of someone who is (simply) bored with the notion of the theatre. Yet it is striking that Lessing's prose itself appears fragmentary in this draft, as if it needed to be revised – to take a definite form – to accommodate how Kat(i)e's vision becomes fragmented. It is as if, in the move between this first draft and the final version, Lessing enacts her own changing relationship to literary form. Even if art can no longer serve the purpose of 'observation' of the world or 'confirmation' of what we think it to be, it can nonetheless observe the process of change – the forming of history – at an individual level.

One of the central questions that is contested in *The Marriages Between Zones Three, Four and Five* is how history is narrated or occluded and the forms in which in survives, including in the rumours, gossip, songs and children's counting games that open the book. In the theatre, Kate Brown begins to think that 'the things happening in the world, the collapse of everything' has changed the shape of events in the play and in the world. In this novel, the arranged marriage at the centre of the book leads to the collapse of the existing order in Zones Three and Four. It is thus as if an event might not just *interrupt* history, by changing the course of events, but interrupt *history*: erasing the whole framework within which the past has been understood.

In *The Human Condition*, Hannah Arendt offers a speculative account of the future: 'The most radical change in the human condition we can imagine would be an emigration of men from the earth to some other planet' (1998: 10). Arendt uses this example to illustrate how contingent some of what we think of as human 'nature' might be: these 'hypothetical wanderers from the earth would still be human', but their condition would be radically different to anything we currently understand as 'the human'. Lessing's novel is speculative in a similar way: it allows for reflection on how the conception of 'human nature' may be historically contingent. For example, she imagines substantially different conditions in each zone. The contrasts between them illustrate how human beings are conditioned in different circumstances, while the movement between the zones shows how difficult it can be to see beyond that conditioning or to survive its collapse.[3]

The narrative, which is told from the perspective of Zone Three, is framed as a corrective: 'One of the motives for this chronicle is an attempt to revive in the hearts and memories of our people another idea of Al·Ith, to re-instate her in her proper place in our history' (1994a: 177) This degeneration in memories of Al·Ith implies repetition; in the action of the novel, Al·Ith is also seeking to recover a 'proper' version of the history of the zones. The novel is also about how each zone recovers (among other things) from a stagnation in storytelling, discovering new songs and tales from other zones and thus remembering more of its collective history.

The relationship between the zones remains one of the novel's most puzzling aspects. When the women of Zone Four make a visit to Zone Three, for example, they experience a feeling of 'bitter exile':

> What they were looking at, the inwardness of this scene, was not pleasure or happiness, words which – no matter how far they had seemed from them down in Zone Four – now seemed paltry and even contemptible qualities – but something they could not begin to understand. They were most powerfully and bitterly crushed down. The gap between this and what Zone Four could even hope for was – hundreds of years. (272)

Phyllis Sternberg Perrakis has argued: 'From a historical perspective, the zones can be seen as analogues for the different ways that human kind has related to the cosmos in different eras' (2003: 80). If so, what does it mean that these different historical periods coexist and can interrupt one another in the novel? Is this an example of two cultures, at different stages of development, observing one another – or does it imply some degree of time travel in the movement between the zones ('hundreds of years')? Either way, the women cannot force the pace of Zone Four's development. They overestimate their own agency; they remain bound, to some extent, by the particular social and political reality of Zone Four.

Within the world of *Marriages* the action is dictated largely by the Providers, whom B. F. Nellist links with an older idea of Providence (2005: 31). Lessing's impulse is thus more spiritual than Arendt's. Lessing's protagonists ultimately seek to relinquish their conditioning *in order* to recover a true understanding of their nature and history. On one reading, the central couple Al·Ith and Ben Ata strive to reach beyond what Idries Shah refers to as 'the commanding self'. Lessing wrote in an article for *The Times* (1994b):

> 'The commanding self' is a Sufi term for the false personality. [The Sufi] contention is that we are all products of ideas put into us by our parents, by our culture, by the time we live in, and that what is real in us is very small (and precious). It is this part the Sufis aim to reach and teach [. . .] Being introduced to the great treasurehouse of Sufi literature taught this writer, at least, a realistic view of her talents.

The novel thus raises provocative questions about human agency. Both Al·Ith and Ben Ata, as queen and king, appear powerful at the start of the novel. Yet they acquire more agency when they relinquish responsibility for their zone and submit to the will of the Providers. Each takes a realistic view of his/her talents. It is this which allows them to see beyond the conditions of their zones and which thus makes certain forms of action and remembrance possible.

One thing that is easy to overlook in *Marriages*, which has a strikingly optimistic tone, is the devastating consequences there are to the changes initiated by the marriages. For example, the encounter with Zone Three ruptures not only the everyday reality of Zone Four but also its under-standing of the past. Jarnti explains to Dabeeb: 'It's not just that *now* we are told that the army is nothing, and that all our old ways we were so proud of were nothing and that the great thing is to build barns and make drains. But that makes all the past nothing, too. Don't you see?' (289). The word 'nothing' recurs throughout this passage. Indeed, this section begins: 'And then – nothing happened.' Action is not possible when the form of history has been so entirely ruptured. Lessing antici-pates later arguments by the philosopher Jonathan Lear who, in *Radical Hope*, reads the phrase 'nothing happened' in a different context. It was used by Plenty Coups, the last great Chief of the Crow Nation, who told his story before he died: 'When the buffalo went away the hearts of my people fell to the ground and they could not lift them up again. After this nothing happened' (2008: 2). Lear sees the phrase as reveal-ing of cultural devastation; nothing *can* happen once everything one has known ceases to exist. Jarnti's whole understanding of the past is erased or irrevocably altered: 'that makes all the past nothing, too'. It is as if Jarnti is able to fully realise what Kate Brown glimpses intermittently in the theatre: that he has been an 'actor' in a cultural drama, which is now exhausted. Indeed, the narrator echoes the words of Othello in stating that both Jarnti and Dabeeb's 'occupations' were 'gone'. For Lear the implications are partly predictive. Plenty Coups and Jarnti may antici-pate how human beings will be forced to adapt following devastating climate change.

One thing that interests both Lessing and Lear is how one might teach oneself (or a child) to be resilient in the face of such cultural devasta-tion. Lear notes: 'A culture does not tend to train the young to endure its own breakdown' (83). In Zone Four, generations of children have been taught not to look up. Jarnti struggles even once this practice is encouraged: 'He would bring a camp stool and sit staring ahead [to the mountains of Zone Three]: for his head could not lift itself on those so long-punished and brought-down muscles' (286). Thus the people who are 'most' or 'best' educated in the virtues of a society might be least equipped to survive beyond it. Two key aspects to survival in *Marriages* appear to be dreams and the work that the narrator himself performs, which allow the transmission of knowledge beyond the individual and his or her historical timescale. However one interprets the metaphor of marriage in this novel, the relationship between the zones is dialogic and pedagogic: each learns from the other, in part because of an encounter with difference. This is a radical departure from Kate Brown's expectations of a trip to the theatre, in which she sought 'confirmation' from 'the sort of play where one observed people like oneself in their recognizable predicaments'. Thus it is through encountering songs and stories from other zones that each of the protagonists begins to understand their 'real' history, which is continually being forgotten or obscured.

These aspects of creative process have their counterpart in Lessing's own. In the typescript for *Marriages* a number of sections appear as insertions. These include five passages of the novel that are crucial to its account of how stories are transmitted: a section in which the narrator interjects in order to reflect on the song and story festival that Al·Ith has ordered in Zone Three, which begins 'And now I propose to interrupt this narrative' (174–7); Al·Ith's dream about sexually initiating her son, Arusi, and its interpretation by Al·Ith, Dabeeb and Ben Ata (214–21); another passage about storytelling in which the narrator speaks directly to the reader, which begins 'And now I must raise my voice, say something' (242–5); a short section cited earlier reflecting on how 'crushed down' the women of Zone Four feel after their visit to Zone Three (272); and the account of Jarnti's feelings cited above about the loss of his occupation after the endless wars cease in Zone Four, which begins 'And then – nothing happened' (286–9). The numbering of the pages in the typescript suggests these were new sections rather than rewrites; so, for example, the sequence involving Al·Ith's dream about Arusi is numbered 189 a–f (in folder 4.1), leaving the numbers before (189) and after (190) unchanged.

Most of these sections are interruptions in content as well as in composition. The two sections in which the narrator speaks directly to the reader, in particular, are didactic and interpretative rather than contributing to the action of the story.[4] They also function both to reclaim the narrative 'I' and to emphasise the collective 'we' of Zone Three (and the collective nature of what lies beyond that Zone). For example:

> This business of the song and story festival Al·Ith had asked for, believing that she would find there information, or at least hints and suggestions of half-forgotten sagacities [. . .] she had been right. But wrong about *where*. Which was, in fact, the ceremony, or commemoration, of the Zone Four women [. . .] After all, this story of Al·Ith has taught us all that what goes on in one Zone affects the others, even when we believe we are hostile, or forget everything that goes on outside our own borders. (174, 176)

The songs and stories have a pedagogic function: they are utilised for 'information', to recover 'half-forgotten sagacities'; they teach the characters about what 'goes on outside our own borders'. The women of the zones form two communities with an interrupted connection to each another, which continues in spite of their inability to attend to it. They discover in this and other incidents the possibility of plural versions of history.

The sense of impersonality in the making of the songs links to an openness in how stories are interpreted in the novel. When Al·Ith dreams that she is sexually initiating Arusi, she and Dabeeb speculate about where the dream 'comes from'. Ben Ata is disgusted: 'He could have no belief now that he could come on a woman who would not, suddenly, present him with problems and thoughts and comparisons that even went right back into history, into the far past' (221). The dream might be read in a variety of ways, including in the psychological explanation that Dabeeb offers: that it is time to wean the child. The idea that a dream might offer us a retelling of something that the people of the zones once were or did (collectively) is congruent with the narrator's theories on the nature of his role: 'We are the visible and evident aspects of a whole we all share, that we all go to form' (242). It is as if storytelling in this novel disrupts the mistaken temporality on which the zones were constructed. Indeed, the narrator makes an explicit comparison between his role and what happens to Al·Ith when she is dreaming: 'Al·Ith dreamed all night of people known and unknown, creatures real and imagined, saw and did not see events and phenomena she had not experienced herself' (244).

This impersonal mode of storytelling reflects Lessing's creative process at this time, as she described it: 'Only I could have written *The Golden Notebook*, but I think Anon wrote this other book [*Marriages*]' (1996: 92). The multiplicity of interpretations within the novel likewise represents a new turn in Lessing's work; less of the 'You see, you see' that Hensher identified. Instead there is a fuller space for the reader to interpret the subject matter differently. Al·Ith's dream may also hint at one source of the interruptions in Lessing's narrative. Lessing frequently commented on the importance of dreams in her own creative process, an emphasis she shares with Anna Wulf, the fictional novelist in *The Golden Notebook*. The recurrence of dreams as interruptions in the novels, including the seal sequences in *The Summer Before the Dark*, suggests that the interruptions might have been prompted by dreams themselves.

The Jungian and Sufi sources and implications of this book have been traced by Perrakis, Müge Galin (1997) and others. My interest here is different. Part of what is evident in the development from *The Summer*

Before the Dark to *Marriages* is an evolution in Lessing's understanding of the work of a storyteller. Here, for example, is a remark from the narrator of *Marriages*:

> We Chroniclers do well to be afraid when we approach those parts of our histories (our natures) that deal with evil, the depraved, the benighted. Describing, we become. We even – and I've seen it and have shuddered – summon. (243)

The revision in an ellipsis, from 'history' to 'nature', may show that Lessing – like Arendt – wishes to emphasise the relationship between the two. It also shows the scale of Lusik's sense that his people barely understand their own history or nature. This has implications for the spiritual and ethical concern with 'evil' in Lessing's later thought, across the *Canopus* novels and in the later *Mara and Dann* (for example). It also points towards a genuinely creative and pluralistic aspect to Lessing's writing in this period: a sense of the writer's capacity to do more than describe; to empathise with radically different others (to 'become') and to 'summon' them, as if out of 'nothing'. Lessing feared 'repetition' and her early work is often bleak in its sense of human futility. *Marriages*, however, illustrates that 'the unexpected, the sidelong, the indirect' (175) may be a catalyst for change. Lessing recovers something like optimism at this stage in her career; a sense of possibility. To be 'interrupted' is often to be taken unawares. As Lessing writes in a deleted prefatory note to the typescript of *Marriages* (folder 4.1): 'I cannot help feeling that some people may be surprised that I have written this book. I can only say that I am quite surprised myself.'

Notes

1. I have examined the majority of Lessing's typescripts held at the Harry Ransom Center at the University of Austin at Texas. Lessing did not keep most of her early drafts. The majority of those typescripts that remain date from the 1970s; most but not all are in the Ransom Center, although that collection stops with *Mara and Dann* (1999).

2. This is not always the case. In an interview with Mervyn Rothstein for the *New York Times* (1988), Lessing refers to an early version of *The Fifth Child*: 'I wrote it twice. The first time I wrote it I thought it was dishonest and too soft . . . So I threw away the first draft.'

3. From a literary point of view, the metaphor of the zones is open to a variety of interpretations, as Perrakis has shown (2003: 80–1).

4. I had drawn on all five of these sections as key passages when teaching this novel, long before I examined the typescripts. The fact that I responded to them as significant (or separable from the novel) may imply that they remain slightly apart from the narrative.

Works Cited

Arendt, Hannah [1958] (1998), *The Human Condition*, Chicago: University of Chicago Press.

—— [1963] (2006), *On Revolution*, London: Penguin.

Coetzee, J. M. (2002), *Stranger Shores: Essays 1986–1999*, London: Vintage.

Derrida's Elsewhere (D'ailleurs Derrida) (2001), dir. Safaa Fathy, DVD, Paris: Éditions Montparnasse.

Diski, Jenni (2014), 'When Doris Lessing rescued me', *The Guardian*, 12 April, <www.theguardian.com/books/2014/apr/12/doris-lessing-rescued-me-jenni-diski> (last accessed 29 October 2015).

Fraser, Antonia (ed.) (2015), *The Pleasure of Reading: 43 Writers on the Discovery of Reading and the Books that Inspired Them*, London: Bloomsbury.

Galin, Müge (1997), *Between East and West: Sufism in the Novels of Doris Lessing*, New York: State University of New York Press.

Hensher, Philip (2001), 'A brave journey in thought', *The Spectator*, 1 September, p. 33 <http://archive.spectator.co.uk/article/1st-september-2001/33/a-brave-journey-in-thought> (last accessed 11 January 2016).

Lawrence, D. H. (2006), *Lady Chatterley's Lover* (with an introduction by Doris Lessing), London: Penguin.

Lear, Jonathan (2008), *Radical Hope: Ethics in the Face of Cultural Devastation*, Cambridge, MA: Harvard University Press.

Lessing, Doris (1979), *Shikasta*, London: Jonathan Cape.

—— [1980] (1994a), *The Marriages Between Zones Three, Four and Five*, London: Flamingo.

—— (1994b), 'On *The Commanding Self* by Idries Shah', *The Times*, 5 May.

—— (1994c), *Under My Skin*, London: Flamingo.

—— [1973] (1995), *The Summer Before The Dark*, London: Flamingo.

—— (1996), *Putting the Questions Differently: Interviews With Doris Lessing, 1964–1994*, London: Flamingo.

—— (2005), *Time Bites: Views and Reviews*, London: Flamingo.

Nellist, B. F. (2005), 'Surviving Change: Doris Lessing, *The Marriage Between Zones Three, Four and Five*', *The Reader*, 17, 30–5.

Perrakis, Phyllis Sternberg (2003), 'Sufism, Jung and the Myth of Kore: Revisionist Politics in Lessing's *Marriages*' in Harold Bloom (ed.), *Doris Lessing: Bloom's Modern Critical Views*, Philadelphia: Chelsea House Publishers, pp. 61–84.

Rege, Josna (1999), 'Considering the Stars: the Expanding Universe of Doris Lessing's Fiction' in Phyllis Sternberg Perrakis (ed.), *Spiritual exploration in the works of Doris Lessing*, Westport: Greenwood Press, pp. 121–33.

Rothstein, Mervyn (1988), 'The painful Nurturing of Doris Lessing's *The Fifth Child*', *New York Times*, June 14 <www.nytimes.com/books/99/01/10/specials/lessing-child.html> (last accessed 11 January 2016).

Sullivan, Hannah (2008), 'Modernist Excision and Its Consequences', *The Papers of the Bibliographical Society of America*, 102.4 (2008), 501–19.

Williams, Raymond (1983), *Keywords: A vocabulary of culture and society*, London: Flamingo.

Chapter 11

Lessing's Witness Literature

Elizabeth Maslen

As this collection testifies, Doris Lessing has always been drawn, from her earliest writings, to commitment literature, witness literature, whether in her fiction or her non-fiction. This article will centre on one of her most challenging and prescient works of reportage in the 1980s, a text that throws light on much that has happened in our contemporary world of conflict and refugee crises. *The Wind Blows Away Our Words* (1987) is based on her visit to Afghan fighters and refugees in Pakistan during the war against the Soviet Union. Lessing's reportage will be situated within the growing tradition of women writing witness literature in response to the traumatic events of the twentieth century, concentrating on an older contemporary, Storm Jameson.

The essential task for those, like Jameson and Lessing, with a legacy of such crises is to break free from the hauntings that they provoke, from becoming trapped in the past, to find, as the psychologist Robert Jay Lifton puts it:

> new inner forms that include the traumatic event, which in turn requires that one finds meaning or significance in it so that the rest of one's life need not be devoid of meaning or significance. Formulation means establishing the lifeline on a new basis. (176)

Lessing's parents, trapped in the past by their experiences of the First World War, never achieved this. But many of Lessing's older women contemporaries, writers like Storm Jameson, set out, in the wake of the First World War, to establish just that: a lifeline 'on a new basis'. However, there was also the pressing need to remember, to reassess, and to ponder on what was in danger of being forgotten or suppressed. For it is all too clear that what appals at one date can be forgotten, its lessons unlearnt. Wolf Gruner recalls, for example, how the massacre of the Armenians by the Ottomans has been 'overshadowed by the Nazi extermination of the European Jews' (197). After 1945, what had been seen in 1930 as 'the bloodiest and most atrocious mystery in history' was lost to view: 'The "industrial enterprise" of Auschwitz would now replace the Kemach Gorge as the symbol of an "unprecedented," horrific, and systematic slaughter of a people by another people' (197–8).

Such overshadowings alert us to what enters the archive and what does not. As Shoair Mavlian acknowledges, the official archive 'once perceived as a neutral historical repository, is far from being so, and is instead a predetermined collection made by those in a position of power' (210). It can be tampered with and rearranged, as the airbrushing of photographs of Trotsky under Stalin, for instance, shows. And, '[a]s time progresses, the archive helps form collective memory, establishing accepted narratives and official histories' (215). However, 'these histories are often contested, and over time [they are] questioned as perceptions alter and archival material is activated, clarified and recontextualised' (215). Lessing is in the tradition of such writers as Virginia Woolf, Rebecca West and many later contemporaries who raise questions about accepted narratives. Woolf's links with Lessing have already been discussed in this volume by Rowena Kennedy-Epstein; but Storm Jameson also has striking similarities to Lessing. Like Lessing, she is an iconoclast, never subscribing unreservedly to any cause or credo, evading the straitjacketing Adam Guy referred to earlier in his chapter, always aware of those whose voices go unheard, always urging her readers to question. Writing on patriotism, for instance, in 1935 she savaged the romanticising of war, for since machines 'deliver the poison gas or a rain of white-hot steel, human courage is as unavailing as human flesh' (1939b: 201). Jameson's reach beyond England tunes in with Lessing's constant insistence on global interconnection:

> For ill or good England is a close part of Europe and will remain so until aeroplanes are forbidden to be built. In Europe the majority of the nations have the misfortune to be foreigners, and are close enough to us to make living with them uncomfortable and dangerous, if it is not regulated. In such circumstances we ought to sit in conference with them the whole time, for our safety's sake. (1939b: 253)

As with Lessing, such powerfully expressed views can be seen as propaganda, especially if they go beyond the accepted perspective of any one group or national norm; but such a charge arguably raises questions about the right to free speech.

As another war threatened and the rhetoric of aggression increased, Jameson drew on her awareness of the already existing European conflict, and on her close involvement with refugees from Nazi oppression, suggesting to women readers, for instance, their responsibility to help shape a future beyond the present conflict. In December 1939 she wrote:

> Do not accept without reflecting on it anything you hear or read. Try to dis-
> cover the deep reasons why this war started. Try . . . to imagine what sort of
> a world would make it unlikely that any nation would want to start another.
> You can see that things have been going wrong for a long time. Try with all
> your wits to see how they can be put right. Right enough to last.
>   On what you think, on what you feel today, depends the future of this land,
> the future of the children in it. (1939a: 34–5)

The attempt to present a view persuasively inevitably meant, for Jameson as for Lessing, the continual exploration of form and style, both in reportage and in fiction. Like Lessing, Jameson always saw aesthetic quality as emerging from content, and experimented both in reportage and in novels that blur the boundaries between fiction and fact. Moreover, like Lessing, Jameson acknowledged how context changes across time and place, and the need for writers to respond accordingly. Like Lessing she was never provincial, always aware of the linkage between public and private, alert to the outside world and the network of consequences that could reach far beyond any one part of it.[1]

In her turn Lessing, like Jameson, was aware how easily one form of 'witness' could become more acceptable than others, and both aimed to show many kinds of witness. These stem from those who have par-ticipated; those who have inherited trauma and are shaped by it; those who stand at some distance, in time or space, meditating on the event; those who see comparisons; those who explore implications for the future. Jameson's and Lessing's wide-ranging interpretation of 'witness' literature was echoed in December 2001, when the Swedish Academy celebrated the centenary of the first award of a Nobel Prize with a symposium on Witness Literature. The participants came from widely differing backgrounds: Holocaust survivors, writers who lived under totalitarian regimes, others with colonial and postcolonial experience. All explore, like Jameson and Lessing, how to bear witness to situations that are likely to be airbrushed out or forgotten. Li Rui, for example, who grew up under the Chinese Cultural Revolution, reflected that:

> no-one can clearly explain why we draw so many conclusions from the same
> event. And not only do the conclusions differ: thinking carefully, we may also
> ask ourselves whether all mortal beings on this earth really live in the same
> world. (77–8)

Nadine Gordimer, having lived in the South Africa of apartheid, wit-nessed, as a white writer, what her black brothers and sisters were suffering. She therefore made a powerful plea for the validity of the writer reflecting on traumatic happenings from the outside, very relevant to Lessing's reportage on Afghanistan. Gordimer suggested that '[i]f witness literature is to find its place, . . . it is in . . . the transformation of events, motives, emotions, reactions from immediacy into the enduring significance that is meaning' (87). Lessing also recognised such problems, which are also shared with the historian, as Peter Englund observes: 'what happens when we turn the past into a narrative? . . . The very form of narrative tempts us to tidy things up' (51). Lessing is fully aware that such narratives must not be left on trust to those in authority, that the truths one reporter may uncover may not be the whole truth. She shares Gordimer's conviction that writers 'can exclude or discard *nothing* in [their] solitary travail towards meaning, downward into the acts of terrorism'. They have to 'seek this meaning in those who commit such acts just as we do in its victims' (91). Gordimer's comments resonate with Lessing's reflection in 1988, meditating on the writer's responsibility:

> I like to think that if someone's read a book of mine, they've had . . . the literary equivalent of a shower. Something that would start them thinking in a slightly different way perhaps. That's what I think writers are for. . . . We spend all our time thinking about how things work, why things happen, which means we are more sensitive to what's going on.

It is in these contexts that I want to explore *The Wind Blows Away Our Words*.

After her 1982 visit to Zimbabwe, newly independent after a bruising civil war, Lessing went, in 1986, to Pakistan. Since the early 1960s, when the Afghan Idries Shah introduced her to Sufism, she had come to know many Afghans. The Soviet invasion of Afghanistan in 1979 inevitably affected them deeply, and Shah himself wrote his only novel on this subject, *Kara Kush* (1986). Like Lessing's *The Golden Notebook* (1962), it shares traits with reportage. The publisher's blurb for the novel claimed that:

> The accounts of battles and raids, precise military details, and the stories of Soviet and red Afghan atrocities were all from primary sources: eye witnesses, participants, defectors, victims, and prisoners. ('Kara Kush')

Similarly, when Lessing was asked by Thomas Frick in the 1988 *Paris Review* interview whether she worried about 'what sort of authority you could bring to such an enormous story, being an outsider visiting for a short time', her response was brisk:

> Do journalists worry about the authority they bring, visiting countries for such a short time? As for me, rather more than most journalists, I was well

briefed for the trip, having been studying this question for some years, knowing Afghans and Pakistanis (as I made clear in the book) and being with people who knew Farsi – this last benefit not being shared by most journalists. (1988)

Lessing travelled with the charity Afghan Relief, to report on fighters resisting the Russians, the role of women in Afghan society, and the living conditions of many thousands of refugees in the far north of Pakistan. Yet on her return, she alleged that the articles she wrote on this were 'refused by all the American and European newspapers they were sent to' (159). Lessing has been accused of paranoia in making such charges, and there is perhaps an element of truth in this; certainly, at least one of the Afghan articles was subsequently published by the *New Yorker* in 1987. However, her charges recall the rejection by Western journals of reports by Jewish correspondents concerning the increasing anti-Semitism in Central Europe during the 1930s. And there are echoes of Dorothy Sayers' experience, when her commissioned paper, 'Living to Work', was rejected by the BBC in 1946 'on the heterogeneous grounds that it appeared to have political tendencies, and that "our public do not want to be admonished by a woman"' (5). Or, indeed, of Muriel Rukeyseyer's novel about the Spanish Civil War, *Savage Coast*, which as Rowena Kennedy-Epstein notes in this volume was written in 1936 but not published until 2013. Again we are reminded that all too often reportage that looks outside the received wisdom of the official archive may be accused of propaganda. So how, after her rejection, does Lessing set about drawing us into reportage?

What she uses are techniques of narrative honed in her earlier work, modulating between storytelling and vivid description, between the comments of a narrator and a wealth of impersonal data. She used those techniques in the non-fictional *Going Home* (1957), and refined them in *The Golden Notebook*: Lessing's reportage techniques can never be divorced from her novels. Moreover, like Orwell in *Homage to Catalonia* (1938), she is adept at using an accessible 'one of us' style, presenting a narrator who is far from omniscient. As for her narrative, she is in tune with Garton Ash who argues, like Englund, that historians and journalists 'have to work like novelists in many ways', because:

> We *imagine*. . . . No good history or reportage was ever written without a large imaginative sympathy with the people written about. Our characters are real people, but we shape them like characters, using our own interpretation of their personalities. (63)

After the rejection of her articles, Lessing must have been more than usually aware of the importance of narrative strategies if she was to

engage a readership. In a number of other works she shows an awareness of such problems: as in *Mara and Dann*, for example, when Mara
tries to persuade friends to prepare for an approaching drought and
finds that '[y]ou can tell someone something true, but if they haven't
experienced anything like it they won't understand' (197). Each enclave
is wrapped up in its own concerns, refusing to see itself as inexorably
linked to the destiny of the larger world. Lessing recalls Brecht, who saw
himself 'like one who seeks to warn the city of an impending flood, but
speaks another language . . . so do we come forward and report that evil
has been done to us' (247). He in turn echoes

> Goethe's adage that 'Everyone hears only what he understands' [that] cap-
> tures how different groups and individuals, including professional historians,
> approach inconvenient historical truths. (Michlic: 167)

And as David Punter shows in his chapter, similar concerns beset the
artists and storytellers of Zone Three in *The Marriages of Zones Three,
Four and Five*, who struggle to arrive at the truth of the legendary marriage that is described, and which is remembered very differently in Zone
Four. Lessing's experience with those rejected articles was nothing new.

So now, in *The Wind Blows Away Our Words*, Lessing does not
plunge straight into the Afghan refugee camps. The first of the book's
four sections offers a lively version of the Cassandra legend, told in the
astringent, colloquial idiom Lessing had used in *Briefing for a Descent
into Hell* (1971) for the meeting of the gods on Olympus; Cassandra's
cheating of her would-be lover Apollo, resulting in her prophecies never
being believed, takes on a wittily updated relevance. But then, having
lured us in with a tale, Lessing turns the tables: 'You could say the
whole world has become Cassandra, since there can be no one left who
does not see disaster ahead' (16) – and readers find themselves in the
contemporary world of felled rain forests, poisoned oceans, Chernobyl
and unheeded warnings. But Lessing keeps the tone mocking, as she
weaves together the Troy legend with modern follies that wilfully put
humanity at risk. She recalls the Trojans' admittance of the wooden
horse even though they could hear the warriors in its belly; and weaves
this legendary strand into the modern world where we so often choose
to remember one version of 'facts' at the expense of others that may
well determine our survival. Lessing also offers a teasing reminder that
Homer's epic shaped historical fact for the sake of the narrative: Troy
had been sacked six times before. Lessing comments:

> Helen does not know this repeated calamity has been blurred to make one,
> generic, calamity . . . Embarrassing really to keep records of this happening,

again and again. And again. As if our glorious ancestors didn't have a grain of common sense between them, or enough to stop it all happening again. And again. You'd think that once would be enough, wouldn't you? (27–8)

Lessing does not labour the underlying relevance.

The second section of the book, much the longest, turns to the Afghan War, but again Lessing does not plunge straight in. She begins by establishing the first-person narrator as an outsider: the kind of technique Orwell used, replacing an omniscient narrator with a questioner, one prepared to admit what they do not understand. So Lessing opens in a colourful, travelogue style, sketching groups of Pakistanis at the Air Pakistan office in London, observing cultural differences. Her destination is Peshawar; she says she has read books about the city, seeing it as 'an enticing town born to be the setting for a Bogart movie' (38); she deliberately creates her narrative persona as a tourist figure, entranced by an entertaining 'take' on the city. But she uses this ploy to explore serious limitations in journalistic reporting on the war, as 'seldom is it mentioned that Peshawar is the centre only for the eastern side of Afghanistan. It is as if the American eastern states claimed to be all America' (38). Journalists, she says, tend to ignore Quetta, the link to western Afghanistan, and if they accept fighters' offers to take them into Afghanistan, they rarely venture beyond the Pushtun border areas: 'it is as if Texas were to be seen as all of the United States' (39).

So right at the start of this key section, Lessing both disarms accusations of hubris by admitting that her view will be limited, and suggests that the West is getting distorted accounts of the war from the professionals. However, she also paves the way for another perspective, describing the 'brown and dusty' landscape around Peshawar. She tells us it is not like the brown and dusty landscapes of Africa, Australia and 'rectangles' in Texas, because this unpromising landscape is cultivated intensively. But the reference to other landscapes reminds us that Lessing can set what she finds within her own global experience, something she will exploit later in the book. She also notes historic changes in the land around Peshawar: 'once it must have spread among forests and rivers [. . .] Perhaps for centuries this plain was full of villages made of mud on river banks and among trees' (40). Such details underpin Lessing's ongoing theme of past history and present events having inevitable relevance for the future. It is in this context that she sets her interviews, reported as if verbatim, with the fighters of the Afghan resistance she meets, the muhjahidin, and their womenfolk.

The book is disturbing to read now, for it is grimly prescient. Lessing records, for example, the hundreds of thousands of refugees flooding into Pakistan from war-torn Afghanistan, telling how these desperate people were at first welcomed by the local Pakistanis, but then, as the numbers continued to grow, caused increasing unease. She tells how most of the muhjahidin she personally encountered were 'sensible, non-fanatical people' and that she did not meet the 'extreme and bigoted mullahs' (42), although many Western TV programmes of the time suggested these were the only kind. She admits that 'Any Moslem country is difficult for a westerner . . . We are full of ignorance and prejudice and so are they'; she points out how the West tends to associate 'the words "Islam", "Moslem" with "Terrorist", or with Fundamentalist Islam'; she did not see Fundamentalism at the time of her visit as 'the most important' strand – though she adds, disturbingly, 'it may, alas, become the most important' (46). She has evidence for this fear, as one of the moderate leaders tells that:

> The people you in the West call Fundamentalists are the most ideological but they are also the best fighters . . . They have allies and followers all over the Moslem world and, long term, this may create difficulties for us all. (55)

Of course, Lessing has the capacity to set such information in a broader context. The muhjahidin belief that the West would send more help if people realised the extent of their suffering reminded her of Africans in the Southern Rhodesia of her youth who said: '"If our brothers in England knew how we were being treated they would help us." The men who said this were the forerunners of the militants who were soon to come on the stage' (71). She recalls how, when she and some others tried to plead their cause in England, they were:

> patronized, put down, laughed at . . . Criticism of South Africa was just beginning in certain limited quarters . . . but Southern Rhodesia, a British colony? – of course we couldn't behave badly! *What! We, the British?* But I do wonder more and more: suppose people had been prepared to listen then in the early 1950s, to the few voices who were shouting warnings – would later disasters have been prevented? The seven years' civil war in Southern Rhodesia for example? (71)

Lessing is never one to compartmentalise if she feels one crisis can throw light on another; she anticipates much that would be discussed at the Nobel Centennial symposium, and indeed much that concerns us now.

Not all this section focuses on the war and its warriors. There are meetings with women who had been left in bombed Afghan villages when their men went to fight; they are eloquent in their descriptions of their flight as refugees, through snow and ice, bombed all the way. They tend to be, Lessing finds, far better storytellers than the men, their tales 'full of life, full of anger' (77), without concern for the stoical public image the men adopt. Lessing explores the life of purdah, noting how some fear their husbands, and how one young woman doctor who practised freely in Kabul, is now trapped in purdah, her education and ability resented by other women. Lessing follows the famous example of previous women travel writers in the East, such as Lady Mary Wortley Montagu and Fanny Parkes, in gaining access to female-only environments so as to gain insight and information not available to a more numerous and apparently authoritative body of male counterparts; and once there she is careful to stress her ignorance among the women, trying to make sense of their narratives. She ponders the history of purdah, how many Moslem women 'have claimed that they feel "free" when veiled' (104). But she also notes how in Iran at that date it was often orthodox women who roamed the streets 'looking for "sisters" who had erred by showing a trace of lipstick, or a loose strand of hair'. 'It is, alas, not only men who imprison women' (104), Lessing comments. However, she admits to seeing the lure of purdah for some; they stay safe and cosseted, while the men protect them. There are echoes here of Jameson's wry comments on those she terms 'parasitic women' (quoted in Maslen, 46), leaving all responsibility to their menfolk.

The final section of the book is again tersely expressed, its title 'The Strange Case of the Western Conscience'. There is little technical subtlety here, rather a deliberately provocative and brutal barrage of numbers and facts. Lessing stresses the shock of encountering, after her experiences among the Afghans, the lack of interest in the West. She recalls an interviewer from a leading journal who, when told of Afghan refugee numbers, simply commented 'that it was all very hard to believe'; the published interview airbrushed any mention of Afghanistan (158). Lessing's response is iconoclastic, hard-hitting, with no attempt at narrative finesse. She offers counts of refugees from different countries, making comparisons between responses to such information from different parts of the world. She reiterates how often her attempts to publicise the Afghans' plight have been rejected and concludes that 'this neatly illustrates the media's way of sheltering behind attitudes they have themselves created' (160). As always, she is not afraid to make her readers uncomfortable; like Gruner, she argues that:

> we have been conditioned to see Hitler's Germany . . . as the archetype of evil for our time; have accepted this continual hammering on one nerve . . . it has probably often happened in the past that a terrible atrocity has become the symbol or shorthand for other, lesser or greater, atrocities, so that they become forgotten. Our minds seem to work like this. (169)

In the end, she suggests the very hugeness of numbers of refugees, of deaths, numb the mind to the fates of individuals: 'Is it possible that our careless, our casual use of these "millions" is one of the reasons for brutality, for cruelty?' (172). A very pertinent question for now, as for then, and one that interrogates the use of huge numbers that characterised her earlier work, of the sort Adam Guy discussed earlier in this book. Has our ever-increasing exposure to the enormity of suffering millions throughout the twentieth (and twenty-first) century dulled our concern for mere individuals?

Lessing often had to contend with disapproving reviews; in this instance Jeri Laber, one of the founders of Human Rights Watch, and co-author of *A Nation is Dying: Afghans under the Soviets*, pointed to an inaccurate date, a mistake about who was prime minister at the time (1988). But as Lessing herself maintained, her reportage is not that of most journalists, who tend not to portray themselves as unreliable narrators; nor is she the kind of historian who attends to details not necessarily central to their overview. Lessing's reportage is a passionate plea to understand the suffering of fellow human beings. And in the end, she and Laber share the same concerns, even if their ways of addressing these are very different.

Lessing has shown her awareness throughout her reportage – and indeed throughout her novels – that views on the whole truth depend on who is speaking; each person will have their agenda, and the lottery of who is interviewed will shape our view of any contest. She is rightly wary of those who, in Timothy Snyder's telling phrase, conflate 'lifestyle with life' (324). She shows how profitably an outsider may bring other experiences to bear: her awareness of the Zimbabwean civil war and its evolution are far from irrelevant to her reflections on where the Afghan war might lead. And her fears for the future increase over the decades: age for her, as for Sartre and Jameson, darkens her vision, and intensifies the urge to warn. Yet pessimism is not nihilism, as Lessing's touch of wry humour near the end of *Walking in the Shade* (1997) demonstrates; she recalls how, in 1962:

> We were all still on the escalator Progress, the whole world ascending towards prosperity ... At the end of a century of grand revolutionary romanticism; frightful sacrifices for the sake of paradises and heavens on earth and the withering away of the state; passionate dreams of utopias and wonderlands and perfect cities; attempts at communes and commonwealths, at co-operatives and kibbutzes and kolkhozes – after all this, would any of us have believed that most people in the world would have settled gratefully for a little honesty, a little competence in government? (368)

And importantly she uses the same epigraph for both volumes of her autobiography, *Under My Skin* (1994) and *Walking in the Shade*. It is taken from Idries Shah's *Caravan of Dreams* (1968):

> The individual, and the groupings of people, have to learn that they cannot reform society in reality, nor deal with others as reasonable people, unless the individual has learned to locate and allow for the various patterns of coercive institutions, formal and informal, which rule him. No matter what his reason says, he will relapse into obedience to the coercive agency while its pattern is within him.

So, Lessing would imply, the way of the Sufi that she learnt from Shah offers both warning and advice for the future forming of history to any who care to listen.

Note

1. For a detailed account of Jameson's commitments in her writings, see Maslen (2014).

Works Cited

Brecht, Bertolt (1976), *Poems 1913–1956*, ed. J. Willett and R. Manheim, London: Eyre Methuen.

Englund, Peter (2002), 'The Bedazzled Gaze: On Perspective and Paradoxes in Witness Literature', in H. Engdahl (ed.), *Witness Literature: Proceedings of the Nobel Centennial Symposium*, Singapore: World Scientific Publishing Co., pp. 45–56.

Garton Ash, Timothy (2002), 'On The Frontier', in H. Engdahl (ed.), *Witness Literature: Proceedings of the Nobel Centennial Symposium*, Singapore: World Scientific Publishing Co., pp. 57–68.

Gordimer, Nadine (2002), 'The Inward Testimony', in H. Engdahl (ed.), *Witness Literature: Proceedings of the Nobel Centennial Symposium*, Singapore: World Scientific Publishing Co., pp. 85–98.

Gruner, Wolf (2014), '"Armenian Atrocities": German Jews and Their Knowledge of Genocide during the Third Reich', in H. Earl and K. A. Schleunes (eds), *Expanding Perspectives on the Holocaust in a Changing World, Lessons and Legacies*, vol. XI, Evanston: Northwestern University Press, pp. 180–207.

Jameson, Storm (1939a), 'In Courage Keep Your Heart', *Woman's Journal*, December 1939, 34–5.

—— [1935] (1939b), 'What is Patriotism?', reprinted as 'On Patriotism', *Civil Journey*, London: Cassell, pp. 248–60.

'Kara Kush', <https://idriesshahfoundation.org/books/kara-kush> (last accessed 8 January 2016).

Laber, Jeri (1988), 'Half a Nation Dead or Displaced', *New York Times*, 24 January 1988, <https://www.nytimes.com/books/99/01/10/specials/lessing-wind> (last accessed 8 January 2016).

Lessing, Doris (1987), *The Wind Blows Away Our Words*, London: Picador.

—— (1988), 'The Art of Fiction No. 102', Thomas Frick, <http://www.the parisreview.org/interviews/2537/the-art-of-fiction-no-102-doris-lessing> (last accessed 31 October 2015).

—— (1997), *Walking in the Shade: Volume Two of My Autobiography, 1949–1962*, London: Flamingo.

—— (2000), *Mara and Dann: An Adventure*, London: Flamingo.

Lifton, Robert Jay (1979), *The Broken Connection: on Death and the Continuity of Life*, New York: Simon & Schuster.

Li Rui (2002), 'Cloned Eyes', in H. Engdahl (ed.), *Witness Literature: Proceedings of the Nobel Centennial Symposium*, Singapore: World Scientific Publishing Co., pp. 77–83.

Maslen, Elizabeth (2014), *Life in the Writings of Storm Jameson*, Evanston: Northwestern University Press.

Mavlian, Shoair (2014), 'The Modern Archive of Conflict', in S. Baker and S. Mavlian (eds), *Conflict. Time. Photography*, London: Tate Publishing, pp. 207–17.

Michlic, Joanna Beata (2014), '"The Many Faces of Memory": How Do Jews and the Holocaust Matter in Postcommunist Poland?', in H. Earl and K. A. Schleunes (eds), *Expanding Perspectives on the Holocaust in a Changing World, Lessons and Legacies*, vol. XI, Evanston: Northwestern University Press, pp. 144–79.

Sayers, Dorothy (1946), *Unpopular Opinions: Twenty-one Essays*, London: Victor Gollancz.

Snyder, Timothy (2015), *Black Earth: The Holocaust as History and Warning*, London: The Bodley Head.

Chapter 12

A Catastrophic Universe: Lessing, Posthumanism and Deep History

Clare Hanson

If he wasn't human, what was he? A human animal, she concluded, and then joked with herself, Well, aren't we all? (*Ben, in the World*, 42)

Human evolution is a major concern of Lessing's fiction from *The Four-Gated City* (1969) to *The Cleft* (2007) and this interest is one of the primary motives for her turn to speculative fiction, a genre which allows her to range imaginatively across evolutionary time. Focusing on her later fiction, this chapter argues that in her *Canopus in Argos* sequence and in fables such as *The Fifth Child* (1988) Lessing engages presciently with the kind of 'deep history' advocated by Dipesh Chakrabarty in his influential discussion of history in the age of the Anthropocene. As the chapters by Adam Guy and David Sergeant earlier in this volume have shown, questions of scale were important to Lessing's career from the beginning, and Chakrabarty's contention that the evidence for anthropogenic climate change requires us to reconfigure the meaning of human history signals another important way in which Lessing engages with this idea. According to Chakrabarty, it demands a change of scale in our thinking, which must now operate at a planetary level, and it unsettles the temporality of historical thought, which must now encompass geological time and the possibility of our own extinction. In addition, because humans have now become a geological force, 'the time honoured distinction between natural and human histories' has been destroyed. In consequence, he suggests, there is a need to conceptualise 'the human' at the level of the species rather than the individual, despite the fact that the concept of the species invokes a collectivity 'that escapes our capacity to experience the world' (222). Although he does not make this point explicitly, Chakrabarty's analysis of the implications of climate change for our understanding of human subjectivity converges with key tenets of posthumanist thought as it has developed over the last two decades. Posthumanism has been seen as a response to climate change and to rapid advances in bio- and info-technologies, developments which seem to point in contradictory directions, either to the 'end of man' or to man's self-transcendence. Accordingly, posthumanism is associated with an ambivalence described by Stefan Herbrechter in terms of 'the cultural malaise or euphoria [. . .] caused by the feeling that arises once you start taking the idea of "post-anthropocentrism" seriously' (3). Nonetheless, philosophers such as Herbrechter and Rosi Braidotti have made a strong case for the ethical value of what they term a 'critical posthumanism', which in Braidotti's words 'inflicts a blow to any lingering notion of human nature, *anthropos* and *bios*, as categorically distinct from the life of animals and non-humans, or *zoe*' (65). She goes on to argue that the task of current critical thought is to enlarge and re-frame subjectivity 'along the transversal lines of post-anthropocentric relations', reconfiguring subjectivity as 'an assemblage that includes non-human agents' (82), while the vitalist philosopher Elizabeth Grosz argues for a posthumanism which affirms the continuity between 'man and all other now or once living species' (17). Lessing's fiction similarly calls in question our assumptions about the relationship between humans and 'all other now or once living species', articulating in this respect a critical posthumanist perspective, yet the posthumanist implications of her fiction are often in tension with her transhumanist interests and are further complicated by her preoccupation with the long reach of geological time.

Human Animals

Lessing engages with 'once living species' most directly in her 1988 novella *The Fifth Child*, which centres on a monstrous child who is a supposed 'evolutionary throwback'. According to Lessing, the story was inspired in part by 'The Last Neanderthal', an essay by the evolutionary anthropologist Loren Eiseley in which he gives an account of meeting a young girl who seems to come from an earlier phase of human history.[1] Eiseley describes her as a 'phantom' and an 'alien' who possesses the physical characteristics of a Neanderthal, being 'short, thickset and massive ... her head, thrust a little forward against the light, was massive-boned. Along the eye orbits at the edge of the frontal bone I could see outlined in the flames an armoured protuberance that, particularly in women, had vanished before the close of the Würmian ice' (174). Alongside suggestions of 'primitive' characteristics, Eiseley notes the 'curious gentleness' that touches the girl and reflects that the Neanderthals' 'low archaic skull vault' was as capacious as our own: he is willing to concede that the Neanderthals possessed some 'human' characteristics but is by definition thereby viewing them though an anthropocentric lens. He also comments that what is significant in his encounter with this primitive 'other' is the co-existence in his mind of 'two stages of man's climb up the energy ladder' (176). The Neanderthals are here positioned as human ancestors rather than the separate species they are now known to have been and the metaphors of climbing and ascent suggest that what precedes the human is inferior and undeveloped, reflecting the orthodoxy of mid twentieth-century anthropology.

Lessing's last Neanderthal differs from Eiseley's in being rendered as a hostile intruder almost from the moment of his conception. When she is pregnant with the eponymous fifth child, Harriet Lovatt experiences his movements as an attack, as though the foetus is 'trying to tear its way out of her stomach'. She imagines she is incubating a chimera, reflecting that 'when the scientists make experiments, welding two kinds of animal together, of different sizes, then I suppose this is what the poor mother feels. She imagined pathetic botched creatures, horribly real to her' (52). She construes her connection with Ben in terms of competition and survival and after his birth the narrative tracks her growing antagonism towards a child who not only looks different, with his low sloping brow, massive shoulders and sallow skin, but behaves differently, stalking birds, crushing flowers and struggling with everyday social interactions. Ben is an ontological riddle and the question of what (not who) he is comes up repeatedly, to be answered by Harriet with the claim that he is a throwback to the Neanderthals, while he is also described as a hybrid who unsettles the boundary between the animal and the human (52). There is a particular focus on the way in which Ben destroys the 'family life' (155) which Harriet and her husband David are so anxious to create and which is the object of particularly scathing critique in this text. Lessing stresses that Harriet and David's 'happy family' (28) depends on hefty financial subsidy from their parents, highlighting the interdependency of capitalism and the bourgeois family. Moreover, when Ben is placed in an institution it is clear that this is to protect the family unit, David arguing forcefully that '"It's either him or us"' (90). By placing Ben and his family in such stark contention the text highlights the exclusions and disavowals inherent in an ideology of 'family life' which entails biological and social homogeneity and where the future is understood in terms of the (re)production of the same.

When Harriet visits Ben in the institution she discovers him drugged, naked, straitjacketed and lying in a pool of urine. She understands that the drugs would soon have killed him and brings him home to prevent his death at the hands, indirectly, of his family. As he readjusts to family life, Harriet speculates about his thoughts and feelings and wonders if he is 'experiencing a misery she could not begin to imagine, because he was for ever shut out from the ordinariness of this house and its people' (116). Despite his violent impulses and brutality, by the time of his adolescence Ben is positioned as a signifier of difference who challenges not just normative family values but the self-identity and exceptionalism of the human:

> [Harriet] felt she was looking, through him, at a race that reached its apex thousands and thousands of years before humanity, *whatever that meant*, took this stage. Did Ben's people live in caves underground while the ice age ground overhead, eating fish from dark subterranean rivers, or sneaking up into the bitter snow to snare a bear, or a bird – or even people, her (Harriet's) ancestors? Did his people rape the females of humanity's forebears? *Thus making new races, which had flourished and departed, but perhaps had left their seeds in the human matrix,* here and there, to appear again, as Ben had? (156, my italics)[2]

It can be argued that through Harriet's perspective on her son, Lessing takes the radical step of relativising the claims of the evolutionary past and the present. To put it another way, what is at stake in this text is not the unmasking of the primitive as it persists in modern man but the deconstruction of the historically specific category of the primitive. This category and the related concept of atavism are intimately bound up with the idea that evolution entails progress, a teleological view that continues to inform evolutionary thought despite the fact that Darwin himself was increasingly sceptical, writing in a letter of 1872 that 'after long reflection I cannot avoid the conclusion that no inherent tendency to progressive development exists'. As Elizabeth Grosz has argued, Darwin's ambivalence about the question of biological progress is associated with a marked decentring of the human in *The Descent of Man* (1871), published twelve years after the *Origin of Species*. Reflecting on the relationship between humans and other species in the later text, Darwin argues that 'the difference in mind between man and the higher animals, great as it is, is certainly one of degree and not of kind' and goes on to suggest that the emotions and faculties which have been used to identify man's uniqueness (love, memory, reason and so on) 'may be found in an incipient, or even sometimes in a well-developed condition, in the lower animals' (quoted in Grosz: 23). Emphasising the continuities between humans and other animals, Darwin nonetheless suggests that characteristics such as morality are differently elaborated in different species, giving as an example the ethics of the beehive in which the killing of worker bees might be perceived as, in his words, 'a sacred duty'. As Grosz argues, he thereby acknowledges a 'fundamental relativity of knowledges, aims, goals, and practices [. . .] and the ways in which each species, from the humblest to the most complex, orients its world according to its interests, capacities, knowledges, and uses' (Grosz: 21).

Ben, in the World (published twelve years after *The Fifth Child*, in 2000) presses critically on the relationship between humans and other species, emphasising the parallel between the cultural derogation of so-called 'primitive man' and the abjection of non-human primates. Ben is now eighteen, although in line with his characterisation as a Neanderthal he appears much older.[3] He has left home and exists on the margins of society, working in the black economy and living from hand to mouth. Unlike *The Fifth Child*, which is focalised primarily through Harriet, this text provides access to an approximation of Ben's consciousness, a move which enables Lessing to convey Ben's acute intuitions and his all too human feelings, while dramatising his detachment from some forms of instrumental reason. For example, he has difficulty in planning ahead, which makes him vulnerable to the designs of others, as demonstrated in the picaresque plot which sees him kidnapped and taken to Brazil, allegedly to star in a film about early man. The inclusion of this subplot underscores the dubious ways in which 'primitive' man has been represented in twentieth-century popular culture, in films such as *One Million Years BC* (1966), *Quest for Fire* (1980) and *The Iceman* (1984) for example. Neanderthals have long had projected onto them the 'animal' qualities which humanist ideology would wish to disavow, such as physical aggression and uncontrolled sexuality and when we see Ben through the eyes of the other characters he appears as a fetish-figure combining immense physical strength with sexual allure: he is a creature of 'seductive strangeness' (82).

The question of the place of the human in relation to other animals is further opened up when Ben comes to the attention of scientists at a biomedical research facility and is captured for the purposes of scientific study. In an account which is all the more powerful for its brevity, Lessing describes the conditions for the animals in the research institute, stressing the needless cruelty of the design of experiments in which, for example, monkeys are arranged in tiers of cages 'so that the excrement from the top cages must fall down on the animals below' (146). This, the narrator suggests, is a scene which can be found across the globe in sites where therapeutic aims become entangled with the power of global biocapital, so that their functions 'blur and blend' (130). Lessing's critique of animal exploitation is uncompromising and her views can be aligned with those of John Sanbonmatsu, who has argued compellingly that 'negation of the animal other is not a side concern to the "real issues" facing human social life but the pivot around which our civilisation itself has formed, the phenomenological *ground* upon which the figure of the human being continues to stand' (9). In elaborating this position Sanbonmatsu draws on Adorno and Horkheimer's critique of the long history in European thought of constructing the human in contradistinction to the animal, the latter being perceived as lacking the powers of reason, memory and forethought. He suggests that Adorno and Horkheimer's thinking may have been influenced by the work of Wilhelm Reich in this respect, in particular *The Mass Psychology of Fascism* (1933), in which Reich argues that:

> Man takes great pains to dissociate himself from the vicious animal and to prove that he is 'better' by pointing to his culture and his civilisation, which distinguish him from the animal ... His viciousness, his inability to live peacefully with his own kind, his wars, bear witness to the fact that man is distinguished from the other animals only by boundless sadism and the mechanical trinity of an authoritarian view of life, mechanistic science, and the machine. (Quoted in Sanbonmatsu, pp. 9–10.)

There is a suggestive convergence between Reich's argument and the critique of human barbarity which pervades Lessing's later fiction. Like Reich, Lessing underscores the disjunction between what Santonmatsu terms our (illusory) 'narratives of inherent human dignity' (12) and the reality of our enslavement of other sentient beings, both human and non-human. The presence of Ben with his ambiguously human/non-human status alongside the experimental animals in *Ben, in the World* makes this point succinctly.

Perhaps the most striking example of Lessing's exploration of animal/human relations occurs in the earlier text, *Memoirs of a Survivor* (1974), which addresses the theme of hybridity in a fiction in which novel animal/human interactions shape a post-apocalyptic future.[4] The focus of this novella is on the unnamed narrator, her young charge Emily and the beast Hugo, a creature who is neither cat nor dog but poised somewhere in between. In her representation of the narrator's reaction to Hugo, Lessing draws attention to the ways in which we differentially construct the 'identity' of non-human animals. For the narrator, only dogs count as a companion species, to borrow Donna Haraway's term, while cats (inscribing a familiar stereotype) are assumed to be alien, hostile creatures:

> Seen thus from the back, Hugo aroused the emotions most dogs do: compassion, discomfort, as if for a kind of prisoner or slave. But then he would turn his head and, expecting to see the warm abject lovingness of a dog's eyes, fellow-feeling vanished away: this was no dog, half humanized. His strong green eyes blazed. Inhuman, cat's eyes, a genus foreign to man, not sorry and abject and pleading. (58)

Yet Hugo's undecidable ontological status disrupts the narrator's anthropocentric assumptions; moreover the text demonstrates that the species with which humans live and interact are hybrids in a different sense, compounded at one and the same time of an ontology that escapes our grasp and a mode of being forged in and through human-animal interactions. As an emblem of such hybridity, Hugo can be seen as a proto-cyborg who invites us to think about the possibility of what Braidotti terms a 'post-human relationality', that is, the forging of more fluid, non-hierarchical human/animal bonds (73). The relationship between Hugo, Emily and the narrator in this text exemplifies a more equitable mode of human/animal relation, as the various actors come to understand their complex co-dependencies to the point where the humans are ready to risk their lives to protect that 'ugly, bristly old beast' (184). The novel concludes with an apotheosis in which Hugo and Emily lead the way into a new world which could be read as figuring (among other things) a post-anthropocentric future:

> Emily [was] quite beyond herself, transmuted, and in another key, and the yellow beast Hugo fitted her new self: a splendid animal, handsome, all kindly dignity and command, he walked beside her and her hand was on his neck. Both walked quickly behind that One who went ahead showing them the way out of this collapsed little world into another order of world altogether. (190)

Human Agents

Such an emancipatory vision resonates with the posthumanist perspective advocated by Braidotti which 'composes the notion of *zoe* as a non-human yet generative life-force' (104). At the same time, Lessing's fiction frequently articulates perspectives which echo transhumanist aspirations. While posthumanism entails the decentring of the humanist conception of the human, transhumanism is concerned with the enhancement of precisely those qualities which have been thought to distinguish man from other species, notably instrumental reason. The term transhumanism was first coined by Julian Huxley in an essay in which he defined it in terms of 'man remaining man, but transcending himself, by realising new possibilities of and for his human nature' (Huxley 1957: 17). Lessing's interest in these ideas may derive in part from her friendship with Naomi Mitchison, who was part of an intellectual circle which crossed the divide between the arts and the sciences and where such issues were debated by writers and by biologists such as Huxley himself, Mitchison's brother the geneticist J. B. S. Haldane, and James Watson (a close friend of Mitchison's son).[5] Huxley's view, advanced in bestselling Pelican books such as *Essays of a Humanist*, is that humans have reached a critical point in their evolution, comparable in significance to the moment when human ancestors first moved from water to dry land. For him, the rapid advance of man's cognitive abilities means that we are moving from a phase of biological evolution to one of 'psychosocial evolution'. Humans are distinguished from other species by their 'rational, knowledge-based imagination' which has allowed them to understand the process of their own evolution; in consequence, he claims, 'man is not merely the latest dominant type produced by evolution, but its sole active agent on earth. His destiny is to be responsible for the whole future of the evolutionary process on this planet' (Huxley 1964: 85, 125). As Alison Bashford has argued, there is a clear line of descent from Huxley's transhumanism to that of twenty-first century transhumanists such as John Harris and Nick Bostrom, the principal difference being that whereas Huxley and other mid-century thinkers see human improvement in terms of change at the level of the population, contemporary transhumanism emphasises the individual's right to self-enhancement.[6] Such a stress on free choice accords with the ideology of neo-liberalism and more crucially, appears to distance twenty-first century transhumanism from the taint of eugenics.

Lessing's Canopeans can be read as the embodiment of the principle of evolutionary self-understanding outlined by Huxley and endorsed by public intellectuals such as Peter Medawar. As the most highly developed species in Lessing's cosmos, the Canopeans act as Huxley's 'agents' of evolution and when they see the potential of the humans (or 'former monkeys') on Shikasta, they implement 'an all-out booster, Top-Level Priority, Forced-Growth Plan' (28), introducing a 'strong and healthy species' (29) to live with them in a symbiosis that will speed up their development. Subsequently, when progress stalls due to a misalignment of cosmic forces, the Canopean eugenicists decide on a boost of their own genes to create a strain with 'improved intelligence' (130). Lessing presents these strategies in terms of population genetics and in this respect, *Shikasta* (1979) can be seen as an attempt to think at the species level which Chakrabarty finds so problematic. For him 'the species' is an abstraction that is incommensurable with subjectively lived experience, whereas in Lessing's text the 'deepest self' is *identified* with species-consciousness, as for example when one of the Canopean agents comments that:

> an individual may be told she, he, is to die, and will accept it. For the species will go on . . . But that a whole species, or race, will cease or drastically

change – no, that cannot be taken in, accepted, not without a total revolution of the deepest self. (55)

The Canopeans believe that species-consciousness will ensure the survival of the Shikastans yet are also aware that 'this is a catastrophic universe, always; and subject to sudden reversals, upheavals, changes, cataclysms, with joy never anything but the song of substance under pressure forced into new forms and shapes' (140). The text here echoes the understanding of geological time promoted in the 1960s and 1970s by writers such as Eiseley, with his account of the origins of man in a 'geo-catastrophic' (82) world, and Stephen Jay Gould, whose theory of 'punctuated equilibrium' (Eldredge and Gould, 256) proposed that evolution was less gradual than was previously thought and that new species could emerge in periods of rapid geological change. By emphasising the Shikastans' vulnerability to the violence and unpredictability of evolution, Lessing underscores the limits of Canopean and/or human power to intervene in the process, the further implication being that the notion of humans as the sole agents of evolution is a hubristic fantasy.

If *Shikasta* is productively ambivalent in its engagement with transhumanist thought, in *The Making of the Representative for Planet 8* (1982; the fourth Canopus novel) Lessing blends transhumanist ideas with Sufi concepts of spiritual death and rebirth. The novella focuses on a planet which the Canopeans have populated with a genetically engineered species which is hit by the sudden advent of an ice age. In an echo of Naomi Mitchison's dystopian novel *Solution Three* (1975), it is implied that it is because the inhabitants of the planet are so well designed for their environment that they are unable to adapt to this cataclysmic event.[7] Guided by Canopean agents, a band of 'Representatives' encourage the other members of their species to resist the encroachment of the ice but when it is clear that the planet faces extinction they embark on a final trek to its coldest point. In a long Afterword, Lessing invites us to read this journey alongside the accounts of Scott's expedition to the Antarctic which fascinated her as a child. She interprets that doomed expedition in terms of the human drive to transcendence and argues that 'this need to break out of our ordinary possibilities – the cage we live in that is made of our habits, upbringing, circumstances [. . .] may well be the deepest one we have' (134). As these comments suggest, what is important for the Representatives (as for the members of Scott's expedition) is to discover and express the capacities latent within them. Moreover, Lessing presents their eventual death not in terms of self-destruction but as an apotheosis in which they morph into beings (or a single being) operating on a higher plane:

one pattern had already sunk back into the physical substance of Planet 8, and another went forward, our eyes changing with every moment so that we were continually part of a new scene, or time [. . .] all our functions and the capacities of our work were in the substance of these new beings, this Being, we now were. (118–19)

When Lessing writes of the essential qualities of the Representatives being re-embodied on distant planets, this can be read in terms of the Sufi belief in the persistence of the soul as it journeys through different worlds or, equally, as a reference to the redistribution of genetic material by Canopean genetic engineers. Indeed, it could be argued that the Canopean belief system is shaped by a blend of mysticism and scientific rationalism which offers evolutionary progress at a cosmic level as compensation for the losses and depredations of individual life. For the Canopeans it is axiomatic that individuality (known to them as 'the degenerative disease') should be sacrificed for the good of the species and, further, that the extinction of the species may be necessary for the greater (cosmic) good. The apotheosis of the Representatives can thus be read as invoking in dramatically condensed form the experience of species extinction. While Lessing is ostensibly writing about an alien species, her protagonists are recognisably human and her interest is in the modulation of human subjectivity as it is incorporated into new life forms, prompting the question 'what new eyes were these that could see our old home thus, as interlocking structures of atoms, and where were we, the Representatives? – *what* were we, and how did we seem to those who could watch us, with their keener, finer sight?' (118).

Human History

Chakrabarty concludes his essay on climate change by making the case for a new kind of history, on the grounds that:

> climate change poses for us a question of a human collectivity, an us, pointing to a figure of the universal that escapes our capacity to experience the world [. . .] It calls for a global approach to politics without the myth of a global identity, for, unlike a Hegelian universal, it cannot subsume particularities. We may provisionally call it a 'negative universal history'. (222)

In calling for a global approach without the myth of global identity, Chakrabarty acknowledges the danger that a supposedly universal history will elide the economic and material differences that structure relations between human beings. Despite this, he contends that the fact that humanity has become a geological agent requires us to forge

a 'new universal history of humans' (221) and he is particularly interested in the problem this poses at the level of the experiential. Climate
change science, he suggests, brings us a self-knowledge which we can
access intellectually but cannot experience. This creates a rupture with
traditional forms of historical understanding which are predicated on
phenomenological knowledge, so that in a study such as Lessing's close
friend E. P. Thompson's *The Making of the English Working Class*
(1963), for example, an understanding of the workers' experience of
capitalism is central to the formation of that history. However, when
an evolutionary biologist such as E. O. Wilson argues that the planetary
future depends on our self-understanding as a species, he invokes a conceptual framework that is incommensurable with traditional historical
understanding. Chakrabarty suggests there can be no phenomenology
of a species and in this sense we cannot know what being a species
is, for 'in species history, humans are only an instance of the concept
species' (220). To meet this conceptual challenge, Chakrabarty argues
for a 'negative human history' which can encompass both the human
and the concept of a universal 'that escapes our capacity to experience
the world'. Such a negative human history would join biological and
historical modes of thought and would create a conversation between
'recorded and deep histories of human beings' (220). Lessing's fiction
can be seen as anticipating Chakrabarty's call for a 'negative universal
history' in that it mediates between historical and biological epistemologies and between recorded and deep history. Prior to *Briefing for a
Descent into Hell* (1971), her fiction focuses on the interiority and subjectivity of her protagonists to create a rich archive of post-war (mainly
female) consciousness. As she writes in 'The Small Personal Voice'
(1957), her aim at this point was to write fiction in the tradition of the
nineteenth-century novel, with its celebration of the individual and affir-
mation of 'faith in man himself' (6). In the 1960s and 1970s however,
responding to the energies of Marxist and psychoanalytic thought,
her fiction develops a hermeneutics of suspicion which is increasingly
directed towards the concept of a fixed human essence. In the *Children
of Violence*, Martha Quest's attempt to forge an authentic self is unsettled by her growing awareness of the incoherence and ideologically
mediated nature of subjectivity, as Kevin Brazil's chapter in this volume
has shown. The critique of the category of the human in Lessing's subsequent fiction can be seen as an extension of this line of thought and in
this respect her trajectory can be aligned with the transition described by
Braidotti, whereby the energies of twentieth-century anti-humanist critical theory have been transformed into twenty-first century posthumanist
thought (26–30).

Focusing on the experiential impact of the Anthropocene, Lessing's fiction not only maps some of the territory discussed by Chakrabarty but also anticipates some of Bruno Latour's arguments about the shift in perception that it entails. Latour suggests that one of the most significant consequences of climate science is that it has undone the dichotomy between subject and object which structures 'the scientific world-view' (2, 14), in which the natural world is construed as lacking in agency, a mere backdrop for the human subject who is understood in terms of rational autonomy. For Latour, now that we can see human action everywhere, the concept of an 'objective nature' has unravelled and in consequence, 'to be a subject is not to act autonomously in front of an objective background but *to share agency with other subjects that have also lost their autonomy*' (5, italics original). Taking this analysis further, he points out the importance of recognising the agency of the non-human world and of reconceptualising our relationship with non-human actors (15). These arguments are helpful for thinking about Lessing's explorations of a posthuman subjectivity in *Shikasta*, as she documents the 'last days' of humanity which are followed by a tentative regeneration of the species. On the cusp of this transition, the Canopean agent Johor observes the Shikastans negotiating between older ways of thinking about the universe (which depend on the subject/object dichotomy highlighted by Latour) and an understanding of their co-dependency with other organisms. Looking at an autumn leaf, on the one hand they see it as 'a brilliant gold, a curled, curved, sculptured thing, balanced like a feather' (254): in other words, as something extrinsic to the human which is fixed and lacking in agency. On the other, they are able to see it as 'a fighting, seething mass of matter in the extremes of tension, growth, destruction, a myriad of species of smaller and smaller creatures feeding on each other' (254), a perspective in which the leaf and the human are co-implicated in a complex mesh of living systems. The second perspective is an uncomfortable but necessary one, Lessing suggests, as the Shikastans must position themselves in relation to planetary space and geological time and must accommodate 'the knowledge that the universe is a roaring engine of creativity, and they are only temporary manifestations of it' (256–7).

Latour notes that in the Anthropocene 'all agents share the same shape-shifting destiny, a destiny that cannot be followed, documented, told, and represented by using any of the older traits associated with subjectivity or objectivity' (15). As these comments suggest, the representation of a decentred humanity requires new forms of representation, which for Lessing entails a creative reworking of the genres of fable and science fiction. In her fables, rather than following tradition and using animals to allegorise human weakness, she creates real or imaginary animals which represent aspects of human potential, as in *Memoirs of a Survivor* and *The Fifth Child*: her subversive use of the form is inseparable from the troubling of the boundary between human and animal. Similarly in her science fiction, Lessing breaks new ground in her radical interrogation of human subjectivity, departing in this respect from the humanist understanding of character which Ursula le Guin advocates in her famous essay 'Science Fiction and Mrs Brown' (1975). Le Guin argues that the kind of characterisation Virginia Woolf defended in 'Mr Bennett and Mr Brown' (1923) is also central to science fiction, as writers of science fiction 'are not interested in what things do, but in how things are. Their subject is the subject, that which cannot be other than the subject: ourselves. Human beings' (109). While such an understanding of character is close to Lessing's position in 'The Small Personal Voice', it is far from the decentring of the human in her science fiction, where subjectivity is reconfigured as relational, transversal and caught up in affective bonds with non-human others. In using science fiction to map such a landscape as early as the 1970s Lessing is again remarkably prescient: the form and themes of her work overlap significantly with twenty-first century dystopias such as Margaret Atwood's *MaddAddam* trilogy (2003–13) and Sarah Hall's *The Carhullan Army* (2007).

Lessing's fiction engages intensely with the transformation in human self-understanding brought about by the Anthropocene and prior to that by the 'Modern Synthesis' of evolutionary biology.[8] In reflecting on species consciousness, her fiction explores the possibility of species improvement in ways which chime with transhumanist thought; yet by demonstrating the failure of the Canopeans' eugenic plans Lessing points to the limits of scientific reason and to the dangers of the human exceptionalism on which transhumanism is grounded. In her fables she deploys the motifs of the hybrid animal and evolutionary throwback to underscore the contingency of the category of the human and suggest the possibility of a reconfiguration of subjectivity along 'transversal' posthumanist lines. In complex and often contradictory ways her fiction thus participates in a conversation about the nature of the human which runs throughout the twentieth century but which has gathered in pace and intensity in the twenty-first. In this respect, her fiction occupies the territory marked out by Chakrabarty, in which knowledge from science and the humanities is conjoined to map a post-humanist, post-anthropocentric landscape. Such cross-disciplinary thinking has become more urgent as knowledge emerging from a range of scientific disciplines, particularly life science and climate science, lays claim to a redefinition of the human. As Braidotti points out, the current crisis in the humanities is in part a consequence of the re-framing of the human in terms set by scientific disciplines. However, she argues that this shift should be seen not as a threat but as an opportunity for developing novel forms of trans-disciplinary thought, for example in environmental and evolutionary studies. Lessing's fiction is an obvious point of departure for such trans-disciplinary work, given the depth of its engagement with evolutionary theory, in particular. Elizabeth Grosz has argued that the humanities have yet to recover from the challenge posed by evolution, which unsettled the concepts of man, reason and consciousness which were the structural underpinnings of these disciplines. The climate-change crisis has added a further dimension to this challenge by positioning humanity as the inadvertent agent of environmental degradation and species decline. As Grosz asks:

> what kind of new understanding of the humanities would it take to adequately map this decentering that places man back within the animal, within nature, and within a space and time that man does not regulate, understand or control? What new kinds of science does this entail? And what new kinds of art? (25)

Her response is to argue for an 'inhuman humanities' grounded in species equality, a perspective which is endorsed by Rosi Braidotti as she develops her concept of '*zoe*-egalitarianism', a philosophy which recognises *zoe* as the generative power that flows across all species (103). Lessing's fiction is entirely congenial with such neo-vitalist, posthumanist philosophical perspectives and, it could be argued, has laid some of the building blocks for the conceptual shift associated with the displacement of anthropocentrism.

Notes

1. Lessing notes of Eiesley's essay, 'It's just the most immensely touching, sad piece. It stuck in my mind, and I said, "If Neanderthals, why not Cro-Magnons, why not dwarves, goblins, because all cultures talk about these creatures?"' (1988).
2. Recent research has confirmed this intuition about the relationship between humans and Neanderthals. As Robin Dunbar notes, between two and four percent of modern European DNA is shared with the Neanderthals, although interbreeding was not a regular affair. See Dunbar (2014), Chapter 7 for further discussion of this issue.
3. Lessing's characterisation of Ben in *The Fifth Child* conforms to what was known in the 1980s about the life cycle of Neanderthals, who developed far more rapidly than humans and had a much shorter lifespan. In *Ben, in the World* she draws on more recent speculation that the large visual system

of the Neanderthals may have been adapted to poor light at high altitudes. Stressing Ben's difficulties with the glittering sun, she invites us to speculate about the nature of a consciousness produced by perceptual systems that are very different from ours.

4. Human/animal relations also feature prominently in *Briefing for a Descent into Hell* (1971), *Mara and Dann* (1999) and *The Story of General Dann and Mara's Daughter, Griot and the Snow Dog* (2005).

5. For a discussion of this group of writers and scientists see Hanson (2012), Chapter 3. Mitchison's influence on Lessing has been insufficiently recognised despite the fact that her science fiction offered a likely prototype for the ambitious speculations of Lessing's *Canopus* sequence. *Memoirs of a Spacewoman* (1967) is particularly close to Lessing's concerns, featuring a scientist-explorer who is an expert in communicating with other species and who volunteers for (disastrous) experiments in cross-species breeding.

6. Nick Bostrom defines transhumanism as follows: 'Transhumanists view human nature as a work-in-progress, a half-baked beginning that we can learn to remold in desirable ways. Current humanity need not be the endpoint of evolution. Transhumanists hope that by responsible use of science, technology, and other rational means we shall eventually manage to become posthuman, beings with vastly greater capacities than present human beings have' (2001).

7. Mitchison's novel warns of the dangers of interfering with the gene pool of species as this can cause them to lose plasticity and adaptability; similarly Lessing stresses the 'congruity' between the inhabitants of Planet 8 and their surroundings in the past and the mismatch between these genetically engineered creatures and their new environment. Although *Solution Three* is dedicated to James Watson, Mitchison's emphasis on the importance of the environment closely echoes the thinking of the geneticist C. H. Waddington, who developed the concept of the 'epigenetic landscape' as a way of theorising potential mechanisms for the impact of the environment on genes and development. The interplay between genes and the environment is one of the central themes of the *Canopus* sequence. See Waddington (1957) for a discussion of epigenetic landscapes.

8. The modern synthesis (also called neo-Darwinism) refers to the synthesis of evolutionary theory with Mendelian genetics in the early twentieth-century. Julian Huxley's *Evolution: The Modern Synthesis* (1942) offers a classic statement of this theoretical framework.

Works Cited

Atwood, Margaret (2004), *Oryx and Crake*, London: Virago.
—— (2010), *The Year of the Flood*, London: Virago.
—— (2014), *MaddAddam*, London: Virago.
Bashford, Alison (2013), 'Julian Huxley's Transhumanism', in Marius Turda (ed.), *Crafting Humans: From Genesis to Eugenics and Beyond*, Taiwan: National Taiwan University Press, pp. 153–68.

Bostrom, Nick (2001), 'Transhumanist Values' <http://www.fhi.ox.ac.uk/trans humanist-values.pdf> (last accessed 23 November 2015).

Braidotti, Rosi (2013), *The Posthuman*, Cambridge: Polity Press.

Chakrabarty, Dipesh (2009), 'The climate of history: four theses', *Critical Inquiry*, 35:2, 197–222.

Darwin, Charles (1872), letter to Alpheus Hyatt (4 December 1872), Darwin Correspondence Project <http://www.darwinproject.ac.uk/entry-8658> (last accessed 23 November 2015).

Dunbar, Robin (2014), *Human Evolution*, London: Pelican.

Eiseley, Loren [1964] (1973), 'The Last Neanderthal', in *The Unexpected Universe*, Harmondsworth: Penguin.

Eldredge, Niles and Stephen Jay Gould [1972] (2014), 'Punctuated Equilibria: An Alternative to Phyletic Gradualism', in Francisco J. Ayala and John C Avise (eds) *Essential Readings in Evolutionary Biology*, Baltimore: Johns Hopkins University Press, pp. 238–72.

Grosz, Elizabeth (2011), *Becoming Undone: Darwinian Reflections on Life, Politics, and Art*, Durham and London: Duke University Press.

Hall, Sarah (2008), *The Carhullan Army*, London: Faber & Faber.

Hanson, Clare (2012), *Eugenics, Literature and Culture in Post-war Britain*, London: Routledge.

Haraway, Donna (2007), *When Species Meet*, Minnesota: University of Minnesota Press.

Herbrechter, Stefan (2013), *Posthumanism: A Critical Analysis*, London: Bloomsbury.

Huxley, Julian (1942), *Evolution: the Modern Synthesis*, London: Allen & Unwin.

—— (1957), *New Bottles for New Wine*, London: Chatto & Windus.

—— [1964] (1969), *Essays of a Humanist*, Harmondsworth: Penguin.

Latour, Bruno (2014), 'Agency at the Time of the Anthropocene', *New Literary History* 45:1, 1–18.

Le Guin, Ursula [1975] (1980), 'Science Fiction and Mrs Brown', reprinted in Susan Wood (ed.) *The Language of the Night: Essays on Fantasy and Science Fiction*, Hastings on Hudson, NY: Ultramarine Publishing, pp. 101–21.

Lessing, Doris (1969), *The Four-Gated City*, London: MacGibbon & Kee.

—— [1971] (1972), *Briefing for a Descent into Hell*, London: Granada Publishing.

—— (1974), *Memoirs of a Survivor*, London: Octagon Press.

—— [1957] (1974), 'A Small Personal Voice', reprinted in *A Small Personal Voice: Essays, Reviews, Interviews*, ed. Paul Schlueter, New York: Alfred A. Knopf, pp. 3–21.

—— [1979] (1981), *Canopus in Argos: Archives Re: Colonised Planet 5 Shikasta*, London: Granada Publishing.

—— [1979] (1981), *Shikasta*, London: Grafton Books.

—— (1982), *Canopus in Argos: Archives The Making of the Representative for Planet 8*, London: Jonathan Cape.

—— (1988), 'The Art of Fiction No. 102', Thomas Frick, <http://www.the parisreview.org/interviews/2537/the-art-of-fiction-no-102-doris-lessing> (last accessed 31 October 2015).

—— (1999), *Mara and Dann: An Adventure*, London: Flamingo.

—— [1988] (2001), *The Fifth Child*, London: Flamingo.

—— [2000] (2001), *Ben, in the World*, London: Flamingo.

—— [2005] (2006), *The Story of General Dann and Mara's Daughter, Griot and the Snow Dog*, London: Harper Perennial.

—— (2007), *The Cleft*, London: Fourth Estate.

Mitchison, Naomi [1962] (1977), *Memoirs of a Spacewoman*, London: New English Library.

—— [1975] (1995), *Solution Three*, New York: The Feminist Press.

Sanbonmatsu, John (2011), 'Introduction', in John Sanbonmatsu (ed.), *Critical Theory and Animal Liberation*, Lanham, MD: Rowman & Littlefield, pp. 1–34.

Thompson, E. P. [1963] (1991), *The Making of the English Working Class*, London: Penguin.

Waddington, C. H. (1957), *The Strategy of the Gene: A Discussion of Some Aspects of Theoretical Biology*, London: Allen & Unwin.

Select Bibliography

This select bibliography of primary and secondary works is intended to supplement the bibliographies provided at the end of individual chapters and to act as a resource for future research on Lessing's work. Lessing's works are listed by their first date of publication in the United Kingdom.

Primary Works

Lessing, Doris (1950), *The Grass is Singing*, London: Michael Joseph.
—— (1951), *This Was The Old Chief's Country: Stories,* London: Michael Joseph.
—— (1952), *Martha Quest*, London: Michael Joseph.
—— (1953), *Five: Short Novels*, London: Michael Joseph.
—— (1956), *Retreat to Innocence*, London: Michael Joseph.
—— (1957), *Going Home*, London: Michael Joseph.
—— (1957), *The Habit of Loving,* London: MacGibbon & Kee.
—— (1958), *A Ripple from the Storm*, London: Michael Joseph.
—— (1959), *Fourteen Poems*, Northwood: Scorpion Press.
—— (1960), *In Pursuit of the English: A Documentary*, London: MacGibbon & Kee.
—— (1962), *The Golden Notebook*, London: Michael Joseph.
—— (1962), *Play With A Tiger: A Play in Three Acts*, London: Michael Joseph.
—— (1964), *African Stories*, London: Michael Joseph.
—— (1965), *Landlocked*, London: MacGibbon & Kee.
—— (1967), *Particularly Cats*, London: Michael Joseph.
—— (1969), *The Four-Gated City*, London: MacGibbon & Kee
—— (1971), *Briefing For a Descent Into Hell*, London: Cape.
—— (1972), *The Story of a Non-Marrying Man and Other Stories*, London: Cape.
—— (1973), *Collected African Stories*, London: Michael Joseph.
—— (1973), *The Summer Before the Dark*, London: Cape.
—— (1974), *A Small Personal Voice: Essays, Reviews, Interviews*, New York, Knopf.
—— (1978), *Collected Stories*, London: Jonathan Cape.

—— (1979), *Shikasta: Re, Colonised Planet 5*, London: Jonathan Cape.

—— (1980), *The Marriages Between Zones, Three, Four, and Five,* London: Jonathan Cape.

—— (1981), *The Sirian Experiments*, London: Jonathan Cape.

—— (1982), *The Making of the Representative for Planet 8*, London: Jonathan Cape.

—— (1983), *Documents Relating to the Sentimental Agents in the Volyen Empire,* London: Jonathan Cape.

—— (1983), *The Diary of a Good Neighbour*, London: Michael Joseph.

—— (1984), *The Diaries of Jane Somers*, London: Michael Joseph.

—— (1984), *If the Old Could*, London: Michael Joseph.

—— (1985), *The Good Terrorist*, London: Jonathan Cape.

—— (1987), *Prisons We Choose To Live Inside*, London: Jonathan Cape

—— (1987), *The Wind Blows Away Our Words*, London: Picador.

—— (1988), *The Fifth Child*, London: Jonathan Cape.

—— (1992), *London Observed: Stories and Sketches*, London: Harper Collins.

—— (1992), *African Laughter: Four Visits to Zimbabwe*, London: Harper Collins.

—— (1994), *Collected Stories Volume 1: To Room Nineteen*, London: Flamingo.

—— (1994), *Collected Stories Volume 2: The Temptation of Jack Orkney*, London: Flamingo.

—— (1994), *Under My Skin: Volume One of My Autobiography, to 1949*, London: Harper Collins.

—— (1995), *Playing the Game*, London: Harper Collins.

—— (1996), *Love, Again*, London: Flamingo.

—— (1996), *Putting the Questions Differently: Interviews with Doris Lessing 1964–1994*, London: Flamingo.

—— (1997), *Walking in the Shade: Volume Two Of My Autobiography 1949–1962*, London: Harper Collins.

—— (1999), *Mara and Dann: An Adventure*, London: Harper Collins.

—— (2000), *Ben, in the World*, London: Flamingo.

—— (2001), *The Sweetest Dream*, London: Flamingo.

—— (2002), *On Cats*, London: Flamingo.

—— (2003), *The Grandmothers*, London: Flamingo.

—— (2004), *Time Bites: Views and Reviews*, London: Fourth Estate.

—— (2005), *The Story of General Dann and Mara's Daughter, Griot and the Snow Dog*, London: Fourth Estate.

—— (2007), *The Cleft*, London: Fourth Estate.

—— (2008), *Alfred and Emily*, London: Fourth Estate.

Secondary Criticism

Abel, Elizabeth (1981), '(E)Merging Identities: The Dynamics of Female Friendship in Contemporary Fiction by Women', *Signs*, 6 (3): 413–35.

Agatucci, Cora (1991), 'Breaking from the Cage of Identity: Doris Lessing and *The Diaries of Jane Somers*', in Janice Morgan, Colette T. Hall and Molly

Snyder (eds), *Redefining Autobiography in Twentieth-Century Women's Fiction*, New York: Garland.

Aghazadeh, Sima (2010), 'Lessing's Narrative Strategies in *The Summer before the Dark*', *Doris Lessing Studies*, 29 (2): 14–20.

—— (2011), 'Sexual-Political Colonialism and Failure of Individuation in Doris Lessing's *The Grass Is Singing*', *Journal of International Women's Studies*, 12 (1): 107–21.

Allen, Orphia Jane (1980), 'Structure and Motif in Doris Lessing's "A Man and Two Women"', *Modern Fiction Studies*, 26: 63–74.

—— (1981), 'Interpreting "The Sun between Their Feet"', *Doris Lessing Newsletter*, 5 (2): 1–2.

—— (1983), 'Interpreting "Flavours of Exile"', *Doris Lessing Newsletter*, 7 (1): 8,12.

Altman, Meryl (1996), 'Before We Said "We" (and After): Bad Sex and Personal Politics in Doris Lessing and Simone de Beauvoir', *Critical Quarterly*, 38 (3): 14–29.

Anderst, Leah (2015), 'Feeling With Real Others: Narrative Empathy in the Autobiographies of Doris Lessing and Alison Bechdel', *Narrative*, 23 (3): 271–90.

Andréu Jiménez, Cristina (1987), 'When Utopia Is No Longer an Island: An Interpretation of Doris Lessing', *Doris Lessing Newsletter*, 11 (1): 9, 12.

Annus, Irén E. (2011), 'The Unheroine: The Figure of the Spinster in Doris Lessing's "The Trinket Box"', in Nóra Séllei and June Waudby (eds), *She's Leaving Home: Women's Writing in English in a European Context*, New York: Peter Lang, pp. 53–62.

Aouadi, Bootheina Majoul (2013), 'The Exegesis of Doris Lessing's *The Cleft*: Rethinking Being and Time', in Sharon R. Wilson (ed.), *Women's Utopian and Dystopian Fiction*, Newcastle upon Tyne, England: Cambridge Scholars.

Appignanesi, Lisa (2002), 'Interview: Doris Lessing', *BookForum*, 9 (1): 28–9.

Arias, Rosario (2005), '"All the World's a Stage": Theatricality, Spectacle and the Flâneuse in Doris Lessing's Vision of London', *Journal of Gender Studies*, 14 (1): 3–11.

—— (2012), '"Aren't You Haunted by All This Recurrence?": Spectral Traces of Traumatized Childhood(s) in Doris Lessing's *The Sweetest Dream*', *Critique*, 53 (4): 355–65.

Arlett, Robert (1987), 'The Dialectical Epic: Brecht and Lessing', *Twentieth-Century Literature*, 33 (1): 67–79.

Arnett, James (2010), 'Free from the Family: Lessing, Klein, and the Unwanted Child', *Doris Lessing Studies*, 30 (1): 13–18.

Auberlen, Eckhard (1989), 'Great Creating Nature and the Human Experiment in *The Golden Notebook* and *Canopus in Argos*', *Doris Lessing Newsletter*, 13 (1): 12–15.

Austin, Diana (2008), '"A Fit Country for Heroes to Live in": Doris Lessing's *The Good Terrorist* as Trauma Text', *Doris Lessing Studies*, 27 (1–2): 23–9.

Barnes, Sophia (2010), 'Stating the Problem: Doris Lessing's *The Golden Notebook* and the Possibility of Representation', *Doris Lessing Studies*, 29 (2): 20–4.

Barnouw, Dagmar (1973), 'Disorderly Company: From *The Golden Notebook* to *The Four-Gated City*', *Contemporary Literature*, 14 (4): 491–514.

Barzilai, Shuli (1988), 'Unmaking the Words That Make Us: Doris Lessing's "How I Finally Lost My Heart"', *Style*, 22 (4): 595–611.

Bazin, Nancy Topping (1980a), 'Androgyny or Catastrophe: The Vision of Doris Lessing's Later Novels', *Frontiers*, 5 (3): 10–15.

—— (1980b), 'The Moment of Revelation in *Martha Quest* and Comparable Moments by Two Modernists', *Modern Fiction Studies*, 26 (1): 87–98.

Bazin, Victoria (2008), 'Commodifying the Past: Doris Lessing's *The Golden Notebook* as Nostalgic Narrative', *Journal of Commonwealth Literature*, 43 (2): 117–31.

Beck, Anthony (1984), 'Doris Lessing and the Colonial Experience', *Journal of Commonwealth Literature*, 19 (1): 64–73.

Bell, Glenna (1992), 'Lessing's "To Room Nineteen"', *Explicator*, 50 (50:3): 180–3.

Bentley, Nick (2014), '"Unanchored Fragments of Print": Lessing's Experiments with Drama and Poetry in the Late 1950s', *Doris Lessing Studies*, 32: 19–26.

Berets, Ralph (1980), 'A Jungian Interpretation of the Dream Sequence in Doris Lessing's *The Summer before the Dark*', *Modern Fiction Studies*, 26: 117–29.

Bertelsen, Eve (1984), 'Doris Lessing's Rhodesia: History into Fiction', *English in Africa*, 11 (1): 15–40.

—— (1985a), 'The Persistent Personal Voice: Lessing on Rhodesia and Marxism', *Doris Lessing Newsletter*, 9 (2): 8–10, 18.

—— (1985b), 'Touching Base: Lessing in Johannesburg, 1956', *Doris Lessing Newsletter*, 9 (2): 16.

—— (1986), 'Doris Lessing', *Journal of Commonwealth Literature*, 21 (1): 134–61.

—— (1991), 'Veldtanschauung: Doris Lessing's Savage Africa', *Modern Fiction Studies*, 37 (4): 647–58.

Bittner, Petra (2001), 'Rhodesia's Lady of Shalott: Post-/Colonial Representation of a Female Protagonist', *Doris Lessing Studies*, 21 (2): 16–20.

Bloom, Harold (ed.) (1986), *Doris Lessing*, New York: Chelsea House.

Boehm, Beth A. (1997), 'Reeducating Readers: Creating New Expectations for *The Golden Notebook*', *Narrative*, 5 (1): 88–98.

Bolling, Douglass (1973), 'Structure and Theme in *Briefing for a Descent into Hell*', *Contemporary Literature*, 14 (4): 550–64.

—— (1977), 'Thoughts on Jack Orkney', *Doris Lessing Newsletter*, Winter 1976: 8–9.

Boschman, Robert (1994), 'Excrement and "Kitsch" in Doris Lessing's *The Good Terrorist*', *ARIEL*, 25 (3): 7–27.

Briggs, Marlene A. (2008), '"Born in the Year 1919": Doris Lessing, the First World War and the *Children of Violence*', *Doris Lessing Studies*, 27 (1–2): 3–10.

Brightwell, Gerri (1994), 'Flags and Filters: The Influence of Color in *The Golden Notebook*', *Doris Lessing Newsletter*, 16 (1): 3, 7, 14–15.

Brock, Richard (2009), '"No Such Thing as Society": Thatcherism and Derridean Hospitality in *The Fifth Child*', *Doris Lessing Studies*, 28 (1): 7–13.

Broderick, Catherine (1983), 'Doris Lessing in Japan', *Doris Lessing Newsletter*, 7 (1): 13–15.

Broner, E. M. (1993), 'Opening *The Golden Notebook*: Remembering the Source', *Doris Lessing Newsletter*, 15 (2): 6–7, 14–15.

Brooks, Ellen W. (1973), 'The Image of Woman in Lessing's *The Golden Notebook*', *Critique*, 15 (1): 101–9.

Brown, Byron K. (2005), '"Aspects of Each Other": Lessing, Laing, and the Question of Authority', *Doris Lessing Studies*, 25 (1): 12–16.

Brown, Lloyd W. (1975), 'The Shape of Things: Sexual Images and the Sense of Form in Doris Lessing's Fiction', *World Literature Written in English*, 14: 176–86.

Brown, Ruth Christiani (1978), 'Martha Quest: An Echo of Psyche's', *Doris Lessing Newsletter*, 2 (2): 8–10.

—— (1983), 'Peace at Any Price: *A Ripple from the Storm*', *Doris Lessing Newsletter*, 7 (2): 7–8, 10.

Brust, Imke (2010), 'The Crisis of an Old Order: Gender, Sexual Relations, and Reproduction in Lessing's *The Cleft*', *Doris Lessing Studies*, 30 (1): 23–7.

Burgan, Mary (1993), 'The "Feminine" Short Story: Recuperating the Moment', *Style*, 27 (3): 380–6.

Burkom, Selma R. (1969), 'A Doris Lessing Checklist', *Critique*, 11 (1): 69–81.

—— (1973), *Doris Lessing: A Checklist of Primary and Secondary Sources*, Troy, NY: Whitston.

Butcher, Margaret K. (1980), '"Two Forks of a Road": Divergence and Convergence in the Short Stories of Doris Lessing', *Modern Fiction Studies*, 26: 55–61.

Cairnie, Julie (2007), 'Doris Lessing, Socialist Realism, and the Plaasroman', *Doris Lessing Studies*, 26 (2): 20–2.

—— (2008), 'Rhodesian Children and the Lessons of White Supremacy: Doris Lessing's "The Antheap"', *Journal of Commonwealth Literature*, 43 (2): 145–56.

Caracciolo, Peter (1984), 'What's in a Canopean Name?', *Doris Lessing Newsletter*, 8 (1): 15.

Carey, John L. (1973), 'Art and Reality in *The Golden Notebook*', *Contemporary Literature*, 14 (4): 437–56.

Carlson, Susan L. (1987), 'Doris Lessing, Women Playwrights, and the Politics of Dramatic Form', *Doris Lessing Newsletter*, 11 (2): 5–7.

Carnes, Valerie (1976), '"Chaos, That's the Point": Art as Metaphor in Doris Lessing's *The Golden Notebook*', *World Literature Written in English*, 15: 17–28.

Cartwright, John F. (1991), 'Bound and Free: The Paradox of the Quest in Doris Lessing's *Children of Violence*', *Commonwealth Novel in English*, 4 (1): 46–61.

Cederstrom, Lorelei (1980a), 'Doris Lessing's Use of Satire in *The Summer Before the Dark*', *Modern Fiction Studies*, 26: 131–45.

—— (1980b), '"Inner Space" Landscape: Doris Lessing's *Memoirs of a Survivor*', *Mosaic*, 13 (3–4): 115–32.

—— (1990), *Fine-Tuning the Feminine Psyche: Jungian Patterns in the Novels of Doris Lessing*, New York: Peter Lang.

Cheng, Yuan-Jung (2007), 'Parody and Pastiche in *The Golden Notebook*', *Doris Lessing Studies*, 26 (2): 4–8.

Chennells, Anthony (1985), 'Doris Lessing: Rhodesian Novelist', *Doris Lessing Newsletter*, 9 (2): 3–7.

—— (2001), 'Postcolonialism and Doris Lessing's Empires', *Doris Lessing Studies*, 21 (2): 4–11.

Chown, Linda E. (1990), *Narrative Authority and Homeostasis in the Novels of Doris Lessing and Carmen Martín Gaite*, New York: Garland.

—— (2005), 'Revisiting Reliable Narration and the Politics of Perspective', *Doris Lessing Studies*, 25 (1): 16–18.

Cleary, Rochelle (1982), 'What's in a Name? Lessing's Message in *The Marriages Between Zones Three, Four and Five*', *Doris Lessing Newsletter*, 6 (2): 8–9.

Cole, Amanda (2005), '"Sucks to You": Lessing in London on Woolf', *Doris Lessing Studies*, 25 (1): 8–11.

Collins, Cornelius (2010), '"A Horizontal, Almost Nationless Organisation": Doris Lessing's Prophecies of Globalization', *Twentieth-Century Literature*, 56 (2): 221–44.

Conboy, Sheila C. (1990), 'The Limits of Transcendental Experience in Doris Lessing's *The Memoirs of a Survivor*', *Modern Language Studies*, 20 (1): 67–78.

Craig, David (1984), 'Middle-Class Tragedy', *Critical Quarterly*, 26 (3): 3–19.

Crater, Theresa (2004), 'Temporal Temptations in Lessing's *Mara and Dann*: Arriving at the Present Moment', *Doris Lessing Studies*, 23 (2): 17–20.

DaCrema, Joseph J. (1989), 'Lessing's "The Black Madonna"', *Explicator*, 47 (3): 55–8.

Davis, Rick (1994), '*The Golden Notebook* as Auto-Vivisection', *Doris Lessing Newsletter*, 16 (1): 1, 10–12.

Daymond, M. J. (1986), 'Areas of the Mind: *The Memoirs of a Survivor* and Doris Lessing's African Stories', *ARIEL*, 17 (3): 65–82.

—— (2001), 'Writing Autobiography and Writing Fiction: Interview with Doris Lessing, London, 28 July 2000', *Current Writing: Text and Reception in Southern Africa*, 13 (1): 7–21.

Dean, Sharon (1981), 'Marriage, Motherhood, and Lessing's "To Room Nineteen"', *Doris Lessing Newsletter*, 5 (1): 1, 14.

—— (1992), 'Lessing's *The Fifth Child*', *Explicator*, 50 (2): 120–2.

De Mul, Sarah (2006), 'The Politics of the Zimbabwean Everyday in Doris Lessing's *African Laughter: Four Visits to Zimbabwe*', *Doris Lessing Studies*, 25 (2): 10–14.

De Rango, Emily (2013), 'Clothing in Doris Lessing's *The Memoirs of a Survivor*', *Explicator*, 71 (4): 259–62.

Dietz, Bernd (1985), 'Entrevista: A Conversation with Doris Lessing', *Doris Lessing Newsletter*, 9 (1): 5–6; 13.

DiSalvo, Jacqueline (1988), 'The Intertextuality of Doris Lessing's *The Good Terrorist* and Milton's *Samson Agonistes*', *Doris Lessing Newsletter*, 12 (1): 3–4.

Dooley, Gillian (2003), '"The Horizon Conquerors": Lessing and Naipaul in Post-War London', *New Literatures Review*, 39: 75–88.

—— (2005), 'The Post-War Novel in Crisis: Three Perspectives', *AUMLA*, 104: 103–19.

—— (2009), 'An Autobiography of Everyone? Intentions and Definitions in Doris Lessing's *Memoirs of a Survivor*', *English Studies: A Journal of English Language and Literature*, 90 (2): 157–66.

Downward, Lisa (2013), 'Is *A Proper Marriage* a Bildungsroman?' *Doris Lessing Studies*, 31 (1–2): 20–3.

Draine, Betsy (1979), 'Changing Frames: Doris Lessing's *Memoirs of a Survivor*', *Studies in the Novel*, 11: 51–62.

—— (1980), 'Nostalgia and Irony: The Postmodern Order of *The Golden Notebook*', *Modern Fiction Studies*, 26: 31–48.

—— (1983), *Substance Under Pressure: Artistic Coherence and Evolving Form in the Novels of Doris Lessing*, Madison: University of Wisconsin Press.

—— (2000), 'From the Margins of Privilege', *Contemporary Literature*, 41 (3): 554–63.

DuPlessis, Rachel Blau (1979), 'The Feminist Apologues of Lessing, Piercy, and Russ', *Frontiers*, 4 (1): 1–8.

Duyfhuizen, Bernard (1980a), 'On the Writing of Future-History: Beginning the Ending in Doris Lessing's *The Memoirs of a Survivor*', *Modern Fiction Studies*, 26: 147–56.

—— (1980b), 'The Doris Lessing Typescripts at the University of Tulsa', *Doris Lessing Newsletter*, 4 (1): 7–8.

Eagleton, Mary (2009), 'The Spectre of the Aged Woman Writer', *Doris Lessing Studies*, 28 (2): 4–9.

Elshtain, Jean Bethke (1980), 'The Post-*Golden Notebook* Fiction of Doris Lessing', *Salmagundi*, 47–8: 95–114.

Fahim, Shadia S. (1994), *Doris Lessing: Sufi Equilibrium and the Form of the Novel*, New York: St. Martin's.

Fand, Roxanne J. (1999), *The Dialogic Self: Reconstructing Subjectivity in Woolf, Lessing, and Atwood*, Selinsgrove, PA: Susquehanna University Press.

Farquharson, Kathy (2009), '"The Last Walls Dissolve": Space versus Architecture in *The Memoirs of a Survivor* and "The Yellow Wallpaper"', *Doris Lessing Studies*, 28 (1): 4–7.

Fenton, Gregory (2013), 'Towards a Communist Narratology: On the Idea of Communism in Lessing's *The Golden Notebook*', *Doris Lessing Studies*, 31 (1–2): 9–15.

Fishburn, Katherine (1985), *The Unexpected Universe of Doris Lessing: A Study in Narrative Technique*, London: Greenwood.

—— (1987), *Doris Lessing: Life, Work, and Criticism*, Fredericton, New Brunswick: York.

—— (1988), 'Wor(l)ds within Words: Doris Lessing as Meta-Fictionist and Meta-Physician', *Studies in the Novel*, 20 (2): 186–205.

—— (1990), 'Back to the Preface: Cultural Conversations with *The Golden Notebook*', *College Literature*, 17 (2–3): 162–82.

—— (1994), 'The Manichean Allegories of Doris Lessing's *The Grass Is Singing*', *Research in African Literatures*, 25 (4): 1.

Franko, Carol (1995), 'Authority, Truthtelling, and Parody: Doris Lessing and "the Book"', *Papers on Language and Literature*, 31 (3): 255.

Frick, Thomas (1988), 'Doris Lessing: The Art of Fiction No. 102', *Paris Review*, 106 n.p.

Gage, Diane Burdick (1978), 'The Relevance of History', *Doris Lessing Newsletter*, 2 (2): 4–5.

Galin, Müge (1997), *Between East and West: Sufism in the Novels of Doris Lessing*, Albany: State University of New York Press.

—— (2007), 'Doris Lessing: The Sufi Connection', *Doris Lessing Studies*, 26 (2): 23–4.

Galván Reula, J. F. (1987a), 'Doris Lessing: A Spanish Checklist of Translations and Criticism', *Doris Lessing Newsletter*, 11 (1): 10–11, 15.

—— (1987b), 'The Spanish Confusion: The Reception of Doris Lessing in Spain', *Doris Lessing Newsletter*, 11 (1): 3–4, 12.

García Navarro, Carmen (2004), 'Doris Lessing Revisited: Some Insights on Lessing's Recent Reception in Spain', *Doris Lessing Studies*, 23 (2): 20–4.

Gardiner, Judith Kegan (1991), 'The Pit without the Pendulum', *Doris Lessing Newsletter*, 14 (1): 1, 12–14.

—— (1983), 'Evil, Apocalypse, and Feminist Fiction', *Frontiers,* 7 (2): 74–80.

—— (1984), 'Gender, Values, and Lessing's Cats', *Tulsa Studies in Women's Literature*, 3 (1–2): 111–24.

—— (1989a), *Rhys, Stead, Lessing, and the Politics of Empathy*, Bloomington: Indiana University Press.

—— (1989b), 'The Exhilaration of Exile: Rhys, Stead, and Lessing', in Mary Lynn Broe and Angela Ingram (eds) *Women's Writing in Exile*, Chapel Hill: University of North Carolina Press, pp. 134–50.

—— (2005), 'Doris Lessing's *The Golden Notebook*', in Brian W. Shaffer (ed.), *A Companion to the British and Irish Novel, 1945–2000*, Oxford: Blackwell, pp. 376–87.

—— (2006), 'Historicizing Homophobia in *The Golden Notebook* and "The Day Stalin Died"', *Doris Lessing Studies*, 25 (2): 14–18.

—— (2009), 'Lessing as Gorgon: "The Stare"', *Doris Lessing Studies*, 28 (2): 13–18.

Garren, Samuel B. (2005), 'The Honeysuckle and the Camellia: A Reader-Response Theory of Literary Interpretation', *Doris Lessing Studies*, 25 (1): 19–22.

Geoffroy, Alain (1989), 'Dreams in Doris Lessing's *The Grass Is Singing*', *Commonwealth Essays and Studies*, 11 (2): 110–20.

Gerber, Nancy (1992), 'Remembering a Lifetime of Cats', *Doris Lessing Newsletter*, 14 (2): 6, 15.

Gerver, Elisabeth (1978), 'Women Revolutionaries in the Novels of Nadine Gordimer and Doris Lessing', *World Literature Written in English*, 17: 38–50.

Graham, Robin (1979), 'Twenty "New" Poems by Doris Lessing', *World Literature Written in English*, 18: 90–8.

Gray, Billy (2004), 'A Conversation with Doris Lessing: "Lucky the Culture Where the Old Can Talk to the Young and the Young Can Talk to the Old"', *Doris Lessing Studies*, 24 (1–2): 1, 23–30.

Gray, Stephen (1985), 'Circular Imperial History and Zimbabwe in *Shikasta*', *Doris Lessing Newsletter*, 9 (2): 11, 16.

—— (1986), 'An Interview with Doris Lessing', *Research in African Literatures*, 17 (3): 329–40.

Greene, Gayle (1985), 'Women and Men in Doris Lessing's *Golden Notebook*: Divided Selves', in Shirley Nelson Garner, Claire Kahane, and Madelon Sprengnether (eds), *The (M)other Tongue: Essays in Feminist Psychoanalytic Interpretation*, Ithaca, NY: Cornell University Press, pp. 280–305.

—— (1987), 'Doris Lessing's *Landlocked*: "A New Kind of Knowledge"', *Contemporary Literature*, 28 (1): 82–103.

—— (1991), '*The Diaries of Jane Somers*: Doris Lessing, Feminism, and the Mother', in Brenda O. Daly and Maureen T. Reddy (eds), *Narrating Mothers: Theorizing Maternal Subjectivities*, Knoxville: University of Tennessee Press, pp. 139–56.

—— (1992), 'Bleak Houses: Doris Lessing, Margaret Drabble, and the Condition of England', *Forum for Modern Language Studies*, 28 (4): 304–19.

—— (1994), *Doris Lessing: The Poetics of Change*, Ann Arbor: University of Michigan Press.

Green, Martin (1982), 'The Doom of Empire: *Memoirs of a Survivor*', *Doris Lessing Newsletter*, 6 (2): 6–7, 10.

Griffin, Michael James, II (2010), 'Reading Textuality and Sexuality in Doris Lessing's *The Golden Notebook* and Luce Irigaray's *This Sex Which Is Not One*', *Doris Lessing Studies*, 29 (1): 19–23.

Grogan, Bridget (2011), '(Im)Purity, Danger and the Body in Doris Lessing's *The Grass Is Singing*', *English Studies in Africa*, 54 (2): 31–42.

Gurr, Andrew (1982), 'The Freedom of Exile in Naipaul and Doris Lessing', *ARIEL,* 13 (4): 7–18.

Hakac, John (1986), 'Budding Profanity in "A Sunrise on the Veld"', *Doris Lessing Newsletter*, 10 (1): 13.

Halisky, Linda H. (1990), 'Redeemeing the Irrational: The Inextricable Heroines of "A Sorrowful Woman" and "To Room Nineteen"', *Studies in Short Fiction*, 27 (1): 45–54.

Hanley, Lynne (1988), 'Alias Jane Somers', *Doris Lessing Newsletter*, 12 (1): 5–6.

—— (1991), *Writing War: Fiction, Gender, and Memory*, Amherst: University of Massachusetts Press.

—— (1994), 'Sleeping with the Enemy: Doris Lessing in the Century of Destruction', in John Richetti et al. (eds), *The Columbia History of the British Novel*, New York: Columbia University Press, pp. 918–38.

Hanson, Clare (1985), 'Free Shorter: The Shorter Fiction of Doris Lessing', *Doris Lessing Newsletter*, 9 (1): 7–8; 14.

—— (1987), 'Doris Lessing in Pursuit of the English; Or, No Small, Personal Voice', *PN Review*, 14 (4 [60]): 39–42.

—— (1988), 'Each Other: Images of Otherness in the Short Fiction of Doris Lessing, Jean Rhys and Angela Carter', *Journal of the Short Story in English*, 10: 67–82.

Hardin, Nancy Shields (1973), 'Doris Lessing and the Sufi Way', *Contemporary Literature*, 14 (4): 565–81.

—— (1977), 'The Sufi Teaching Story and Doris Lessing', *Twentieth Century Literature*, 23 (3): 314–26.

Hargreaves, Tracy (2012), '"To Find a Form That Accommodates the Mess": Truth Telling from Doris Lessing to B. S. Johnson', *Yearbook of English Studies*, 42 (1): 204–22.

Harris, Jocelyn (1991), 'Doris Lessing's Beautiful Impossible Blueprints', in James Acheson (ed.), *The British and Irish Novel Since 1960*, New York: St. Martin's, pp. 32–47.

Harvey, Stephanie (1993), 'Doris Lessing's "One off the Short List" and Leo Bellingham's "In for the Kill"', *Critical Survey*, 5 (1): 66–76.

Hayes, Carol (1984), 'British Progress', *Doris Lessing Newsletter*, 8 (1): 9–11.

Hayes, Tricia (1979), 'Adolescent Awakenings in the Fiction of Doris Lessing', *Doris Lessing Newsletter*, 3 (1): 9–10.

Henke, Suzette A. (1983), 'Lessing's *Golden Notebook* and Engels' *Origin of the Family*', *Doris Lessing Newsletter*, 7 (2): 6.

—— (1994), 'Doris Lessing's *Golden Notebook*: A Paradox of Postmodern Play', in Lisa Rado (ed.), *Rereading Modernism: New Directions in Feminist Criticism*, New York: Garland, pp. 159–87.

—— (2008), 'Reading Doris Lessing's *Golden Notebook* as a Feminist Narrative', *Doris Lessing Studies*, 27 (1–2): 11–16.

Henstra, Sarah (2007), 'Nuclear Cassandra: Prophecy in Doris Lessing's *The Golden Notebook*', *Papers on Language and Literature*, 43 (1): 3–23.

Hidalgo, Pilar (1987), '*The Good Terrorist*: Lessing's Tract for the Times', *Doris Lessing Newsletter*, 11 (1): 7–8.

—— (2005), 'Doris Lessing and A. S. Byatt: Writing *The Golden Notebook* in the 1990s', *Doris Lessing Studies*, 25 (1): 22–5.

Hilson, Mica (2010), '"The Odd Man Out in the Family?": Queer Throwbacks and Reproductive Futurism in *The Fifth Child*', *Doris Lessing Studies*, 30 (1): 18–22.

Hinz, Evelyn J. (1973), 'The Pietà as Icon in *The Golden Notebook*', *Contemporary Literature*, 14 (4): 457–70.

Hite, Molly (1988a), 'Doris Lessing's *The Golden Notebook* and *The Four-Gated City*: Ideology, Coherence, and Possibility', *Twentieth Century Literature*, 34 (1): 16–29.

—— (1988b), '(En)Gendering Metafiction: Doris Lessing's Rehearsals for *The Golden Notebook*', *Modern Fiction Studies*, 34 (3): 481–500.

Hoffeld, Laura (1979), '*The Summer before the Dark* and *The Memoirs of a Survivor*: Lessing's New Female Bondings', *Doris Lessing Newsletter*, 3 (2): 11–12.

Hogeland, Lisa Marie (1983), 'Coda to: "An Edge of History": The Implicit Feminism of Doris Lessing's *The Four-Gated City*', *Doris Lessing Newsletter*, 7 (2): 11–12.

Holmquist, Ingrid (1980), *From Society to Nature: A Study of Doris Lessing's Children of Violence*, Gothenburg: Acta Gothoburgensis.

Howe, Florence (1973), 'A Conversation with Doris Lessing (1966)', *Contemporary Literature*, 14 (4): 418–36.

Hsieh, Meng-Tsung (2010), 'Almost Human but Not Quite? The Impenetrability of Being in Doris Lessing's *Ben, in the World*', *Doris Lessing Studies*, 29 (1): 14–19.

Hunter, Eva (1985), 'Plus ça Change', *Doris Lessing Newsletter*, 9 (2): 17.

—— (1991), 'Friendship and Aging in Doris Lessing's *Diaries of Jane Somers* and Lisa Alther's *Other Women*', *Doris Lessing Newsletter*, 14 (1): 8, 10–11, 15.

Hunter, Melanie (1997), '"A Question of Wholes": Spiritual Intersection, Apocalyptic Vision in the Work of Doris Lessing', *Doris Lessing Newsletter*, 18 (2): 1, 8–10.

Hynes, Joseph (1994), 'Doris Lessing's *Briefing* as Structural Life and Death', *Renascence*, 46 (4): 225–45.

Ichikawa, Hiroyoshi (1977), 'Dorisologist or Lessing Freak?', *Doris Lessing Newsletter*, 1, 8–9.

Ingersoll, Earl G. (1993), 'The Doris Lessing Interviews', *Doris Lessing Newsletter*, 15 (2): 4–5.

—— (1994a), 'Interviewing Doris Lessing', *Doris Lessing Newsletter*, 16 (2): 3, 11, 15.

—— (1994b), 'Writing for Balance: A Conversation with Doris Lessing', *Ontario Review*, 40: 46–58.

—— (2005), 'Doris Lessing's "Playing the Game"', *Doris Lessing Studies*, 25 (1): 5–8.

—— (2010), 'Dystopia/Utopia in Doris Lessing's *Canopus in Argos* Novel *The Marriages between Zones Three, Four, and Five*', *Doris Lessing Studies*, 29 (2): 9–14.

Jackson, Tony (2002), 'R. D. Laing, Doris Lessing and Cold War Madness', *Doris Lessing Studies*, 22 (2): 11–17, 24.

Jiger, Virginia (1983), '"The Grammar of Journey": Doris Lessing and Janet Frame', *Doris Lessing Newsletter*, 7 (1): 11–12.

Jones, Norman C. (1983), 'Acculturation and Character Portrayal in Southern African Novels', *African Literature Today*, 13: 180–200.

Joyner, Nancy (1974), 'The Underside of the Butterfly: Lessing's Debt to Woolf', *Journal of Narrative Technique*, 4: 204–11.

Kaplan, Carey (1983), 'A Womb with a View: The House on Radlett Street in *The Four-Gated City*', *Doris Lessing Newsletter*, 7 (1): 3–4.

Kaplan, Carey and Ellen Cronan Rose (eds) (1988), *Doris Lessing: The Alchemy of Survival*, Athens: Ohio University Press.

Kaplan, Sydney Janet (1973), 'The Limits of Consciousness in the Novels of Doris Lessing', *Contemporary Literature*, 14 (4): 536–49.

Karl, Frederick R. (1972), 'Doris Lessing in the Sixties: The New Anatomy of Melancholy', *Contemporary Literature*, 13 (1): 15–33.

—— (1976), 'The Four-Gaited Beast of the Apocalypse: Doris Lessing's *The Four-Gated City*', in Robert K. Morris (ed.), *Old Lines, New Forces: Essays on the Contemporary British Novel, 1960–1970*, London: Associated University Press, pp. 181–99.

Kay, Helen (1982), '"Realities . . . rooted in Geography": An Analysis of *The Grass Is Singing* in Relation to *Going Home*', *Doris Lessing Newsletter*, 6 (1): 3–4, 11.

Kellermann, Henryk (1989a), 'Fiction and Politics: The Narrative Method in Doris Lessing's *The Wind Blows Away Our Words*', *Doris Lessing Newsletter*, 13 (1): 16–17.

—— (1989b), '*The Fifth Child*: An Interview with Doris Lessing', *Doris Lessing Newsletter*, 13 (1): 3–7.

Kelly, Rebecca (1986), 'Doris Lessing's *The Summer before the Dark*: One Woman or Another?' *Doris Lessing Newsletter*, 10 (1): 11–12.

Kendrix, Piper (1995), 'A Visit to Zimbabwe Complicates Student Reading of African Laughter', *Doris Lessing Newsletter*, 17 (1): 3, 6–7, 15.

Khanna, Lee Cullen (1983a), 'Canopus in the Classroom', *Doris Lessing Newsletter*, 7 (1): 9–10.

—— (1983b), 'Truth and Art in Women's Worlds: Doris Lessing's *Marriages between Zones Three, Four, and Five*', in Marleen Barr and Nicholas D. Smith (eds), *Women and Utopia*, Lanham, MD: University Press of America, pp. 121–33.

Kim, Soo (2007), '"But Let's Preserve the Forms": Doris Lessing's *The Golden Notebook* as a Hegelian Modernist Novel', *Doris Lessing Studies*, 26 (2): 14–20.

King, Holly Beth (1980), 'Criticism of Doris Lessing: A Selected Checklist', *Modern Fiction Studies*, 26: 167–75.

Kinkead-Weekes, Mark (1993), 'Sharp Knowing in Apartheid?: The Shorter Fiction of Nadine Gordimer and Doris Lessing', in Abdulrazak Gurnah (ed.), *Essays on African Writing, 1: A Re-Evaluation*, Oxford: Heinemann, pp. 88–110.

Klein, Carole (1996), 'The Quest for Doris Lessing', in Frederick R. Karl (ed.) *Biography and Source Studies*, New York: AMS, pp. 27–35.

—— (2000), *Doris Lessing: A Biography*, New York: Carroll & Graf.

Klein, Susan M. (2002), 'First and Last Words: Reconsidering the Title of *The Summer Before the Dark*', *Critique,* 43 (3): 228–38.

Knapp, Mona (1984), *Doris Lessing*, New York: Ungar.

—— (1986a), 'Canopuspeak: Doris Lessing's *Sentimental Agents* and Orwell's *1984*', *Neophilologus*, 70 (3): 453–61.

—— (1986b), 'Lessing on the Continent: How Germany Finally Lost Its Heart', *Doris Lessing Newsletter*, 10 (1): 8–9, 13.

—— (1989), 'Opera through the Lessing/Glass', *Doris Lessing Newsletter*, 12 (2): 12.

Krouse, Agate Nesaule (1973), 'A Doris Lessing Checklist', *Contemporary Literature*, 14 (4): 590–7.

—— (1976), 'Doris Lessing's Feminist Plays', *World Literature Written in English*, 15: 305–22.

—— (1978), 'Lessing in Feminist Literary Criticism', *Doris Lessing Newsletter*, 2 (1): 4, 8–9.

Krouse, Tonya (2006), 'Freedom as Effacement in *The Golden Notebook*: Theorizing Pleasure, Subjectivity, and Authority', *Journal of Modern Literature*, 29 (3): 39–56.

—— (2007), 'Doris Lessing, Metaphysics, and Sexuality', *Doris Lessing Studies*, 26 (2): 24–6.

Kurzweil, Edith (1998), 'An Evening with Doris Lessing', *Partisan Review*, 1: 11–29.

Lacey, Lauren (2006), 'Genealogy and Becoming in the *Canopus in Argos: Archives* Series', *Doris Lessing Studies*, 25 (2): 18–23.

Latz, Anna (1997), 'The Quest for Freedom in *Love, Again*', *Doris Lessing Newsletter*, 18 (2): 3, 6–7, 13–14.

LeBeau, Cecilia Harmann (1977), 'The World behind the Wall', *Doris Lessing Newsletter*, Fall: 7, 10.

Lee, Amy (2004), '*The Summer before the Dark*: The Void of Motherhood', *Doris Lessing Studies*, 24 (1–2): 15–18.

Lee, Hermione (2009), 'A Conversation with Doris Lessing', *Wasafiri*, 24 (3): 18–25.

Lefcowitz, Barbara F. (1975), 'Dream and Action in Lessing's *The Summer before the Dark*', *Critique*, 17 (2): 107–20.

Leonard, Suzanne (2004), 'Playing in the Shadows: Aging and Female Invisibility in *The Summer before the Dark*', *Doris Lessing Studies*, 24 (1–2): 11–15.

Leonard, Vivien (1980), '"Free Women" as Parody: Fun Games in *The Golden Notebook*', *Perspectives on Contemporary Literature*, 6: 20–7.

Lightfoot, Marjorie J. (1975), 'Breakthrough in *The Golden Notebook*', *Studies in the Novel*, 7: 277–84.

Linfield, Susie (2001), 'Against Utopia: An Interview with Doris Lessing', *Salmagundi*, 130–1: 59–74.

Lukens, Rebecca J. (1978), 'Inevitable Ambivalence: Mother and Daughter in Doris Lessing's *Martha Quest*', *Doris Lessing Newsletter*, 2 (2): 13–14.

McCallister, John (2001), 'Knowing Native, Going Native: African Laughter, Colonial Epistemology, and Post-Colonial Homecoming', *Doris Lessing Studies*, 21 (2): 12–15.

McCormick, Kay (1985), 'The Child's Perspective in Five African Stories', *Doris Lessing Newsletter*, 9 (2): 12–13, 18.

Magie, Michael L. (1977), 'Doris Lessing and Romanticism', *College English*, 38 (6): 531–52.

Majumdar, Nivedita (2002), 'The Politics of Authenticity: A Reading of *The Golden Notebook*', *Doris Lessing Studies*, 22 (2): 1, 4–8.

Mandl, Bette (1981), '*Martha Quest*: The Dynamics of Mood', *Doris Lessing Newsletter*, 5 (2): 3–4.

—— (1985), 'The Politics of Representation in *The Marriages between Zones Three, Four and Five*', *Notes on Contemporary Literature*, 15 (2): 4–5.

Marchino, Lois A. (1972), 'The Search for Self in the Novels of Doris Lessing', *Studies in the Novel*, 4: 252–61.

—— (1978), 'Life, Lessing, and the Pursuit of Feminist Criticism', *Doris Lessing Newsletter*, 2 (2): 1, 15–16.

Marder, Herbert (1980), 'The Paradox of Form in *The Golden Notebook*', *Modern Fiction Studies*, 26: 49–54.

Markow, Alice B. (1974), 'The Pathology of Feminine Failure in the Fiction of Doris Lessing', *Critique*, 16 (1): 88–100.

Marshall, Leni (2004), 'Changing Bodies, Changing Minds: *The Diaries of Jane Somers*', *Doris Lessing Studies*, 24 (1–2): 19–22.

Maslen, Elizabeth (1984), 'Doris Lessing: The Way to Space Fiction', *Doris Lessing Newsletter*, 8 (1): 7–8, 14.

—— (1986) 'Doris Lessing's *The Good Terrorist*: Socialist or Anti-Socialist', *Red Letters*, 19: 24–34.

—— (1994), *Doris Lessing*. Plymouth: Northcote House.

Matheson, Sue (1986), 'Lessing on Stage: An Examination of Theatrical Metaphor and Architectural Motif in *The Memoirs of a Survivor*', *Doris Lessing Newsletter*, 10 (2): 8–9.

Miller, Jane (1998), 'Doris Lessing and the Millennium', *Raritan*, 18 (1): 133–45.

Monteith, Moira (1991), 'Doris Lessing and the Politics of Violence', in Lucie Armitt (ed.), *Where No Man Has Gone Before: Women and Science Fiction*, London: Routledge, pp. 67–82.

Mooney, Jane (1984), '*Shikasta*: Vision or Reality', *Doris Lessing Newsletter*, 8 (1): 12–14.

Morgan, Ellen (1973), 'Alienation of the Woman Writer in *The Golden Notebook*', *Contemporary Literature*, 14 (4): 471–80.

Morphet, Fionna (1985), 'The Narrowing Horizon: Two Chapter Openings in *The Grass Is Singing*', *Doris Lessing Newsletter*, 9 (2): 14–15.

Myler, Kerry (2013), 'Madness and Mothering in Doris Lessing's *The Four-Gated City*', *Doris Lessing Studies*, 31 (1–2): 15–20.

Nagurski-Bernstein, Irene (1985), 'On a Soviet Edition of Doris Lessing Stories: No Witchcraft for Sale', *Doris Lessing Newsletter*, 9 (1): 12.

Newman, Robert D. (1984), 'Doris Lessing's Mythological Egg in *The Memoirs of a Survivor*', *Notes on Contemporary Literature*, 14 (3): 3–4.

Noble, Michael (1997), '"This Tale Is Our Answer": Science and Narrative in Doris Lessing's *Canopus*', *Doris Lessing Newsletter*, 18 (2): 4–5, 12, 15.

Page, Malcolm (1977), 'Lessing's Unpublished Plays: A Note', *Doris Lessing Newsletter*, Fall: 3, 6.

—— (1980), 'Doris Lessing as Theatre Critic, 1958', *Doris Lessing Newsletter*, 4 (1): 4, 13.

Peel, Ellen (1982), 'Communicating Differently: Doris Lessing's *Marriages between Zones Three, Four and Five*', *Doris Lessing Newsletter*, 6 (2): 11–13.

—— (1986), 'Feminist Narrative Persuasion: The Movement of Dynamic Spatial Metaphor in Doris *Lessing's The Marriages between Zones Three, Four, and Five*', *Sociocriticism*, 4–5: 115–42.

—— (1987), 'Leaving the Self Behind in *Marriages*', *Doris Lessing Newsletter*, 11 (2): 3, 10.

—— (1989), 'The Self Is Always an Other: Going the Long Way Home to Autobiography', *Twentieth-Century Literature*: 35 (1): 1–16.

Perrakis, Phyllis Sternberg (1981), 'Doris Lessing's *The Golden Notebook*: Separation and Symbiosis', *American Imago*, 38 (4): 407–28.

—— (1992), 'Sufism, Jung and the Myth of Kore: Revisionist Politics in Lessing's *Marriages*', *Mosaic*, 25 (3): 99–120.

—— (1995), 'The Female Gothic and the (M)Other in Atwood and Lessing', *Doris Lessing Newsletter*, 17 (1): 1, 11–15.

—— (2004), 'Journeys of the Spirit: The Older Woman in Doris Lessing's Works', *Doris Lessing Studies*, 24 (1–2): 39–43.

—— (2007), 'Navigating the Spiritual Cycle in *Memoirs of a Survivor* and *Shikasta*', in Phyllis Sternberg Perrakis (ed.), *Adventures of the Spirit: The Older Woman in the Works of Doris Lessing, Margaret Atwood, and Other Contemporary Women Writers*, Columbus: Ohio State University Press, pp. 47–82.

Perrakis, Phyllis Sternberg (ed.) (1999), *Spiritual Exploration in the Works of Doris Lessing*, London: Greenwood Press.

Pezzulich, Evelyn (2004), 'Coming of Age: The Emergence of the Aging Female Protagonist in Literature', *Doris Lessing Studies*, 24 (1–2): 7–10.

Pickering, Jean (1980), 'Marxism and Madness: The Two Faces of Doris Lessing's Myth', *Modern Fiction Studies*, 26: 17–30.

—— (1990), *Understanding Doris Lessing*, Columbia: University of South Carolina Press.

Port, Cynthia (2004), '"None of It Adds Up": Economies of Aging in *The Diary of a Good Neighbour*', *Doris Lessing Studies*, 24 (1–2): 30–5.

Porter, Dennis (1974), 'Realism and Failure in *The Golden Notebook*', *Modern Language Quarterly*, 35: 56–65.

Pratt, Annis (1974), *Doris Lessing: Critical Studies*, Madison: University of Wisconsin Press.

Pruitt, Virginia (1981), 'The Crucial Balance: A Theme in Lessing's Short Fiction', *Studies in Short Fiction*, 18 (3): 281–5.

Pulda, Molly (2010), 'War and Genre in Doris Lessing's *Alfred and Emily*', *Doris Lessing Studies*, 29 (2): 3–9.

Rapping, Elayne Antler (1975), 'Unfree Women: Feminism in Doris Lessing's Novels', *Women's Studies*, 3: 29–44.

Raschke, Debrah (2001), 'The "Heart of the Kingdom": Colonial Politics in Lessing's *The Fifth Child*', *Doris Lessing Studies*, 21 (2): 20–6.

—— (2009), 'Knowledge and Sexual Construction in Lessing's *The Memoirs of a Survivor* and *The Fifth Child*', *Doris Lessing Studies*, 28 (1): 13–16.

Raschke, Deborah, Phyllis Sternberg Perrakis and Sandra Singer (eds) (2010), *Doris Lessing: Interrogating the Times*, Columbus: Ohio State University Press.

Rege, Josna (2004a), 'The Child Is Mother of the Woman: Exchange between Age and Youth in Doris Lessing', *Doris Lessing Studies*, 24 (1–2): 3–7.

Rege, Josna (ed.) (2004b), 'Coming to Age', *Doris Lessing Studies*, 24 (1–2): 1–47.

Reid, Martha (1980), 'Outsiders, Exiles, and Aliens in the Fiction of Doris Lessing', *Doris Lessing Newsletter*, 4 (2): 3–4, 14.

Reilly, Terry (2008), 'Free Women and Freeman: The Language of Lobotomy in *The Golden Notebook*', *Doris Lessing Studies*, 27 (1–2): 17–22.

—— (2014), 'Doris Lessing and Moidi Jokl: A Reassessment', *Doris Lessing Studies*, 32: 5–7.

Ridout, Alice (2010), '"The View from the Threshold": Doris Lessing's Nobel Acceptance Speech', *Doris Lessing Studies*, 29 (1): 4–8.

—— (2014), 'Of Pigeons and Expats: Doris Lessing, Sam Selvon, and Zadie Smith', *Doris Lessing Studies*, 32: 26–9.

Ridout, Alice and Susan Watkins (eds) (2009), *Doris Lessing: Border Crossings*, London: Continuum.

Ridout, Alice, Roberta Rubenstein and Sandra Singer (eds) (2015), *Doris Lessing's* The Golden Notebook *After Fifty*, New York: Palgrave Macmillan.

Rigney, Barbara Hill (1978), *Madness and Sexual Politics in the Feminist Novel: Studies in Bronte, Woolf, Lessing, and Atwood*, Madison: University of Wisconsin Press.

Roberts, Sheila (1993), 'Sites of Paranoia and Taboo: Lessing's *The Grass Is Singing* and Gordimer's *July's People*', *Research in African Literatures*, 24 (3): 73–85.

Rohmann, Gerd (1989), 'Lessing in Two Germanies', *Doris Lessing Newsletter*, 13 (1): 18–21.

Rose, Ellen Cronan (1976a), 'The End of the Game: New Directions in Doris Lessing's Fiction', *Journal of Narrative Technique*, 6: 66–75.

—— (1976b), *The Tree Outside the Window: Doris Lessing's Children of Violence*, Hanover: University Press of New England.

—— (1980), 'Twenty Questions', *Doris Lessing Newsletter*, 4 (2): 5.

—— (1989), 'Crystals, Fragments and Golden Wholes: Short Stories in *The Golden Notebook*', in Clare Hanson (ed.), *Re-Reading the Short Story*, New York: St. Martin's, pp. 126–37.

Rosen, Ellen I. (1978), 'Martha's "Quest" in Lessing's *Children of Violence*', *Frontiers* 3 (2): 54–9.

Rosenfeld, Aaron S. (2005), 'Remembering the Future: Doris Lessing's "Experiment in Autobiography"', *Critical Survey*, 17 (1): 40–55.

—— (2007), 'She Was Where?: Lessing, Woolf and Their Radical Epistemologies of Place', *Doris Lessing Studies*, 26 (2): 8–14.

Rosner, Victoria (1999), 'Home Fires: Doris Lessing, Colonial Architecture, and the Reproduction of Mothering', *Tulsa Studies in Women's Literature*, 18 (1): 59–89.

Rountree, Catherine (2008), 'A Thing of Temperament: An Interview with Doris Lessing, London, May 16, 1998', *Jung Journal*, 2 (1): 62–77.

Rowland, Susan (2000), '"Transformed and Translated": The Colonized Reader of Doris Lessing's *Canopus in Argos* Space Fiction', in Abby Werlock (ed.), *British Women Writing Fiction*, Tuscaloosa: University of Alabama Press, pp. 42–55.

Rubenstein, Roberta (1975a), 'Doris Lessing's *The Golden Notebook*: The Meaning of Its Shape', *American Imago*, 32: 40–58.

—— (1975b), 'Outer Space, Inner Space: Doris Lessing's Metaphor of Science Fiction', *World Literature Written in English*, 14: 187–97.

—— (1979a), *The Novelistic Vision of Doris Lessing: Breaking the Forms of Consciousness*, Urbana: University of Illinois Press.

—— (1979b), 'The Room of the Self: Psychic Geography in Doris Lessing's Fiction', *Perspectives on Contemporary Literature*, 5: 69–78.

—— (2001), 'Feminism, Eros, and the Coming of Age', *Frontiers: A Journal of Women Studies*, 22 (2): 1–19.

—— (2014), *Literary Half-Lives: Doris Lessing, Clancy Sigal, and Roman à Clef*, New York: Palgrave Macmillan.

Ryf, Robert S. (1975), 'Beyond Ideology: Doris Lessing's Mature Vision', *Modern Fiction Studies*, 21: 193–201.

Sage, Lorna (1983), *Doris Lessing*, London: Methuen.

Sarvan, Charles (1978), 'D. H. Lawrence and Doris Lessing's *The Grass Is Singing*', *Modern Fiction Studies*, 24: 533–7.

Savkay, Canan (2010), 'Lessing's Engagement with Platonic Idealism in *Briefing for a Descent into Hell*', *Doris Lessing Studies*, 29 (1): 9–14.

Saxton, Ruth Olsen (1987), 'Garments of the Mind: Clothing and Appearance in the Fiction of Doris Lessing', *Doris Lessing Newsletter*, 11 (1): 13.

—— (2004), 'Sex over Sixty? From *Love, Again* to *The Sweetest Dream*', *Doris Lessing Studies*, 24 (1–2): 44–7.

Saxton, Ruth and Jean Toibin (eds) (1994), *Woolf and Lessing: Breaking the Mold*, New York: St. Martin's Press.

Scanlan, Margaret (1980), 'Memory and Continuity in the Series Novel: The Example of *Children of Violence*', *Modern Fiction Studies*, 26: 75–85.

—— (1990), 'Language and the Politics of Despair in Doris Lessing's *The Good Terrorist*', *Novel*, 23 (2): 182–98.

Schleuter, Paul (1973), *The Novels of Doris Lessing*, Carbondale: Southern Illinois University Press.

—— (1975), *A Small Personal Voice: Essays, Reviews, Interviews*, New York: Random House.

—— (1978), 'On Lessing Scholarship', *Doris Lessing Newsletter*, 2 (1): 6, 12.

—— (1981), '*Memoirs of a Survivor*', *Doris Lessing Newsletter*, 5 (2): 5–6.

—— (1985), 'Lessing's Unpublished Rhodesian Materials', *Doris Lessing Newsletter*, 9 (1): 13.

—— (1987), 'The Other Doris Lessing: Poet', in Lawrence B. Gamache and Ian S. MacNiven (eds), *The Modernists: Studies in a Literary Phenomenon*, Rutherford: Fairleigh Dickinson University Press, pp. 249–60.

—— (2002), 'Lessing Critics: The Earlier Generation', *Doris Lessing Studies*, 22 (2): 18–23.

Schneider, Karen (1995), 'A Different War Story: Doris Lessing's Great Escape', *Journal of Modern Literature*, 19 (2): 259–72.

Schulte, Bornd (1989), 'Doris Lessing, Author of "New" English Literature', *Doris Lessing Newsletter*, 13 (1): 8–11.

Schweickart, Patrocinio P. (1985), 'Reading a Wordless Statement: The Structure of Doris Lessing's *The Golden Notebook*', *Modern Fiction Studies*, 31 (2): 263–79.

Seligman, Dee (1978a), 'Checklist of Doris Lessing Criticism', *Doris Lessing Newsletter*, 2 (1): 5, 12.

—— (1978b), 'Dissertations on Doris Lessing', *Doris Lessing Newsletter*, 2 (1): 7.

—— (1978c), 'Lessing Short Story Bibliography', *Doris Lessing Newsletter*, 2 (1): 5.

—— (1979a), 'Lessing on Tape', *Doris Lessing Newsletter*, 3 (2): 5.

—— (1979b), 'Published Interviews with Lessing', *Doris Lessing Newsletter*, 3 (2): 5.

—— (1980), 'The Four-Faced Novelist', *Modern Fiction Studies*, 26: 3–16.

Seligman, Dee (ed.) (1981), *Doris Lessing: An Annotated Bibliography of Criticism*, Westport: Greenwood.

Serafin, Anne (1980), 'In Search of Doris Lessing', *Doris Lessing Newsletter*, 4 (1): 5–6.

Sheiner, Marcy (1987), 'Thematic Consistency in the Work of Doris Lessing: The Marriage between Martha Quest and Zones Three, Four, and Five', *Doris Lessing Newsletter*, 11 (2): 4, 14.

Singer, Sandra (1986), 'Unleashing Human Potentialities: Doris Lessing's *The Memoirs of a Survivor* and Contemporary Cultural Theory', *Text & Context*, 1 (1): 79–95.

—— (2004), 'Awakening the Solitary Soul: Gendered History in Women's Fiction and Michael Cunningham's *The Hours*', *Doris Lessing Studies*, 23 (2): 9–12.

Singleton, Mary Ann (1976), *The City and the Veld: The Fiction of Doris Lessing*, Lewisburg: Bucknell University Press.

Sizemore, Christine W. (1984), 'Reading the City as Palimpsest: The Experiential Perception of the City in Doris Lessing's *The Four-Gated City*', in Susan Merrill Squier (ed.), *Women Writers and the City: Essays in Feminist Literary Criticism*, Knoxville: University of Tennessee Press, pp. 176–90.

—— (1989), *A Female Vision of the City: London in the Novels of Five British Women*, Knoxville: University of Tennessee Press.

—— (1993), 'Neanderthals, Human Gorillas and Their Fathers: Crossing Scientific Boundaries in Doris Lessing's *The Fifth Child* and Maureen Duffy's *Gor Saga*', *Doris Lessing Newsletter*, 15 (1): 3, 7, 10, 14–15.

—— (1994), 'Teaching Doris Lessing in a Commonwealth Literature Course', *Doris Lessing Newsletter*, 16 (2): 6–7.

—— (2004), 'Patterns of Aging in the Ninth Stage of Life: *The Diary of a Good Neighbour*', *Doris Lessing Studies*, 24 (1–2): 36–8.

—— (2008), '*In Pursuit of the English*: Hybridity and the Local in Doris Lessing's First Urban Text', *Journal of Commonwealth Literature*, 43 (2): 133–44.

Smith, Angela (1984), 'In a Divided Mind', *Doris Lessing Newsletter*, 8 (1): 3–4, 14.

Snitow, Ann Barr (1983), 'Houses like Machines, Cities like Geometry, Worlds like Grids of Friendly Feeling: Doris Lessing-Masterbuilder', *Doris Lessing Newsletter*, 7 (2): 13–14.

Solinger, Frederick J. (2014), 'Nostalgia for the Future: Remembrance of Things to Come in Doris Lessing's *Martha Quest*', *ARIEL*, 45 (3): 75–99.

Soos, Emese (1976), 'Revolution in the Historical Fiction of Jean-Paul Sartre and Doris Lessing', *Perspectives on Contemporary Literature*, 2 (1): 23–33.

Spacks, Patricia M. (1971), 'Free Women', *Hudson Review*, 24: 559–73.

Sperlinger, Tom (2009), 'Doris Lessing's Work of Forgiveness', *Cambridge Quarterly*, 38 (1): 66–72.

—— (2012), 'A Writer without Qualities: Recent Work on Doris Lessing', *Contemporary Women's Writing*, 6 (2): 177–84.

Spiegel, Rotraut (1980), *Doris Lessing: The Problem of Alienation and the Form of the Novel*, Frankfurt: Peter Lang.

Spilka, Mark (1975), 'Lessing and Lawrence: The Battle of the Sexes', *Contemporary Literature*, 16 (2): 218–40.

Sprague, Claire (1977), 'Olive Schreiner: Touchstone for Lessing', *Doris Lessing Newsletter*, Winter 1976: 4–5, 9–10.

—— (1979), 'Doris Lessing's Reasoner Letters', *Doris Lessing Newsletter*, 3 (1): 6–8.

—— (1980), '"Without Contraries Is No Progression": Lessing's *The Four-Gated City*', *Modern Fiction Studies*, 26: 99–116.

—— (1982), 'Doubletalk and Doubles Talk in *The Golden Notebook*', *Papers on Language and Literature*, 18 (2): 181–97.

—— (1983), 'Naming in *Marriages*: Another View', *Doris Lessing Newsletter*, 7 (1): 13.

—— (1989), 'Genre Reversals in Doris Lessing: Stories Like Novels and Novels Like Stories', in *Re-Reading the Short Story*, ed. Clare Hanson, New York: St. Martin's, pp. 110–25.

—— (1992a), '"Anna, Anna, I Am Anna": The Annas of Doris Lessing's *The Golden Notebook*', in *The Anna Book: Searching for Anna in Literary History*, ed. Mickey Pearlman, Westport: Greenwood, pp. 151–8.

—— (1992b), 'Lessing's *The Grass Is Singing, Retreat to Innocence, The Golden Notebook* and Eliot's "The Waste Land"', *Explicator*, 50 (3): 177–80.

—— (2004), 'Race, Sex, and Radical Politics in Doris Lessing's World War II Zambesia/Rhodesia/Zimbabwe', *Doris Lessing Studies*, 23 (2): 6–9.

Sprague, Claire (ed.) (1990), *In Pursuit of Doris Lessing: Nine Nations Reading*, Basingstoke: Macmillan.

Sprague, Claire and Tiger, Virginia (eds) (1986), *Critical Essays on Doris Lessing*, Boston: Hall.

Stamberg, Susan (1984), 'An Interview with Doris Lessing', *Doris Lessing Newsletter*, 8 (2): 3–4, 15.

Stimpson, Catharine R. (1983), 'Doris Lessing and the Parables of Growth', in Elizabeth Abel, Marianne Hirsch and Elizabeth Langland (eds), *The Voyage In: Fictions of Female Development*, Hanover: University Press of New England, pp. 186–205.

Stitzel, Judith (1977), 'The Uses of Humor', *Doris Lessing Newsletter*, Fall: 2–3.

—— (1979), 'Reading Doris Lessing', *College English*, 40 (5): 498–504.

Stone, Laurie (1987), 'Narratives: The Doris Lessing Standard', *Doris Lessing Newsletter*, 11 (2): 9.

Stout, Janis P. (1990), 'A Quest of One's Own: Doris Lessing's *The Summer before the Dark*', *ARIEL*, 21 (2): 5–19.

Style, Colin (1986), 'Doris Lessing's "Zambesia"', *English in Africa*, 13 (1): 73–91.

Suárez-Lafuente, María S. (1987), 'The Effect of Nature in Doris Lessing's African Stories', *Doris Lessing Newsletter*, 11 (1): 5–6.

Sukenick, Lynn (1973), 'Feeling and Reason in Doris Lessing's Fiction', *Contemporary Literature*, 14 (4): 515–35.

Sullivan, Alvin (1980), '*The Memoirs of a Survivor*: Lessing's Notes toward a Supreme Fiction', *Modern Fiction Studies*, 26: 157–62.

Sullivan, Daniel (2011), 'Monstrous Children as Harbingers of Mortality: A Psychological Analysis of Doris Lessing's *The Fifth Child*', *Lit: Literature Interpretation Theory*, 22 (2): 113–33.

Swingewood, Alan (1978), 'Structure and Ideology in the Novels of Doris Lessing', in Diana Laurenson (ed.), *The Sociology of Literature: Applied Studies*, Keele: Keele University Press, pp. 38–54.

Tayeb, Lamia (2009), 'Arabian Nights Fairy-Tale Turned Postcolonial Parable: Narrative Manoeuvres in Doris Lessing's *Mara and Dann*', *Doris Lessing Studies*, 28 (2): 18–25.

Taylor, Jenny (ed.) (1982), *Notebooks/Memoirs/Archives: Reading and Rereading Doris Lessing*, London: Routledge.

—— (1984), 'Notebooks/Memoirs/Archives: The True Story', *Doris Lessing Newsletter*, 8 (1): 5–6, 15.

Thomson, Rosemarie Garland (1999), 'Learning Something Else: Embracing the Dying Body in Doris Lessing's *The Diary of a Good Neighbour*', *Iris*, 38: 44–7.

Thorpe, Michael (1973), *Doris Lessing*, London: Longman for British Council.

Tiger, Virginia (1979), 'Lessing's Stories: A Review', *Doris Lessing Newsletter*, 3 (2): 13–14.

—— (1980), 'Doris Lessing', *Contemporary Literature*, 21 (2): 286–90.

—— (1990), '"Taking Hands and Dancing in (Dis)Unity": Story to Storied in Doris Lessing's "To Room Nineteen" and "A Room"', *Modern Fiction Studies*, 36 (3): 421–33.

—— (1992), 'Lessing through New Lenses', *Doris Lessing Newsletter*, 14 (2): 1, 11–13.

—— (1993), '"The Words Had Been Right and Necessary": Doris Lessing's Transformations of Utopian and Dystopian Modalities in *The Marriages Between Zones Three, Four, and Five*', *Style*, 27 (1): 63–80.

—— (2008), '"Crested, Not Cloven": *The Cleft*', *Doris Lessing Studies*, 27 (1–2): 33–5.

—— (2009), 'Life Story: Doris, Alfred and Emily', *Doris Lessing Studies*, 28 (1): 22–4.

Torrents, Nissa (1980), 'Doris Lessing: Testimony to Mysticism', *Doris Lessing Newsletter*, 4 (2): 1, 12–13.

Tyler, Lisa (1993), 'Classical, Biblical, and Modernist Myth: Doris Lessing's "Flavours of Exile"', *Doris Lessing Newsletter*, 15 (2): 3, 10–11, 13.

—— (1994a), '"Our Mothers" Gardens: Doris Lessing's "Among the Roses"', *Studies in Short Fiction*, 31 (2): 163.

—— (1994b), 'Self-Hatred and the Demonic in Doris Lessing's Fiction', *Doris Lessing Newsletter*, 16 (2): 4–5, 13–15.

Verleun, Jan (1985), 'The World of Doris Lessing's *The Summer before the Dark*', *Neophilologus*, 69 (4): 620–39.

Visel, Robin (1988), 'A Half-Colonization: The Problem of the White Colonial Woman Writer', *Kunapipi*, 10 (3): 39–45.

—— (2008), '"Then Spoke the Thunder": *The Grass Is Singing* as a Zimbabwean Novel', *Journal of Commonwealth Literature*, 43 (2): 157–66.

—— (2010), 'Liberation and Taboo: Normative Sexuality in Lessing's Fiction', *Doris Lessing Studies*, 30 (1): 3–7.

Vlastos, Marion (1976), 'Doris Lessing and R. D. Laing: Psychopolitics and Prophecy', *PMLA*, 91 (2): 245–58.

Walder, Dennis (2008), '"Alone in a Landscape": Lessing's African Stories Remembered', *Journal of Commonwealth Literature*, 43 (2): 99–115.

Walker, Melissa (2008), 'An Eye towards Recovery: Trauma, Nostalgia, and the Bush in *African Laughter*', *Doris Lessing Studies*, 27 (1–2): 29–32.

Wallace, Diana (2006), '"Women's Time": Women, Age, and Intergenerational Relations in Doris Lessing's *The Diaries of Jane Somers*', *Studies in the Literary Imagination*, 39 (2): 41–59.

Wang, Joy (2009), 'White Postcolonial Guilt in Doris Lessing's *The Grass Is Singing*', *Research in African Literatures*, 40 (3): 37–47.

Warnock, Jeanie (2004), 'Unlocking the Prison of the Past: Childhood Trauma and Narrative in Doris Lessing's *The Memoirs of a Survivor*', *Doris Lessing Studies*, 23 (2): 12–16.

Waterman, David (2003), 'Group Allegiance and Coerced Identity: Doris Lessing's *The Sentimental Agents in the Volyen Empire*', *CEA Critic*, 65 (3): 31–42.

—— (2006), *Identity in Doris Lessing's Space Fiction*, Youngstown, NY: Cambria.

Watkins, Susan (2006a), '"Grande Dame" or "New Woman": Doris Lessing and the Palimpsest', *Lit: Literature Interpretation Theory*, 17 (3–4): 243–62.

—— (2006b), 'Writing in a Minor Key', *Doris Lessing Studies*, 25 (2): 6–10.

—— (2010), *Doris Lessing*, Manchester: Manchester University Press.

Watson, Barbara Bellow (1976), 'Leaving the Safety of Myth: Doris Lessing's *The Golden Notebook* (1962)', in Robert K. Morris (ed.), *Old Lines, New*

Forces: Essays on the Contemporary British Novel, 1960–1970, Rutherford, NJ: Fairleigh Dickinson University Press, pp. 12–37.

Watson, Irene G. (1989), 'Lessing's "To Room Nineteen"', *Explicator*, 47 (3): 54–5.

Waxman, Barbara Frey (1985), 'From Bildungsroman to Reifungsroman: Aging in Doris Lessing's Fiction', *Soundings* 68 (3): 318–34.

Weinhouse, Linda (1993), 'Doris Lessing and the Convention of Self', *Commonwealth Novel in English*, 6 (1–2): 94–111.

—— (2009), 'Re-Mapping Centre and Periphery', *Doris Lessing Studies*, 28 (2): 9–13.

Wellington, Charmaine (1989), 'Mary Finchley in *The Summer before the Dark*: A Present Absence', *Doris Lessing Newsletter*, 12 (2): 6–7, 13.

Wells, Sherah (2010), 'The Self Which Surfaces: Competing Maternal Discourses in *A Proper Marriage*', *Doris Lessing Studies*, 30 (1): 7–12.

Welnhouse, Linda (1985), 'Lessing's Play of the 1950s: *Each His Own Wilderness*', *Doris Lessing Newsletter*, 9 (1): 10–11.

White, Thomas I. (1983), 'Opposing Necessity and Truth: The Argument against Politics in Doris Lessing's Utopian Vision', in Marleen Barr and Nicholas D. Smith (eds), *Women and Utopia*, Lanham, MD: University Press of America, pp. 134–47.

Wilson, Raymond J., III (1982), 'Doris Lessing's Symbolic Motifs: The *Canopus* Novels', *Doris Lessing Newsletter*, 6 (1): 1, 9–11.

Wilson, Sharon R. (2009), 'Postcolonial Identities in *The Golden Notebook*', *Doris Lessing Studies*, 28 (1): 17–21.

—— (2013), 'Storytelling in Lessing's *Mara and Dann* and Other Texts', in Sharon R. Wilson (ed.), *Women's Utopian and Dystopian Fiction*, Newcastle: Cambridge Scholars, pp. 23–9.

Wright, Derek (1993), 'Thin Iron and Egg-Shells: The Wall Motif in the Novels of Doris Lessing', *Commonwealth Novel in English*, 6 (1–2): 69–79.

Yelin, Louise (1998), *From the Margins of Empire: Christina Stead, Doris Lessing, Nadine Gordimer*, Ithaca, NY: Cornell University Press.

Zak, Michele Wender (1973), '*The Grass Is Singing*: A Little Novel about the Emotions', *Contemporary Literature*, 14 (4): 481–90.

Notes on Contributors

Sophia Barnes teaches in the School of Letters, Art and Media at the University of Sydney, Australia. She has previously published in *Doris Lessing Studies* and is currently preparing a monograph manuscript titled, *We Must Go On Writing: Doris Lessing and Mikhail Bakhtin.*

Nick Bentley is Senior Lecturer in English at Keele University. He is author of *Martin Amis* (2015); *Contemporary British Fiction* (2008); *Radical Fictions: The English Novel in the 1950s* (2007); editor of *British Fiction of the 1990s* (2005); and co-editor of *The 2000s: A Decade of Contemporary British Fiction* (2015).

Kevin Brazil is a Lecturer in Late Twentieth and Twenty-First Century British Literature at the University of Southampton. His work is published or forthcoming in the *Journal of Modern Literature, Modernism/modernity*, and *Tate Papers*, and he is currently working on a monograph on the post-war novel and visual art.

Cornelius Collins teaches at Fordham University in the Bronx, NY. The current President of the Doris Lessing Society, he has published essays on Lessing and Don DeLillo and is writing a manuscript titled, *The Fiction of Apocalypse: Globalization Narratives of Collapse and Decline after the Cold War.*

Adam Guy teaches at the University of Oxford. His research focuses on the early impact of the *nouveau roman* in Britain. He has published on B. S. Johnson and Christine Brooke-Rose, and is working on a monograph based on his doctoral thesis.

Clare Hanson is Professor of Twentieth Century Literature at the University of Southampton. She has published widely on twentieth-century women's writing and on literature and science. Her books include *A Cultural History of Pregnancy* (2004) and *Eugenics, Literature and Culture in Post-war Britain* (2012). She is working on a study of genetics and the literary imagination.

Rowena Kennedy-Epstein is Lecturer in Women's Writing of the 20th and 21st Centuries at the University of Bristol. She recovered and edited Muriel Rukeyser's novel *Savage Coast* (2013). Her scholarship appears in *Modern Fiction Studies, The Journal of Narrative Theory* and *Modernism/modernity*. Her current book explores radical politics and experimentation in women's writing.

Laura Marcus is Goldsmiths' Professor of English Literature at New College, University of Oxford. She is the author of *Dreams of Modernity: Psychoanalysis, Literature, Cinema* (2014); *Auto/biographical Discourses: Theory, Criticism, Practice* (1994); *Virginia Woolf* (2004 and 2010); and *The Tenth Muse: Writing about Cinema in the Modernist Period* (2007).

Elizabeth Maslen is a Senior Research Fellow of the Institute of English Studies, University of London. Recent books include *Life in the Writings of Storm Jameson* (2014) and a revised and enlarged edition of *Doris Lessing* in the Writers and their Work series (1994 and 2014).

David Punter is a writer, poet and academic, currently Professor of English at the University of Bristol. He has published thirty books on Romantic and Gothic literature, modern and contemporary writing, literary theory and psychoanalysis, including *The Literature of Pity* (2014). *The Gothic Condition* will be published later this year.

David Sergeant is Lecturer in English post-1850 at Plymouth University. He is the author of *Kipling's Art of Fiction 1884–1901* (2013), essays on Robert Burns, Ted Hughes and R. L. Stevenson, and a collection of poetry, *Talk Like Galileo* (2010).

Tom Sperlinger is Reader in English Literature and Community Engagement at the University of Bristol and author of *Romeo and Juliet in Palestine* (2015). He has published articles on Lessing, George Eliot and adult education.

Index

Adorno, Theodor W., 45
  'Commitment', 22
  Minima Moralia, 54
Afghanistan, 1, 155, 158–60
Africa, 7, 15–16, 76, 88, 93–4
Alfred and Emily, 2–3, 7–8, 39–40
amnesia, 130, 133
animals, 104–5, 165, 167–9, 176, 178n
Anthropocene, 97, 111, 114–15, 164,
  175–6
Anzieu, Didier, *Le Corps de l'oeuvre*,
  92–4
apocalypse, 14, 121–2
Apter, Emily, *Against World Literature*,
  18
Arendt, Hannah, 2–3
  *Between Past and Future: Eight
    Exercises in Political Thought*, 3–4
  The Human Condition, 142–3, 145–6
  On Revolution, 142–3
autobiography, 27, 40, 43, 45, 74–5,
  89–91, 93, 162
autodidact education, 53, 73, 77, 139

Banks, Lynn Reid, *The L-Shaped
  Room*, 30
Beckett, Samuel, 10, 47
  Watt, 103–4
Ben, in the World, 168–9, 177–8n
Bentley, Nick, 45
Berger, John, 45–6
Best, Stephen and Sharon Marcus,
  'Surface Reading: An Introduction',
  5, 79
Boehm, Beth A., 78

Bortoft, Henri, 115–17, 126n
  *Taking Appearance Seriously: The
    Dynamic Way of Seeing in Goethe
    and European Thought*, 115
  *The Wholeness of Nature: Goethe's
    Way of Science*, 115–16
Bostrom, Nick, 171
  'Transhumanist Values', 178n
Braidotti, Rosi, *The Posthuman*, 165,
  170, 174, 176–7
Brecht, Bertolt, 45, 157
Briefing for a Descent into Hell, 105,
  118, 157, 174, 178n
British New Left, 26, 40, 74
Burgess, Anthony, 137
  A Clockwork Orange, 27, 30
Butler, Judith, *Giving an Account of
  Oneself*, 42

Canopus in Argos: Archives (novel
  sequence), 140–1, 164
  *Documents Relating to the
    Sentimental Agents in the Volyen
    Empire*, 3
  *The Making of the Representative for
    Planet 8*, 7, 122, 172
  *The Marriages Between Zones Three,
    Four and Five*, 128, 134–5,
    139–40, 145–50
  *The Marriages Between Zones Three,
    Four and Five* (typescript), 148,
    150
  Shikasta: Re, Colonised Planet 5, 24,
    111, 119, 121, 128, 132–3, 137,
    140, 171–2, 175

capitalism, 30–1, 36, 57, 103, 114, 120, 166, 174
Carson, Anne, 68
Cha, Theresa Hak Kyung, *Dictee*, 68
Chakrabarty, Dipesh, 'The Climate of History: Four Theses', 121, 164, 171, 173–6
character, 40–2, 46–8, 50–1
Children of Violence (novel sequence), 40–54, 78, 100–1, 118, 139, 174
   The Four-Gated City, 6–7, 24, 40, 43, 53, 104–6, 111–25, 140, 164
   Landlocked, 40, 50, 53, 125n
   Martha Quest, 40–4, 48–50, 98, 107
   A Proper Marriage, 40, 48–9, 52
   A Ripple From the Storm, 26, 33, 35, 40, 44
cinema *see* film
cinema mind *see* film
Clark, Timothy, 111
The Cleft, 7, 129, 164
climate change, 117–21, 123, 147, 164, 173–4
Coetzee, J. M., 137
Cohen, Albert K., *Delinquent Boys: The Culture of the Gang*, 34
Cold War, 13, 46–7, 58, 61–3, 75
Colletta, Lisa, 103
colonisation, 46, 97
commitment, 10–13, 16–17, 20, 22, 24, 44, 46, 48, 57, 74, 77, 111, 152
communism, 6, 12–13, 33, 74, 97, 122
creative process, 95, 137, 138–9, 148–9
Critchley, Simon, 98–9, 101–2, 104–8

Darwin, Charles, 167
daydreaming, 88–90, 93
deep history, 164, 174
Delaney, Shelagh, *A Taste of Honey*, 30
Derrida, Jacques, 7, 131–3, 140
didacticism, 5, 62, 97–8, 107, 120, 139, 148
Didion, Joan, *The White Album*, 97–8, 139
Dimock, Wai Chee, *Through Other Continents: American Literature Across Deep Time*, 6, 14
Diski, Jenny, 137–8
Drabble, Margaret, 6

dreams, 53–4, 68, 84–5, 87–91, 93–5, 125, 128, 140, 143–4, 147–9, 161
Dunbar, Robin, *Human Evolution*, 177n
Duncan, Greta, and Roy Wilkie, 'Glasgow Adolescents', 27
dystopia, 85, 172, 176

ecocriticism, 114–15, 119, 121, 123
Eiseley, Loren, 'The Last Neanderthal', 165–6
empathy, 48, 86, 112–14
Englund, Peter, 155–6
environmental crisis, 5, 111–25
Esty, Jed, 'Global Lukács', 47–8
eugenics, 171
evolution, 3, 5, 118–19, 150, 161, 164–5, 167, 171–4, 176–7
experimental literary forms, 56–8, 62, 67–8, 95

Fanon, Frantz, *Black Skin, White Masks*, 88, 94
fascism, 57–8, 60, 169
Felski, Rita, 5
   Beyond Feminist Aesthetics: Feminist Literature and Social Change, 52–3
   The Limits of Critique, 52
   Uses of Literature, 79, 82
feminism, 4, 53, 56–63, 68, 80–1
Ferrebe, Alice, *Masculinity in Male-Authored Fiction*, 30–1
The Fifth Child, 129, 150n, 164–8, 176, 177–8n
film, 4, 58, 84–96, 102, 168
First World War, 114, 152
Fowles, John, *Wormholes: Essays and Occasional Writings*, 95–6
Freud, Sigmund, 89, 128, 133–4
   'The Ego and the Id', 93
   'A Metaphysical Supplement to the Theory of Dreams', 93
   'The Psychical Mechanism of Forgetfulness', 130
Frow, John, *Character and Person*, 41
future, 1, 6–8, 35–6, 43, 51–2, 85, 95, 106–7, 123, 128–34, 139–40, 143–5, 154, 158, 161–2, 169–71, 174

Galin, Müge, 149
Garton Ash, Timothy, 156
Gelder, Ken, *The Subcultures Reader*, 34
genre, 1, 4, 8, 57–9, 68, 95, 107, 121, 125, 142, 164, 175–6
Going Home, 47, 156
The Golden Notebook, 1, 4, 5, 11, 28, 31, 34–7, 43–4, 48, 56–69, 71–82, 89–96, 101–3, 106, 149, 155–6
The Good Terrorist, 122
Gordimer, Nadine, 'The Inward Testimony', 154–5
Gothic, 20, 85
The Grass is Singing, 84–90, 138
Greene, Gayle, 74, 98
Grosz, Elizabeth, *Becoming Undone: Darwinian Reflections on Life, Politics, and Art*, 165, 167–8, 177
Gruner, Wolf, 152

Hall, Stuart, 'Politics of Adolescence?', 27
Haraway, Donna, *The Companion Species Manifesto*, 111–12
Hardin, Nancy Shields, 107
Heidegger, Martin, 'The Age of the World Picture', 24
Heise, Ursula, 119
Hejinian, Lynn, 60
Hensher, Philip, 138–9, 149
Herbrechter, Stefan, *Posthumanism: A Critical Analysis*, 165
Hirsch, Marianne, *Family Frames: Photography, Narrative, and Postmemory*, 40
Hoggart, Richard, *The Uses of Literacy: Aspects of Working Class Life*, 27–8
Holocaust, 154
humanism, 1, 15–16, 45, 46
humour, 97, 109, 161
Huxley, Julian, *New Bottles for New Wine*, 170

imagination, 7, 95, 115, 117, 119–20, 171
individual and collective (relationship between), 5, 51, 89, 139

insanity *see* madness
Iran *see* Persia
irony, 16, 49–50, 72, 97–9, 135
Iser, Wolfgang, 43, 77–8

Jameson, Fredric, 120, 122
    The Political Unconscious, 5
Jameson, Storm, 152–4, 160–1
jazz, 26, 31–2

Kincaid, James R., 100
Kullman, Michael, 'The Anti-Culture Born of Despair', 26

Laber, Jeri, 161
Latour, Bruno, 'Agency at the Time of the Anthropocene', 175
Lawrence, D. H., 58
    Lady Chatterley's Lover, 138
Le Guin, Ursula
    The Dispossessed, 122
    'Science Fiction and Mrs Brown', 176
Lear, Jonathan, *Radical Hope*, 147–8
Li Rui, 154
Lifton, Robert Jay, *The Broken Connection: on Death and the Continuity of Life*, 152
Lukács, Georg, 45–8, 53

McGurl, Mark, 'The Posthuman Comedy', 5
McVeigh, Emily, 2, 40
madness, 61, 117
Mannheim, Karl, 'The Problem of Generations', 29
Mara and Dann, 7, 111, 123–4, 140, 150, 157
Marcus, Jane, 57, 68
Marcus, Sharon *see* Best, Stephen
Margolin, Uri, 'Introducing and Sustaining Characters in Literary Narrative: A Set of Conditions', 41
marriage, 2, 40, 84–6, 88, 140, 145, 147–8, 157
Marxism, 1–3, 46, 50–2, 74–5, 122, 126n, 134–5, 174
Mavlian, Shoair, 153

The Memoirs of a Survivor, 7, 105, 108–9, 121–2, 128–31, 140, 169–70, 176
Miller, J. Hillis, *Fiction and Repetition: Seven English Novels*, 52
Mitchison, Naomi, 170–2, 178
  Solution Three, 172
morality, 26, 28, 42, 45, 50, 103, 167
Moretti, Franco, 'Conjectures on World Literature', 6
Mulvey, Laura, *Visual and Other Pleasures*, 94
Murdoch, Iris, 'What I See in Cinema', 90
myth, 7, 10, 27, 40–1, 53–4, 64–5, 72, 93, 134–5

Neanderthal, 165–6, 168, 177–8n
Ngai, Sianne, *Ugly Feelings*, 50
Nobel Prize, 7, 97, 154
Notley, Alice, *The Descent of Alette*, 68
novel sequences, 40–4

Oksenberg Rorty, Amelie, *The Identities of Persons*, 42
oral storytelling, 7, 124

patriarchy, 56–7, 64, 66–8
patriotism, 153
Perrakis, Phyllis Sternberg, 140–1, 146, 149, 150n
Persia, 39
phenomenology, 114–15, 117, 174
Play With a Tiger, 26–31
Plenty Coups, 147
Plotz, John, 72, 75
postcolonialism, 6, 17, 47, 154
posthumanism, 1, 97, 103–7, 164–77, 178n
Prisons We Choose to Live Inside, 109
psychoanalysis, 4, 51, 90–3

radical women's writing, 56–69, 90
reading practices, 4, 5–6, 43, 49, 52–3, 60, 67–8, 71–4, 76–82, 114, 124–5, 139
realism, 1, 11–12, 22, 40–1, 44–8, 53, 67, 90, 93, 95, 98–101, 107, 111, 121, 124, 134–5

refugees, 77, 152–3, 156–61
repetition, 3, 39–41, 51–4, 68, 100–2, 118, 140, 142–3, 145, 150
reportage, 1, 5, 58, 152–8, 161
revolution, 35, 37, 60, 67, 142, 154, 161, 172
Romains, Jules, *Les hommes de bonne volonté*, 42
Roy, Arundhati, *Walking with the Comrades*, 60
Royle, Nicholas, *The Uncanny*, 134
Rubenstein, Roberta, 5–6
  Literary Half-Lives: Doris Lessing, Clancy Sigal, and Roman à Clef, 75
Rukeyser, Muriel, 58–9
  'The Collected Poems', 58
  Savage Coast (Costa Brava), 58–9
  The Usable Truth, 58, 68
  'We Came for Games', 63

Sale, Roger, 97–8
Sanbonmatsu, John, *Critical Theory and Animal Liberation*, 168–9
Sartre, Jean-Paul, 10–14, 16–17, 22
  What is Literature?, 14
satire, 98, 100–3, 105, 138
Sayers, Dorothy, 'Living to Work', 156
scale, 3, 5–6, 14, 16–17, 19, 23–4, 105, 111–25, 128, 130, 132, 140, 148, 150, 164
science fiction, 80, 111, 121, 132, 175–6
Segal, Lynne, 30–1
Shah, Idries, 107, 111, 115, 118, 120, 122–3, 125n, 143, 146, 155, 168
  Caravan of Dreams, 162
Sharpe, Ella Freeman, 93
short stories, 1, 17–24, 105–6
Sillitoe, Alan, 30
Singer, Sandra, 27, 30, 64
Snow, C. P., 48
  The Two Cultures, 46
Snyder, Timothy, 161
South Africa, 18–20, 22, 100, 154, 159
Southern Rhodesia, 34, 62, 82, 84, 109, 138, 155, 159, 161
Spark, Muriel, *The Ballad of Peckham Rye*, 30

Sprague, Claire, *Rereading Doris Lessing: Narrative Patterns of Doubling and Repetition*, 40
Stimpson, Catharine R., 46
The Story of General Dann and Mara's Daughter, Griot and the Snow Dog, 7
style, 44, 97, 100, 124, 137, 139, 154, 156, 158
Sufism, 98, 107, 109, 111, 118, 125, 143, 146, 149, 155, 162
Sullivan, Hannah, 137
The Summer Before the Dark, 107–9, 139–45, 149
The Summer Before the Dark (typescript), 143–5
The Sweetest Dream, 122

Taylor, Alfred, 2, 40
Taylor, Jenny, *Notebooks/ Memoirs/ Archives: Reading and Rereading Doris Lessing*, 45
telepathy, 120, 134–5
terrorism, 155
theatre, 141–8
Thompson, E. P. (Edward), 75
    The Making of the English Working Class, 174
Time Bites, 143
time travel, 6, 128–35, 140, 146
Tobin, Jean, 66–7
typewriter, 137–8

Under My Skin, 89, 138, 144, 162
utopia, 2, 7, 116, 120–3, 141

visionary writing, 2, 6, 68–9, 90, 97

Waddington, C. H., *The Strategy of the Gene*, 178n
Walking in the Shade, 27, 39–40, 91, 161–2
Walkowitz, Rebecca L., *Cosmopolitan Style: Modernism Beyond the Nation*, 13
Watkins, Susan, 4–5, 6
Wells, H. G., 'The Door in the Wall', 130
Wilkie, Roy *see* Duncan, Greta
Williams, Raymond, *The Long Revolution*, 32, 45
Wilson, Colin, *The Outsider*, 32
The Wind Blows Away Our Words, 152, 155–62
witness literature, 152–62
Woolf, Virginia, 56–8, 153
    'Mr Bennett and Mr Brown', 176
    A Sketch of the Past', 89
    Three Guineas, 57–8
working-class identity, 26, 76
world literature, 5–6, 18

youth culture, 2, 26–37, 105

Zimbabwe *see* Southern Rhodesia